# Christian Ethics
*in* Conversation

# Christian Ethics
# *in* Conversation

A Festschrift in Honor of Donald W. Shriver Jr.,
13th President of Union Theological Seminary
in the City of New York

EDITED BY
ISAAC B. SHARP AND
CHRISTIAN T. IOSSO

*Forewords by M. Craig Barnes and Serene Jones*

CASCADE *Books* · Eugene, Oregon

Cascade Books
An Imprint of Wipf and Stock Publishers
199 W. 8th Ave., Suite 3
Eugene, OR 97401

www.wipfandstock.com

PAPERBACK ISBN: 978-1-7252-7360-3
HARDCOVER ISBN: 978-1-7252-7361-0
EBOOK ISBN: 978-1-7252-7362-7

*Cataloguing-in-Publication data:*

Names: Sharp, Isaac B., editor. | Iosso, Christian T., editor. | Barnes, M. Craig,
foreword. | Jones, Serene, 1959–, foreword.

Title: Christian ethics in conversation : a festschrift in honor of Donald W. Shriver
Jr., 13th president of Union Theological Seminary in the city of New York / edited
by Isaac B. Sharp and Christian T. Iosso ; forewords by M. Craig Barnes and Serene
Jones.

Description: Eugene, OR : Cascade Books, 2020 | Includes bibliographical references.

Identifiers: ISBN 978-1-7252-7360-3 (paperback) | ISBN 978-1-7252-7361-0
(hardcover) | ISBN 978-1-7252-7362-7 (ebook)

Subjects: LCSH: Shriver, Donald W., Jr. (Donald Woods), 1927-.

Classification: BX4827.S535 C49 2020 (paperback) | BX4827.S535 C49 (ebook)

Manufactured in the U.S.A.    09/30/20

# Contents

# Forewords

*[handwritten: past glory]*
*[handwritten: New church and social challenges]*
*[handwritten: prophetic stand]*

*[handwritten: Civil rights struggles and of 1960's and post Viet Nam era of 1970's  16 years]*

## IN HONOR OF DONALD SHRIVER

As these essays will make clear, Dr. Donald Shriver led Union Theological Seminary through some very difficult years. At any point along the sixteen years of his presidency, decisions could have been entirely guided by an irretrievable past glory. That would have left it irrelevant to the new theological, ecclesiastical, and social challenges that were multiplying by the end of the last century. But President Shriver kept steering into the wind, even amid severe internal conflict and dire financial challenges, with a clear vision of ensuring that Union Seminary would continue to be as faithful in its present as it was in its past.

Union Seminary's current prophetic standing in our country is a tribute to his indefatigable devotion to turn the school's face forward. Today, President Serene Jones is leading Union into a future that not even Don Shriver could have imagined. But that's the way it hopefully works with the succession of leadership. We are always standing on the shoulders of those who came before us. *[handwritten: essays depict the challenge Shriver faced]*

As a seminary president who is a generation behind Don Shriver, I have learned from the examples of those who have gone before me in offering leadership to theological education. It seems we are all always honoring a tradition where the theological giants once roamed, and trying to ensure it can be reformed for a new day. No one was more focused on that goal than President Shriver. He was called to take Union beyond the so-called glory days of Reinhold Niebuhr and Paul Tillich into a future inscribed by the Civil Rights struggles of the 1960s and the post–Vietnam War era of the 1970s.

These essays depict the challenges Don Shriver faced as he navigated relentless choices that were certain to disappoint someone. Some of these challenges just come with the job. One of my predecessors at Princeton Seminary described his presidency as playing multiple chess games at the same time with faculty, students, trustees, donors, alumni, and the larger church. They're all very interested in your moves on someone else's board. And they tend to think there is a moral imperative behind every choice, even if you're really just trying to pay the bills. The media, and now social media, is always waiting to pass around commentary over the fallout that inevitably follows when hard choices are made.

Some of the essays in this Festschrift celebrate the wisdom of President Shriver's choices, but such triumphal crowns are only bestowed by historical perspective. The challenge of being a seminary president is that the choices have to be made in real time. Often they come fast when you're not prepared, they come with competing advice, and even as you make the choices you realize they have more implications than you can now see. It will be a long time before you know if they really were wise decisions.

In the meantime, a president has to "absorb the hostility," as Don Shriver would sometimes remark. I haven't had the opportunity to talk to him about his use of that phrase, but I assume what he means is the president of a school is not allowed to be reactive. We can never tell a disgruntled professor, "I'm working my ass off for you so give me a break." I tried that once, and it was clearly not my best moment in leadership. Instead, school presidents learn to cultivate a non-anxiousness that frees them to say, "Your opinion is important, but there are lots of other opinions that we have to consider. I'll let you know what we decide." Someone has to break the cycle of hostility and complaint, and it falls to the leader to model that for the whole school. Don Shriver is legendary for his gift of self-restraint through more trials than most presidents will ever see.

While spending their best energies insuring the health and future of their schools, seminary presidents are also called to be a public witness of their theological tradition's deepest convictions. I don't know of anyone who did that better than Don Shriver. One of the essays in this book is written by Professor Cornel West, who affirms all that this southern, white, seminary president did to help Union Seminary model the very values to which he testified in his many public engagements.

Every seminary president lives with competing temptations either to be absorbed by the internal demands of leading a school or to be absorbed by the opportunities to speak in the public realm. It is especially tempting to be on the road when things are difficult at home. But as Professor Gary Dorrien's essay reveals, Don Shriver saw the struggles within his own campus as a lab school for the larger dynamics being played out in society. It was by attending to the challenges of leading a school out of its proud

*Institutional leadership is hard work*

liberal WASP past that he found the courage to struggle with what it means to speak credibly and prophetically into today's multicultural society. That's why he hired Cornel West and many others who brought a new voice to Union Theological Seminary.

At their best seminary presidents inherit a theological and institutional tradition, look around to account for the new challenges and opportunities, and then exhaust themselves to ensure the seminary is heading toward a future filled with hope. Along the way, the financial viability of the school, the unity of the faculty, and the spiritual and theological formation of the students is always on the president's desk if not heart. It's a hard job. And those of us who have it look to sources of inspiration. I am grateful that Dr. Donald Shriver is one of mine.

—M. Craig Barnes, President, Princeton Theological Seminary

*Countless tributes*

## THE PROPHET, PASTOR, PUBLIC PRESIDENT

For those of us who know him, the countless tributes in this volume are not the least bit surprising. As any one of the stellar and diverse essayists featured herein could tell you, Don Shriver is a rare treasure. His illustrious career includes stints not only as an esteemed pastor, long-term activist, and accomplished scholar in the field of Christian social ethics, but also as an incisive public intellectual and Christian statesperson. He has borne invaluable witness to the rapidly vanishing possibility of an unflinchingly self-critical version of U.S. American citizenship, and his shining example of an "honest patriotism" is second only to his exemplary courage as a denominational and ecumenical leader. All people of faith would do well to learn from the ongoing legacy of a life so richly *and* prophetically lived; such examples are few and far between.

Don Shriver has even more to teach those of us who have been called to the endlessly challenging job of the seminary presidency. As my esteemed colleague M. Craig Barnes so poignantly captures in his introductory tribute, in addition to making the difficult choices necessary for any institution hoping to keep the lights on, seminary presidents must inevitably face the additional challenge of serving a variety of particularly passionate constituencies with deeply held (and often competing) convictions about each and every institutional decision. There is no one that I know of who has navigated the communal complexities of the job with as much grace and success as Don Shriver.

Institutional leadership is incredibly hard work, academic institutions bring their own distinct set of challenges, and faith-based academic

*denominational and ecumenical leader*

*prophetic lived faith*

institutions often merely up the ante. Many scholar-activists and pastor-academics capable of rising to the task of leading a school don't take that step. If his astounding career as a renowned scholar, devoted activist, beloved pastor, and eminent social ethicist was rare, rarer still was Don Shriver's willingness to answer the vocational call to lead an independent seminary in the middle of one of the rockiest episodes in our nation's history. Union Theological Seminary is very lucky that he did.

Under Don Shriver's courageous servant leadership, not only did Union survive upheavals in its institutional life, the school was in fact transformed into a thriving contemporary version of itself that few observers could have anticipated. President Shriver garnered the respect of the Union faculty and the board of trustees during a tense season—no small task in either case—and oversaw the building of an all-star faculty that was the envy of seminaries and theological schools the world over. Never content to rest on his laurels, he also continued his work as a public intellectual and theologian while serving as President of Union—a remarkable achievement in its own right.

For me, as for so many others, Don Shiver's profound public example is made all the more meaningful by his personal generosity and private support. For a current seminary president, the close proximity of a previous president can be a challenge. I am incredibly fortunate that Don Shriver is nothing of the sort. In my role as the current President of Union, I count his support, his advice, his guiding wisdom, his pastoral care, and his willingly-shared knowledge of Union's history among the most important supports that I consistently receive.

As Don is so fond of admitting, no one, especially presidents, can accomplish his or her goals alone. In this regard, it is essential that I also thank Don's life-long partner, Peggy, for her long-standing service to Union, to the church, and to the City of New York. An accomplished professional in her own right, Peggy never hesitated to be fully present to the Union community and to Don, whatever the occasion might be. Along with Don, she has also been a constant and loving friend and supporter. They are deep partners, a blessed twosome, and without question, Union is better for their partnership. I for one am thankful for their lessons as well as the strong models their lifework has to offer. I am far more grateful, though, for their learned support and, most of all, for the grace of their warm friendship.

—Serene Jones, President, Union Theological Seminary in the City of New York

*how a progressive seminary
can be redreamed*

# Editorial Preface

## A FESTSCHRIFT OR A TOOLBOX?

One purpose of these essays is to help in the task of "ecumenical and inter-professional formation for prophetic Christianity." That phrase is from Donald W. Shriver Jr., and honoring his leadership—particularly his presidency of Union Theological Seminary in New York City—is what has brought this diverse group of contributors together. This is not a usual academic Festschrift, where colleagues in a given field or institution contribute in appreciation for a completed career. Some do focus on Union Seminary, though partly in a "how to" kind of way, showing how a progressive seminary can be maintained and re-dreamed at the same time. Our hope was that Union's experience and learning would be applicable to other seminaries and divinity schools.

But other essays relate to the ongoing struggle for reconciliation among people who have hurt one another, both on the individual level and as nations, races, and regions. The contributors here are coworkers and sometimes coauthors in the broad field of social and moral transformation. Donald Shriver, in any case, did not stop work at his formal retirement and continued his vocation of peacemaking internationally and in relation to the criminal justice system. A conference he led in 2013, for example, helped reform rules in New York State to keep younger prisoners out of general population and restrict the de facto torture of prolonged solitary confinement. Among the participants from overseas were Christopher Marshall, with whom Shriver had examined the rehabilitation system of New Zealand, and Derick Wilson, a practitioner of peace education and restorative justice involved in the reconciliation process in Northern Ireland. Before that, in 2010, his writing and speaking were instrumental in the formation

xiii

of an international network, the Ara Pacis Initiative (named for a Roman altar to peace), devoted to forgiveness between historic enemies.[1]

In 2020, some of the largest divisions in the United States reflect tragically unfinished business between the races, classes, and genders, work on which Donald Shriver and Union Seminary have both been long active. Dean Thompson traces Don's drive to broaden the Christian social vision from his church beginnings in the segregated Navy town of Norfolk, Virginia, through his work on labor justice and civil rights, to his remarkably frequent appearance in the Letters column of *The New York Times* from the 1970s to the 2010s. Those enduring commitments and visibility gave him the capacity to guide Union Seminary through the financial and identity pressures that mirrored the social changes of those years.

How can people of faith and conscience be prepared to contribute prophetic energy to the vast social and environmental reconstruction that is needed today? Lessons are drawn here on (1) the formation of leaders for a diverse and creative church, (2) the ways that theology and ethics must bridge to other disciplines, and (3) the prophetic calling of the church itself, faced with ethno-nationalism around the world and, in the US context, the identification of many "Evangelical Christians" with an amoral and virtually a-religious leader. There are also (4) key areas where Don Shriver's books and projects provide entree points for understanding current and future struggles.

I came to know President Shriver when he chaired the Presbytery of New York City's Social Concerns Committee, which met in his office at Union in the early 1980s. While navigating all the academic and administrative issues Gary Dorrien insightfully describes, President Shriver also served on and chaired the Presbyterian Church's Advisory Committee on Social Witness Policy (ACSWP). In this he helped unite traditions of social teaching in a denomination that had only reunited in 1983 (after splitting over slavery in 1860); he had served on the national mission board of the "Southern" Presbyterian Church in the U.S. when he was in North Carolina and Georgia. He was instrumental in strengthening the church's labor policy and its welcome of immigrants to a more racially and economically inclusive community, and had also chaired a major Ecumenical Consultation for his denomination.[2] In the mid-1980s, as an anti-apartheid activist,

---

1. For a brief report highlighting Donald Shriver's role, see Iosso, "Forgiveness Lesson."

2. The "Report of the Ecumenical Consultation," held on October 27–31, 1975, was subsequently approved by the 1976 General Assembly of the Presbyterian Church, U.S., and demonstrates the ecumenical leadership Shriver brought to the Union presidency. It contains an extensive record of that church's ecumenical history and renewed commitments.

it seemed natural to be arrested with Dr. Shriver and others for blocking the South African consulate, though not too many seminary presidents (or faculty) did likewise. Nor was I surprised in 2003 when Donald Shriver and three other faith leaders made televised apologies to the Iraqi people for the invasion that had begun to tear their country apart.

Having been inspired to attend Union Seminary partly by Dr. Shriver, I was also prepared to see him co-teaching with professors from Columbia University and Jewish Theological Seminary. One of those courses was on business ethics, co-taught for eight years with economist James Kuhn, then Vice-Dean of Columbia Business School. From that collaboration they co-authored, *Beyond Success: Corporations and Their Critics in the 1990s* (1991). As a denominational corporate social responsibility staffer, I had been one of those critics, and they had invited me to address their class. Several essays in this book testify to the fruitfulness of those co-teaching ventures. Don Shriver has called his teaching method that of intentional conversation, but it was also to model conversations between communities and disciplines, illuminating the moral and—for those with imaginations—faith elements within different professional vocations.

Because of my involvement with Donald Shriver in his service to the church, Presbyterian and ecumenical, and my appreciation for his collaborative work on economic and urban ethics not fully represented elsewhere in this book, I would draw attention to several key areas of engagement.

Donald Shriver's work on economic ethics and values goes back to one of the components in his "Experimental Study of Religion and Society," begun at North Carolina State University early in his career. An initial Study-Research Group on Ethics and Decision-Making in the Textile Industry developed into the major interdisciplinary, *Spindles & Spires: A Re-study of Religion and Social Change in Gastonia*. Though published in 1976, this updating of Liston Pope's *Millhands & Preachers: A Study of Gastonia* (1942) was done with two sociologists and large teams of student interviewers from 1964 to 1975, and looked carefully at the role of values, ideology, and black as well as white churches. Dean Knudsen, one of those coauthors, wrote, "for the intellectual challenges and exchanges we shared . . . that was one real highlight of my academic career."[3]

---

3. Knudsen, email to Donald Shriver, November 1, 2017. Knudsen also provides a brief account of the critical interplay among the coauthors who "shared a general (Protestant Christian) faith but with unique traditions and theological positions . . . (which) often led to basic but conflicting . . . assumptions about human nature and society . . ." Their book benefited from research on both social structure and belief as determinants of human behavior.

During that period Shriver also wrote an ethics introduction for the famed Presbyterian Covenant Life curriculum series, *How Do You Do, and Why?* (1967), and an adult education book, *Rich Man, Poor Man* (1972), which lifted up enduring concerns for the use of money by individuals and institutions, the impact of competition on character, and costs of inequality. He contributed chapters to strategic action books by both Presbyterian denominations, "Bread for Life: The Churches and Rural Economic Development," in *The Church and the Rural Poor* (1975), and "Questions Christians Ask about World Hunger," in *Beyond Survival: Bread and Justice in Christian Perspective* (1977). He underlined the international dimension of these matters in lectures to the Mar Thoma Church in India, published as *The Gospel, the Church, and Social Change* (1978).

*Beyond Success*, with Kuhn, is a major effort to "redefine the managerial story" as a way for business executives to find value, and shared values, within the sometimes oppositional "new constituencies" that have challenged corporate autonomy and power over the past fifty years.[4] A key part of the movement for corporate social responsibility has been based in church investment agencies, but the book looks at unions, consumer groups, and environmental organizations as well. Beyond expressing the democratic values of "associationalism" held by most US Americans, these groups are increasingly entrepreneurial in shaping the public debate that, in turn, shapes regulation and taxation. Whether stockholders or stakeholders, they want more than the procedural or universal justice of either Robert Nozick or John Rawls. Critical constituencies seek "justice as a social good that all members of society should enjoy."[5] Shriver and Kuhn show the corporation to be a social enterprise that cannot hide behind abstract economic defenses of "the market" or of individualistic relativism. Not only are large businesses interdependent with government and cultural forces, but they depend upon—or should depend upon—communal structures and the "old individualism" based on ideas of calling, character and virtue.[6]

Alongside Kuhn's account of how businesses actually seek to temper the free market and maintain authoritarian styles, Shriver uses Alisdair MacIntyre to argue for moral narratives that combine principle and purpose and accountability to larger communities. A manager is a professional to the degree that they serve a public good beyond wealth and power alone. To illustrate how outside constituencies can improve business practice, even

---

4. Kuhn and Shriver, *Beyond Success*, 21, vii.

5. Kuhn and Shriver, *Beyond Success*, 90.

6. Kuhn and Shriver, *Beyond Success*, 205.

painfully, they look at the boycott of Nestle products over its marketing of infant formula in poorer countries.

The Nestle boycott case famously involved marketing formula as a symbol of modernity to consumers who were often without clean water or who would dilute the formula when funds were low, causing widespread malnutrition. Nestle management was largely insulated from shareholder initiatives under Swiss law, and held—dogmatically—that its responsibility was only to make a good product, regardless of its end use. Finally, after great reputational erosion, the Nestle managers recognized a larger "web of responsibility"—and Shriver and Kuhn use that phrase of Carol Gilligan's to make explicit some feminist values in the analysis.[7] Their final chapters recommend various ways to change the "balance of social power," while recognizing that hierarchy and "moral mazes" will remain a big part of business culture.[8]

Toward the end of the 1990s Shriver was effectively asked, "so how is globalization affecting your hopes?" In a response to David Krueger's upbeat case in *The Business Corporation & Productive Justice* (1997), Shriver points to the continued worship of profitability, inequality, and short-term disregard for "the biophysical limits of earth."[9] In later conversation I witnessed in the Society of Christian Ethics with Max Stackhouse, a longtime dialogue partner and chief proponent of globalization as new form of civil society, Shriver judged the neo-liberal market framework inadequate to protect the common good, despite economic advances in China, India, and other places. This was consistent with Shriver's contribution to the denominational social policy, "God's Work in Our Hands (1995)," which became a linchpin for more egalitarian or communally oriented compensation policy, and his leadership on "Building Community among Strangers (1999)," which looked at the challenges of overcoming class, race, gender, and religion-based divisions in a US society increasingly affected by globalization.[10]

To turn briefly to Donald Shriver's work on urban ethics is to note two more collaborative efforts. The former is his book with sociologist, Karl A. Ostrom, *Is There Hope for the City?* (1977). Part of the Westminster series Biblical Perspectives on Current Issues, it contains an exegetical case for the proposition that "for its historical development, the Christian Church

---

7. Kuhn and Shriver, *Beyond Success*, 293.

8. Kuhn and Shriver, *Beyond Success*, 281, 263.

9. Krueger, Shriver, and Nash, *Business Corporation*, 110.

10. These and other social policy statements are excerpts from the *Minutes of the General Assembly* of the Presbyterian Church (U.S.A.), Louisville, KY, in the years given.

is unimaginable apart from *both* Jerusalem and Rome."[11] It also treats the church in Geneva and Puritan Boston, before moving to the current day, partly through imagined dialogue, and partly with data from an "Urban Policy Study" analyzing Raleigh, Durham, and Chapel Hill in 1971. There may be hope for the city if its abandonment by white flight and other disinvestment is reversed, and if a sense of meaning for the urban People of God can be restored.

The second book came out of both Don and Peggy Shriver's involvement in a creative ecumenical study center that was started in 1976 at Wesley Seminary in Washington, DC, The Churches' Center for Theology and Public Policy. Coauthored with Ronald D. Pasquariello and Alan Geyer, both theologically trained public policy experts, *Redeeming the City: Theology, Politics, and Urban Policy* (1982) draws partly on Shriver and Ostrom's 1977 book for its Biblical vision. The bulk of the book is a critique of federal urban policy under Presidents Carter and Reagan with some international and state level comparisons. That race and poverty are so intertwined was seen to call for not only more justice in planning and development, but also a "symbolic consensus," at least among Christians about the values at stake.[12] The book then includes excerpts from then-recent statements by eleven denominations.

Noting these collaborative ventures is to honor Donald Shriver's energy for integrating Christian ethical reflection and practical challenges in almost every area of life!

Not all the persons contacted in the several years of this book's development could write for us, but I thank them nonetheless, and those whose work we could not use in the form available. I spoke with several "Southern" Presbyterian pastors who participated with Donald Shriver in the Fellowship of Concern that did so much to change the theology and ethics of that denomination. I contacted educators who worked with Don on a pioneering internet course on "World Citizenship" in which he reached back for a long interview with his own former professor, Robert Bellah. And among former co-teachers, Ellis Cowling, University Distinguished Professor at North Carolina State University and an expert on natural resource use, spoke of the concept of "transdiscipinarity," his term for bringing natural and social scientific perspectives to bear together without blurring methodologies. We deeply regret the limits required for publication on the number and length of contributions.

---

11. Shriver and Ostrom, *Is There Hope for the City?*, 48, their italics.

12. Pasquariello, Shriver, and Geyer, *Redeeming the City*, 121.

Peggy Shriver was very encouraging from the first, and captures some of the work of institution-building in the poem "Circling Back to Campus":

> Buildings made by human hands have worn and crumbled some,
> While bold new structures, giving shape to bolder dreams, appear.[13]

In discussion of this book, Donald Shriver has said that his calling in both church and seminary was "to reconcile and teach reconciliation." Those broad co-teaching interests show how much he wanted to explore what reconciliation would look like in a range of disciplines, but they of course did not exhaust his own wide-ranging historical approach to Christian ethical scholarship and engagement. Just as Don's work in reconciliation brought him onto the platform near Martin Luther King Jr. in his early college years, and onto the screens of Iraqi televisions in the early 2000s, so prophetic Christianity must be ecumenical, inter-racial, and international. That is the message of this book, and these essays tell us much about how it can be embodied.

—CHRISTIAN T. IOSSO, PhD, UNION THEOLOGICAL SEMINARY IN THE CITY OF NEW YORK, 1991

## BIBLIOGRAPHY

Iosso, Christian. "Forgiveness Lesson for General Assembly." *Presbyterian Outlook*, June 23, 2010, 18–19.

Knudsen, Dean. Email to Donald Shriver, November 1, 2017 and November 20, 2017, letter.

Krueger, David A., Donald W. Shriver Jr., and Laura L. Nash. *The Business Corporation & Productive Justice*. Nashville: Abingdon, 1997.

Kuhn, James W., and Donald W. Shriver Jr. *Beyond Success: Corporations and Their Critics in the 1990s*. New York: Oxford University Press, 1991.

Pasquariello, Ronald D., Donald W. Shriver Jr., and Alan F. Geyer. *Redeeming the City: Theology, Politics, And Urban Policy*. New York: Pilgrim, 1982.

Shriver, Donald W., Jr., and Karl A. Ostrom. *Is There Hope for the City?* Philadelphia: Westminster, 1977.

Shriver, Peggy. *The Dancers of Riverside Park and Other Poems*. Louisville: Westminster John Knox, 2001.

13. Shriver, *Dancers of Riverside Park*, 107.

## A CONVERSATION WITH THE FUTURE

Much of what you will read in the following pages will make far more sense to those with at least a passing knowledge of the history of the institution housed in the gothic castle situated between Reinhold Niebuhr Place and 122nd street in Manhattan. Good stories, like good histories, need context after all. For the uninitiated, then, the description of Union Theological Seminary as a place that "publicly prides itself on being the home of liberals, radicals, and cutting-edge innovators" should paint at least enough of a picture to begin getting a feel for the school's oeuvre.[14]

Institutions, of course, are conservative beasts by their very nature and precious few that last long are as radical as they fancy themselves. But radicalism is also contextual and viewpoint-dependent; radicals are judged on a sliding scale. When viewed against the backdrop of much of the U.S. American theological mainstream—a context that, on the whole, arguably has become more conservative in the past several decades than ever before— Union's reputation as an incubator for against-the-grain thinking begins to look well earned indeed. You would be hard pressed, for instance, to find a Christian institution in this country that has nurtured and produced (much less tolerated) as many activists, feminists, liberationists, pacifists, socialists, womanists, and other political, social-ethical, and theological troublemakers as the fiercely independent school that sits at 3041 Broadway in New York City. There simply is no other place quite like it.

Perspicacious readers undoubtedly have begun to anticipate by now some of the particular challenges that inevitably come along with such a unique reputation. The school, for one of the more obvious instances, has never been an easy one to lead. As an institution with a treasured tradition of anti-institutionalism, Union Theological Seminary indeed has often been the perfectly paradoxical stuff of many an administrator's worst nightmares.

This was certainly the case when Donald W. Shriver Jr. became the thirteenth president of the periodically anarchic school in 1975. As Gary Dorrien masterfully narrates in chapter 2, the newly appointed president would soon learn that the board had initially offered the job to another candidate who (perhaps wisely) had turned them down based on the (essentially accurate) sense that the place was functionally "ungovernable."[15] To make matters worse, as Milton McGatch methodically recounts in chapter 3, for a variety of reasons both internal and external, Union was in such bad

---

14. Shriver, "President as Pilgrim," 132.
15. Shriver, "President as Pilgrim," 117.

financial straits when Shriver arrived in the mid-1970s that many observers believed it was on the brink of total collapse . . .

The school, needless to say, would not ultimately fall into financial ruin. And as the aforementioned chapters by Dorrien and McGatch will attest, to his immense credit, President Shriver was an enormous part of the reason why it would not—a judgment seconded and sustained time and again throughout the following pages in reflections offered by Bill Crawford, James Forbes, Thomas Johnson, Larry Rasmussen, Phyllis Trible, Janet Walton, and Cornel West. For a revealing vignette capturing the true extent of the personal investment that the struggling school exacted from its dedicated leader, look no further than Lionel Shriver's essay "The Fourth Child," which will banish any lingering doubts about the depths of the president's devotion to keeping the place afloat.

As various stories scattered throughout this collection will make clear, pulling Union back from the brink of the abyss was neither easy nor simple. Rife with any number of challenges that look insurmountable even in retrospect, the Shriver era was a particularly thorny time in the life of the school, even for a place with such a "persistently cantankerous history."[16] In retrospect, the history of the sixteen-year period from his arrival in 1975 to his retirement from the presidency in 1991 reads like an ongoing series of crises narrowly averted, conflicts delicately navigated, and criticisms painfully weathered.

Fortunately, he did not have to go it alone. Dr. Shriver will be the first to admit that the rescue mission was never anything less than a team effort. His roster of supporting players, many of whom are featured or mentioned throughout these pages, was impressive by any measure. As anyone who has ever met them also knows, the Shrivers are a two-for-one-package: you do not get Donald W. Shriver Jr. without the path breaking denominational leader, brilliant poet, and consummate partner Peggy Shriver. In fact, without Peggy you likely don't get a Shriver presidency *at all*—more on that later—and you certainly do not get one in which it is possible to invest the time and energy necessary for successfully steering the school through sixteen tumultuous years. For this reason and more it is neither inaccurate nor inappropriate to suggest that Peggy Shriver is as big a reason that Union did not go to ruin on the Shrivers' watch as the man with the title—an assessment he would no doubt cosign.

The Shriver's partnership and the support of an all-star cast of Union faculty, board members, and administrators go a long way toward explaining both how the Shriver presidency helped Union survive and how President

16. Shriver, "President as Pilgrim," 133

Shriver survived the Union presidency. In my view, however, there is at least one more contributing factor worth mentioning that certainly didn't hurt and that also helps clarify why it is that a Festschrift for a Christian ethicist includes chapters by, among others, a biologist, a diplomat, a Jewish seminary chancellor, and an engineer and a dentist.

At its best, Christian social ethics is an interdisciplinary pursuit that draws freely upon the collective wisdom and expertise of a variety of intellectual traditions and fields of study—from history, political science, philosophy, critical theory, and theology to sociology, economics, ecology, and community organizing—with the ultimate goal of bending the structures of society toward justice.[17] The danger of course is dilettantism, which perhaps is why most (good) social ethicists stick with one or sometimes two subdisciplinary lanes, and the temptation toward intellectual arrogance seems especially strong among those whose goal is no less than justice anyway. But with diligent study, adequate training, and a bit of luck, the potential upshot of the ethicist-as-interdisciplinary-justice-seeker model is a field whose worthy goals are paired with the intellectual humility to acknowledge that, in reality, making use of the best tools and learning from the best practices that a variety of professional and academic disciplines have to offer is probably the best way to reach its lofty aims. This is Christian ethics in and as conversation, this is the Shriver approach to social ethics, and this a way of doing ethics that undergirds and makes possible this volume and everything in it.

The following essays offer ample proof of the importance of interdisciplinary, cross-cultural, and inter-faith conversations for Donald W. Shriver's career and lifework. But while working on this book, I came across another instance in which a different kind of conversation concretely informed the Shriver-ian ethic that I cannot resist pointing out, because, at least in my eyes, it might just be the most striking example of all.

In 1996 *Theological Education* invited Dr. Shriver to reflect on his tenure as a seminary president. The resulting essay, "The President as Pilgrim," unceremoniously narrates the countless "peaks and valleys" of his years leading the school, highlighting several of the most defining problems of the era and acknowledging a few of the ways in which the institution met and overcame these challenges on his watch. Over the course of that retrospective account, it becomes increasingly and abundantly clear what an enormous asset a conversational approach to Christian ethics truly was

---

17. A definition I learned from my doctoral advisor, Gary Dorrien. For better-stated versions, see Dorrien, *Economy, Difference, Empire*, x; and Dorrien, *Social Ethics in the Making*, 1.

for his work as president, especially when having to reckon with the school's persistent—and, at the time, potentially catastrophic—financial struggles.

With the interdisciplinary skills that came along with his training as a social ethicist, for instance, President Shriver was well suited for distinguishing between competing goods. Recognizing that there would be some unquestionably difficult trade-offs that would ultimately be worth it, he also knew that there were some goods without which the others would not matter. When it came to the most difficult financial decisions, in his retelling, there were thus two specific strategic moves that he could not and would not ever endorse: moving the school out of its historic location in Morningside Heights and jettisoning either the MDiv of PhD program. For President Shriver, the rationale was simple. The nonnegotiable commitment to staying put and to retaining both major degree programs grew directly from his stubborn insistence on forcing the school to face up to the problem of how best to "give voice to the voiceless."[18] And refusing to entertain either alternative was simply the only reasonable result of engaging in a kind of conversation that many institutions seem either incapable or unwilling to attempt, a conversation with those who are perhaps most voiceless of all: future generations.

Union was responsible to its future students, Union would not be Union if it sacrificed either its home or its most historically significant programs, and that was that. In President Shriver's judgment, there was no way around it:

> Liberation theology speaks much of giving voice to the voiceless, but environmentalists have taught us to think generationally about the future . . . nothing seems to divide presidents and boards from faculty and students so much as this division of responsibility. Boards, in fact, need on occasion to protect presidents from their natural preoccupation with today's crisis, pushing them to see that crisis in relation to a long-range future and to get prepared, if necessary, for some decisions that bring pain to the present generation for the sake of a future one. There is no doubt among most observers of Union in the seventies and eighties that, had we simply yielded to our natural collective resistance to hard and painful budget decisions, the school would have gone out of existence, to the loss, a president has to believe, of some potential theological students who at this moment are only ten years old.[19]

18. Shriver, "President as Pilgrim," 136.
19. Shriver, "President as Pilgrim," 136–37.

I was eight years old when President Shriver wrote those words. Last May, I walked across the stage with a degree from a program at a school on a campus saved in part by a president's willingness to make administrative decisions in light of their potential effects on those who could not yet speak. I thus consider my small contribution to this volume a rare opportunity: the chance to close a circle with a gesture of thanks to someone whose work made it possible for me to pursue the degree that, in turn, equipped me for work like this.

—Isaac B. Sharp, PhD, Social Ethics, Union Theological Seminary in the City of New York, 2019

## BIBLIOGRAPHY

Dorrien, Gary. *Economy, Difference, Empire: Social Ethics for Social Justice.* New York: Columbia University Press, 2010.

———. *Social Ethics in the Making: Interpreting an American Tradition.* Malden, MA: Wiley-Blackwell, 2009.

Shriver, Donald W., Jr. "The President as Pilgrim." *Theological Education* 32, supplement 3 (1996) 115–51.

# Acknowledgments

My (Isaac's) thanks go first to the faculty, staff, and administration of Union Theological Seminary. Without the help and support of Serene Jones, Jody West, and Virginia R. Fischer in the Office of the President, and Fred Davie and Jennifer Smokonich in the Office of the Executive Vice President, this volume would not exist. My sincerest thanks as well to Emily Odom for her work connecting the dots as Director of Alumni/ae Relations and for the incredibly generous donation that she and her husband John made in support of the project upon her departure from her post at Union.

My personal involvement with the project would never have come about without the direct investment of Gary Dorrien, to whom I owe a debt of gratitude that I will never be able to repay. He took a chance on me as a doctoral student when nobody else would and I count the unwavering support and dedication he offers to *all* of his doctoral students one of the most precious gifts I have ever received and will ever receive.

Thanks as well to Dean Thompson, who became a one-man advisory board at several crucial junctures in the final stages of the project and whose timely advice and encouragement always came as a boon.

I must express my gratitude directly to George Callihan, our Editorial Administrator at Wipf and Stock, for his patient guidance through the administrative maze that multi-contributor works like these inevitably present. Thanks also to Charlie Collier for the willingness to step in as editor at such an advanced stage of the game.

For welcoming me into their home on a near-biweekly basis for the last year and for the many rich conversations that we had therein, special thanks once more go to the Shrivers and to their invaluable assistant Brenda Brathwaite. I am deeply grateful for the chance to work on this project and for the added blessing of getting to know them that came along with it.

My deepest gratitude of course belongs to Katie. Nothing that I have ever done would have been possible without her and it wouldn't have been worth it even if it were.

I (Chris) second Isaac's eloquent thanks to Union's current leadership, staff, and faculty. I would thank the initial group who shared with me the conviction that Donald Shriver's inspiring leadership and intellectual connectivity deserved more attention; Dean Thompson, Stephen Phelps, and Richard Knox, a pastor-ethicist who has worked on Dr. Shriver's bibliography. Eric Mount effectively joined that initial group, sharing with Dean long acquaintance with the Shrivers and personal knowledge of what it was to be a prophet in the South. It has been a great gift to this Northerner to see the deep love and honest regional patriotism in all three of these scholar-leaders. Along with the Shrivers, the Thompsons and the Mounts reflect so much of the heart of the church I am privileged to serve.

I am also indebted to Gary Dorrien and Eris McClure for their hospitality during visits, and for Gary's strong anchoring role, as described by and preceding Isaac's fine work. For the generosity of all involved, particularly Don and Peggy, I am very grateful.

Donald Shriver was a leader in the strong group of Presbyterian ethicists who give vital support for an institutional capacity for social ethics in the Presbyterian Church (U.S.A.), in the Advisory Committee on Social Witness Policy. The General Assembly's 2018 statement on political ethics was titled, "Honest Patriotism," partly in recognition of a shared debt to his role.

The contributors to this book have also, at least for me, changed Union. Their willingness to write, and what they have written, speak not only of struggle and survival, but of a shared growth in wisdom and forbearance. I hope the readers will experience some of that changed spirit as well, whether or not they studied at that seminary. Finally, of my own three thesis advisors, one, James Kuhn, is no longer with us, but Donald Shriver and Larry Rasmussen are, and I rejoice in that!

# Early Work

*More than ~~the~~ sixty years*

# 1

# An "Unsilent Southerner"

## and Colleagues Confront the Scourge of Racism

*Dean K. Thompson*

## I.

From his early Davidson College years to his years of old age, Donald Shriver's spiritual, ecclesial, academic, pastoral, moral, prophetic, and political lives have been passionately intertwined with racial justice visions, commitments, collaborations, and conflicts. His initial book of edited sermons was *The Unsilent South: Prophetic Preaching in Racial Crisis* (1965). Surely it curiously represented what one of Shriver's revered mentors, H. Richard Niebuhr, was fond of calling a moral act of self-definition. Today, that gripping collection dramatically points us to its visionary editor, an almost indefatigable "unsilent southerner" and public theologian who, for more than sixty years, taught, preached, lectured, published, marched, and stood up against what Martin Luther King Jr. strategically castigated as the "scourge" of racism. Shriver spent one-half of those years in the South, and one-half in the North. Throughout his "twofold" pilgrimage, he remained humbly aware that traces of racism resided in the recesses of his own being, as in all humans. Thus, he intentionally relied on the honest counsel of African

3

American colleagues and students as "a curative influence" and also to hold him accountable for his sometimes-inescapable microaggressions.[1] In his northern career, he was fond of quoting the wonderful words of his beloved colleague James H. Cone—words that captured the spirit of his entire ministry: "To be Christian and human means developing a perspective on life that includes all people."[2]

Shriver's childhood and youth took place in a segregated Norfolk, Virginia, neighborhood and school system. His father supported "states' rights" decision-making perspectives on racial matters and was critical of later civil rights marches and demonstrations. Looking back on those times, Don finds it fascinating that the white Norfolk citizens in his community had no recognizable sympathy for African Americans, living near white schools, who were bussed daily to their schools five miles away. No one ever challenged the practice. Ironically, grave concerns erupted only when white children became impacted by desegregation bussing efforts. Mary Oakes, a black domestic employee, cared for Don and his sister five and one-half days per week. She had a room, her own dishes and silverware, but was never asked to sit at the family table. Don was unaware of her dire poverty until she died from a leaky gas stove in 1949. "I was never raised to know how many injustices she suffered from."[3] And although the household of his first eighteen years was deeply nurturing, the loudest arguments he remembers, in returning home, time and again, were over civil rights issues.

The church's ecumenical youth gatherings provided a spiritual/relational gateway for Shriver's multiple ongoing involvements in racial justice and civil rights efforts. Integrated conferences, discussion groups, and worship experiences, undergirded by the church's biblical/theological witness against discrimination and degradation, dramatically transformed his upbringing in a segregated society through new relationships with African American students. Those settings enabled him to believe that the church can provide a "revolutionary critique of racism" through the people it brings together in meetings.[4] In the summer of 1948, as an officer in a regional Presbyterian youth organization, he attended an ecumenical conference at Lake Junaluska in western North Carolina. It was his watershed "occasion for racial repentance,"[5] he recalls:

1. Shriver, interview by Crowder, July 11, 2016.
2. Shriver, "Churches and Future of Racism," 156, 159.
3. Shriver, interview by Crowder, July 11, 2016.
4. Shriver, interview by Crowder, July 11, 2016.
5. Shriver, *On Second Thought*, 44.

. . . It was the first time in my life when I sat at a Communion
table in the company of African American peers, and the first
presided over by an African American minister, Lucius Pitts.
During the week of the conference, he had carefully shared with
us some of the struggles of southern black people to survive
the terrors of a segregated, discriminating society. In the communion service, as he intoned the benediction, 'brothers and
sisters, go in peace,' something had happened to me beyond
mere knowledge that something terribly wrong had been done
to the black people of American society. I had participated in a
meeting of white and black people around a table prepared long
ago as a door into a different kind of society.[6]

Shriver's ecumenical youth conference Communion epiphany fed into
his election as moderator of the Assembly's Youth Council of the Presbyterian Church, U.S. in 1950; his election as chair of the United Christian
Youth Movement in 1951, where he met Peggy Ann Leu, his future wife; and
his election as a delegate to the Third World Conference of Christian Youth,
held in South India in 1952.

As a result of his budding leadership roles, Shriver frequently recruited
mentors Pitts and James McBride Dabbs, of the prophetic Southern Regional
Council, to serve in tandem as empowering youth conference leaders. A
major personality within the SRC, Dabbs became highly regarded as one of
the South's foremost advocates for integration. Organized in 1944 to promote racial equality and opposition to racial violence, the SRC was among
the South's leading progressive bodies—a bi-racial but mostly white coalition
composed of men and women, educators, lawyers, newspaper editors, and
Christian ministers. Dabbs was president of the SRC, 1957–1963, traveling
and speaking widely, while exhibiting passionate commitments for youth
and students, and holding memberships in the National Student Association
(NSA) and Students for a Democratic Society (SDS). Dabbs also supported
the Delta Ministry and the Fellowship of Southern Churchmen, whose
leaders included Howard Kester, Miles Horton, and Nelle Morton. Many
of those involvements and relationships flowed crucially into Shriver's own
developing racial visions and quests for justice and mercy. Dabbs, who died
in 1970, abided with Shriver as an important mentor/colleague throughout
the national civil rights era. And across his adult years, Don's speeches and
teachings have underlined Dabbs's remarkable insight regarding his region's
segregationist folkways. Southern society didn't want us to talk about justice,
said Dabbs, because, then, we would have to confront injustice.

6. Shriver, *On Second Thought*, 44–45.

## II.

Yet, talking about justice and confronting injustice persisted as indispensable components in a momentous period of American history. Shriver points to the pivotal event that separated our segregationist past from our integrationist possibilities as May 10, 1954, the Brown vs. the Board of Education, Topeka, Kansas, decision of the U.S. Supreme Court on desegregation. The 1954 Southern Presbyterian Church General Assembly also officially declared: "Enforced segregation of the races is discrimination which is out of harmony with Christian theology and ethics."[7] However, as Shriver has observed, when that same General Assembly sent down to its presbyteries (regional governing bodies) a recommendation to approve reunion with Northern Presbyterians, vehement resistance to Brown throughout the South became a powerful force in making reunion impossible for nearly three decades hence.

A Davidson College history major, Shriver joined several of his peers in attending Union Theological Seminary in Richmond, Virginia, now Union Presbyterian Seminary. There, Ernest Trice Thompson, an eminent church historian, was a source of foundational substance, strength, and direction for Don's own maturing and fervent dedication to racial equality. Thompson would eventually teach more students of ministry than any professor in the history of Southern Presbyterianism. Among his many contributions was his persistent and influential opposition to his denomination's traditional advocacy for "the spirituality of the church"—meaning that the church had no calling to address political and social matters. Thompson insisted that, while the church is surely spiritual, it does not have a non-political character and should not isolate itself from the world of moral and political issues. Shriver's senior year at Union, under the prophetic tutelage of Thompson and other teachers committed to desegregation and anti-racism, was the initial year of the Civil Rights Movement, 1955–1968.

Both mentor Thompson and mentee Shriver, alongside many trusted colleagues, became strategic and unsilent Southern collaborators for racial justice throughout that epoch. As a competent and confident cadre of progressive allies, they heralded and followed the brave leadership of Martin Luther King Jr., who had commenced his public ministry at the Dexter Avenue Baptist Church, Montgomery, Alabama, in May 1954, the same month of the Brown decision, and who, on December 5, 1955, as the head of the Montgomery Improvement Association, delivered a speech calling for a bus boycott that ignited the torch for the Civil Rights Movement.

7. Shriver, *Unsilent South*, 15.

Incarcerated with Ralph Abernathy in April 1963 for nonviolent demonstrations against segregation, King composed a nation-shaking "Letter from Birmingham City Jail" that was spread across the world and became monumental among protest literature. Shriver was personally touched that King's classic epistle had expressed thanks to unsilent southerners Ralph McGill, Lillian Smith, Harry Golden, and his mentor James McBride Dabbs for writing about "our struggle in eloquent, prophetic and understanding terms."[8]

An exemplary leader among Shriver's unsilent pastor friends was J. Randolph Taylor, then pastor of The Church of the Pilgrims, Washington, D.C. At the behest of Walter Fauntroy, who helped coordinate Dr. King's historic March on Washington, August 28, 1963, Taylor joined the local planning committee and was instrumental in recruiting Southern Presbyterians to participate, even though the Inter-Church Relations Committee of the Presbyterian Church, U.S. had issued a "pastoral letter" news release urging members not to attend the mass demonstration. Many Presbyterian leaders acceded to Taylor's prophetic call, including Carl R. Pritchett, pastor of the Bethesda, Presbyterian Church in nearby Maryland, whose soul-wrenching sermon, "The March on Washington," was published by Don Shriver.[9] Three months later, Shriver, Taylor, Ernest Trice Thompson, F. Wellford Hobbie, and Vance Barron led others in founding A Fellowship of Concern whose six hundred members advocated racial reformation, and offered pastoral care and financial support to Southern Presbyterian ministers who were being harassed or who had lost their pastorates for preaching and teaching against racism and segregation.

On May 7, 1964, a delegation led by Taylor represented A Fellowship of Concern in a meeting with U.S. Senators Hubert H. Humphrey, Thomas Kuchel, and Paul Douglas. They presented a plea containing 435 signatures from southern states and the District of Columbia. Their statement requested an end to the filibuster against the impending Voting Rights Act. Senator Humphrey later observed that of the many presentations he had heard regarding the Voting Rights Act, "none was more moving and meaningful" than the one lifted up by A Fellowship of Concern.[10]

Less than two months before his tragic death in 1968, Dr. King sent a letter to the office of A Fellowship of Concern, First Presbyterian Church, Staunton, Virginia, thanking its membership for an apparently generous

8. King, "Letter from Birmingham City Jail," 298. See also Calhoun, *With Staff in Hand*, 140–41.

9. Pritchett, "March on Washington," 99–108.

10. Thompson, "SFTS Celebrates J. Randolph Taylor's Presidency."

contribution to the Southern Christian Leadership Conference, which he served as president. "SCLC has continued adherence to Negro-white unity, nonviolence and responsible militant action," he wrote.[11]

> We know these principles have won landmark victories and will continue to be effective tactics to realize justice and equality . . . When our staff works in the rural South to register voters or educate illiterates, or when it organizes in the teeming ghettos of the North, it is strengthened by the undergirding of your support. We are proud that you are one of us in this, the great Democratic crusade of our era.[12]

A Fellowship of Concern was clearly embedded in the heart and soul of Don Shriver's collection of sermons, *The Unsilent South* (1965), which had been lifted up courageously from Presbyterian pulpits between the years of 1957 and 1964. The nineteen chosen from the 125 persons who had submitted manuscripts likely were members of the prophetic Fellowship, or recipients of its pastoral care, or both. Unsurprisingly, Shriver dedicated the volume to Ernest Trice Thompson "and all others who hunger and thirst after righteousness."[13] Thompson, who was referred to as "Dr. E.T." by students and many admirers, had touched the lives of these published biblical/theological expositors in manifold ways. He was sensitively aware of the price they and other kindred preachers had paid, and the risks they had taken as faithful stewards of the boundary-breaking teachings of Jesus and the Old Testament prophets before him. In the Foreword, Thompson informed readers "that a number of the preachers—four, to be exact—were forced out of their pulpits because of the words which they had spoken. But many of us know in detail," he reported, "the stories of ministers who, because of similar faithfulness, have suffered disappointment, frustration, the alienation of friends, rejection and hatred of their neighbors, disruption of congregations, economic pressure, harassment, and the threat of physical violence."[14]

In the book's introduction, Shriver held that God had fortified these preaching mentors by means of the Bible, the Holy Spirit, the church, and history "in their dynamic interrelationship."[15] These preachers served in a regional context where the institution of slavery had imposed "a quarantine

---

11. King, Letter to A Fellowship of Concern, February 9, 1968.

12. King, Letter to A Fellowship of Concern, February 9, 1968.

13. Shriver, *Unsilent South*, 6.

14. Thompson, "Foreword," 9–10.

15. Shriver, *Unsilent South*, 18.

on the mention of social issues in church gatherings."[16] Drawing on King's "Letter from Birmingham City Jail," Shriver praised these several prophets for rightly criticizing the church for living as a "thermometer" rather than as a "thermostat" of society. He also commended their invaluable involvement "in an attempt to act justly and mercifully, truthfully and lovingly, boldly and humbly, as a prophet and as a priest, as a churchman and as a citizen, as a servant of all . . . and as a slave of none."[17]

After a soft-spoken Unitarian Universalist minister, James Reeb, was murdered in Selma, Alabama, due to his participation in a civil rights march, Shriver traveled there with seven other members of A Fellowship of Concern, where they attended a memorial service in the Brown Memorial Church. Then, the delegation, including Ernest Trice Thompson, Randy Taylor, Wellford Hobbie, and James Luther Mays, joined Dr. King, Walter Reuther, president of the United Automobile Workers, and other nationally prominent leaders, marching three-abreast to the county courthouse where they spoke out for voting rights. At day's end, Shriver and friends listened to a car radio broadcasting President Johnson's urgent plea to Congress for the Voting Rights Act. Of that impassioned speech, Shriver recalled that, "Its most memorable moment came when, in his Texas drawl, the President quoted the song that we sang in Selma that very day: 'We *shall* overcome,' he said, with emphasis."[18]  *Selma March*

Because of Shriver's participation in the Selma march, some Presbyterian elders in Raleigh, North Carolina, unsuccessfully sought to have him fired from his campus ministry position at North Carolina State University. As an employee of the Presbyterian Synod of North Carolina, he felt protected from their plot. A similar mid-1960s racist bullying experience happened to one of Shriver's closest friends, George Telford, then a university minister in Auburn, Alabama, when several Presbyterian elders charged him with "race mixing." Telford had pastorally orchestrated a worship service and dinner conversation for white Auburn University students and black students from nearby Spellman College. A governing synod committee appointed to investigate the complaint and chaired by Albert C. Winn, an eminent minister, theologian and Southern Presbyterian leader, vindicated Telford's campus ministry and interracial decisions. Telford said that the synod's investigation had affirmed "the unsegregatable communion of the saints."[19]

16. Shriver, *Unsilent South*, 16.

17. Shriver, *Unsilent South*, 17, 19, and 166.

18. Shriver, "Churches and Future of Racism," 152.

19. Shriver, "Two saints"; Shriver, Letter to Dean K. Thompson, March 10, 2015; Shriver, interview by Crowder, July 11, 2016.

Malcolm Calhoun—a champion of civil rights, a revered and tireless bureaucratic servant-leader, and a political catalyst in the councils, boards, agencies, and assemblies of the Southern Presbyterian Church—invited Martin Luther King Jr. to speak at his denomination's Christian Action Conference scheduled to meet at the Montreat Conference Center, Montreat, North Carolina, in August 1965. Don Shriver, who served with Calhoun and others on the PCUS Christian Action Committee, which was responsible for the gathering, admired the self-effacing Calhoun as a Presbyterian minister who had "the backbone of a prophet."[20] Historian John Herbert Roper likewise praised Calhoun as a "Southern reformist" who gave his energies to a "frontal assault" against Jim Crow segregation.[21] Calhoun attended the Selma memorial service for the martyred James Reeb, and also marched there with Shriver and friends who had come as a delegation from A Fellowship of Concern. Shortly thereafter, he was among the proponents, indeed, a behind-the-scenes architect for, the 1965 General Assembly's approval of civil disobedience as a "last resort" measure regarding racial injustices.[22]

Dr. King's commitment to speak at the annual Christian Action Conference was aided by Andrew Young, James McBride Dabbs, and Frank Porter Graham, former president of the University of North Carolina, U.S. senator, and U.N. ambassador. However, many opposed the invitation at the 1965 General Assembly, just a few months before the Montreat gathering. During the plenary debates, Dr. L. Nelson Bell, a retired missionary surgeon and the father-in-law of the renowned evangelist Billy Graham, spoke for those who feared King's visit would foster dangerous divisiveness. Bell expressed grave concern for "ministers in the South . . . living with this [race] problem everyday and who are earnestly trying to solve it."[23] He suggested that the General Assembly Division of Christian Action should write to Dr. King and explain that his speech would seriously increase the racial tensions faced by southern ministers. Bell argued that he was pleading on behalf of several Alabama pastors, including his own son who warned that King's presence and oratory would "pour oil on the flame. . . and would set us back."[24] However, the General Assembly Standing Committee on Church Relations unanimously upheld the invitation, and the elected commissioners adopted the Standing Committee's report 311–120.

20. Shriver, "Preface," xv.
21. Roper, "Introduction," xi.
22. Calhoun, *With Staff in Hand*, 118–28.
23. Calhoun, *With Staff in Hand*, 131.
24. Calhoun, *With Staff in Hand*, 131.

On August 21, Dr. King arrived a day late in Montreat, because of his peacemaking efforts at the Watts uprisings in Los Angeles. His great contemporary, Malcolm X, had been assassinated (February 21); and American combat troops had arrived in Vietnam (March 8). Malcolm Calhoun received death threats for his leadership. The Ku Klux Klan threatened to disrupt the packed auditorium, and placed flyers on the automobile windshields of conferees, stating: "J. Edgar Hoover calls Martin Luther King the greatest liar in America."[25] Gayraud S. Wilmore, an eminent Presbyterian historian, theologian, and interpreter of black religion and the black church, gave three addresses at the conference, one of them filling in at a time frame originally scheduled for King. By design, the meetings were attended by many high school and college students.

King's speech, "The Church on the Frontier of Racial Tension," rang forth as a preeminent example of his preeminent oratory:

> It may be true that you cannot legislate integration, but you can legislate desegregation.
>
> It may be true that morality cannot be legislated, but behavior can be regulated.
>
> It may be true that the law cannot change the heart, but it can restrain the heartless.
>
> It may be true that the law cannot make a man love me, but it can restrain him from lynching me.
>
> . . . We shall overcome because the arc of the universe is long, but it bends toward justice.
>
> We shall overcome because Carlyle is right: 'No lie can live forever.'
>
> We shall overcome because William Cullen Bryant is right: 'Truth, crushed to earth, will rise again.'[26]

Eerily, presciently, he extolled the sacrificial lifeblood of civil rights martyrs:

> Before the victory is won, some, like Mrs. Viola Liuzzo, or Rev. James Reeb, Jimmy Lee Jackson, Medgar Evers, and many others, may have to face physical death. If physical death is the price that some must pay to free their children from a permanent death of the spirit, then nothing can be more redemptive.[27]

---

25. Calhoun, *With Staff in Hand*, 137.
26. King, "Church on Frontier of Racial Tension," 11, 23.
27. King, "Church on Frontier of Racial Tension," 23.

With the Watts uprisings as his dramatic backdrop, King addressed some of the root causes of poverty. And in a following question and answer period, he offered a window into his coming prophetic opposition to the nation's Vietnam warfare. " . . . I cannot sit idly by as a minister of the gospel and as a concerned citizen and not say something about Vietnam,"[28] he declared:

> I think it is an absolute necessity for people of good will, for people of moral integrity, to speak on this issue and bring again the insights of our Christian faith to bear on the problem of war . . . I said to President Johnson yesterday, ' . . . I have to speak and take a stand on this issue, and I want you to understand that I will do it whenever I feel that the moment is a propitious moment to do it.'[29]

As a panelist at the final session of the conference, Don Shriver spoke with inspiring appreciation about how King and Dabbs had been able to shake hands at a session with the press the day before, in what was the latter's "natural ecclesiastical habitat" of Montreat, "the citadel of our particular denomination."[30] He expressed personal gratitude that King had praised Dabbs and other prophetic southern writers in his "Letter from Birmingham City Jail." Shriver mused: "I'm not sure that before yesterday, Martin Luther King knew quite in the fullness of the fact that James McBride Dabbs is a Southern Presbyterian."[31] Shriver also lauded another brave civil rights figure, Dr. Ernest Bradford, who had traveled from Selma's Northern Heights Presbyterian Church. "At the same time, in the same place, was Ernest Bradford who is one of Dr. King's men on the fighting line in Selma, Alabama," Shriver thankfully observed.[32] "He is a Southern Presbyterian pastor. Somehow it is right . . . that these men should meet in Montreat."[33]

However, in the aftermath of the unity-building hope bestowed upon the Christian Action Conference by Dr. King, Gayraud Wilmore, Malcolm Calhoun, and others, a backward-looking and interestingly-named Harmony Presbytery, in the Synod of South Carolina, represented many who held fiercely to cherished segregationist convictions—to what Ernest Trice Thompson frequently labeled as "the dead hand of the past."[34] Harmony

---

28. King, "Church on Frontier of Racial Tension," 33.

29. King, "Church on Frontier of Racial Tension," 33, 34.

30. Calhoun, *With Staff in Hand*, 141.

31. Calhoun, *With Staff in Hand*, 141.

32. Calhoun, *With Staff in Hand*, 141.

33. Calhoun, *With Staff in Hand*, 141.

34. See Thompson, "Conflict and Change (1914–1945)," 176. See also Thompson, "Ernest Trice Thompson," 7.

Presbytery dispatched a blistering overture of resentment to the 1966 PCUS General Assembly, requesting that the planners responsible for bringing Drs. King and Wilmore to the conference "be censured and reprimanded for their action."[35] King was ridiculed as one who aligned "race against race," and "as a civil rights agitator and political figure rather than as a religious leader."[36] Wilmore was especially reviled for his conference address asserting that although "the Church cannot and should not 'program' interracial marriages . . . neither should the Church place the least impediment in its way."[37]

Recalling the vociferous nature of more than a few critics, the mild-mannered, unflappable Calhoun peacefully reported: "In any case, our Division went ahead with its work, more inspired by Dr. King than intimidated by reactionary opposition."[38] Yet, many of us, in the grass-roots situations of those crisis-crossroads days, who were struggling with the tugs and pulls between inspiration and reactionary opposition, were also standing in the need of more systematic Christian nurture and educational materials. How in the world should Christians equip one another in the art of moral decision-making amid whirlwind contexts infused with threatening tensions and disagreements, and pulls and pushes in multiple directions?

A generative and wide-ranging response to that question came forward in the mid-1960s, when the Board of Christian Education of the Southern Presbyterian Church recruited Don Shriver to produce a study book on ethics and moral decision-making for Christian youth through its landmark educational series for congregations, branded as *The Covenant Life Curriculum*. During that period, president James I. McCord of Princeton Theological Seminary judged that *The Covenant Life Curriculum* and *The Faith and Life Curriculum*, of the Northern Presbyterian Church, were arguably the most outstanding, sweeping, intergenerational educational projects for congregations undertaken by American Presbyterians.

Published in 1966 as *How Do You Do—And Why?*, Shriver's volume and extensive leaders' guide provided critical ethical guidance for teenagers throughout the South. I say this out of a memorable caldron of personal experience. When I was a year-long seminary intern at First Presbyterian Church, Hickory, North Carolina, 1967–1968, my wife Rebecca Thompson and I used Shriver's study for teenagers in sustaining our youth group through twelve months of social unrest, which reached a boiling point,

35. Calhoun, *With Staff in Hand*, 142.
36. Calhoun, *With Staff in Hand*, 142.
37. Calhoun, *With Staff in Hand*, 136.
38. Calhoun, *With Staff in Hand*, 142.

immediately after the murder of Dr. King in Memphis, when U.S. National Guard troops were brought in to preserve peace, assisted by an interracial collection of community adults and youth.

It is historically noteworthy that Don Shriver, whose breakthrough march toward justice and mercy was set forth from interracial youth meetings, studies, and worship services in 1948, was requested, a generation later during the Civil Rights Movement, to provide a similar hands-on ministry for youth. Grounded in Shriver's own deep biblical theology and faith, our students in Hickory and their peers throughout the Southern Presbyterian Church were asked to wrestle with these developmental topics: becoming a "fellowship of forgiven sinners"; the ministry of reconciliation; the barriers of age, class and race; life in a Christian family; human sexuality; peer group relations; human behavior that divides; outlooks on work, money and poverty; war and peace; the "politics of God" and human politics; and the impact of Christ's resurrection on our hopes for now and the future.[39]

Near the center of *How Do You Do—And Why?* is a section titled "The barrier of race," where Shriver confronted the "disease" of racial prejudice with a winsome blending of the pastoral and the prophetic.[40] He challenged young people to see themselves as valuable participants and leaders in the church's "mission of transformation" in a social order where taxis, restaurants, cemeteries, schools, toilets, hotels, waiting rooms, and drinking fountains were segregated by both custom and law.[41] He pointed to the tenth chapter of Acts as a revealing case study of the Holy Spirit's power to defeat racial prejudice between Jews and Gentiles in the early Christian church. Moreover, he would employ this passage in teaching and preaching against racial prejudice throughout his career. Although Christ's disciple Peter, a Jew, had professed contempt for uncircumcised, Sabbath-breaking, pork-eating Gentiles, the Holy Spirit had moved him, through an empowering vision, to visit and eat with a Gentile leader and believer named Cornelius in his home, where they came to see one another as brothers, and where Peter remained with the previously disdained Gentile family for days.

The same Holy Spirit who had broken down the dividing walls between Peter and Cornelius in ancient times, said Shriver, also promised to help contemporary youth break down their own separating customs, where God's people of different colors had been taught not to eat together in their homes and in the fellowship halls of their churches. Citing Dr. King's sober imperatives in "Letter from Birmingham City Jail," Shriver cautioned:

39. Shriver, *How Do You Do, and Why?*, 51, 156, 179–89.
40. Shriver, *How Do You Do, and Why?*, 94–95, 98.
41. Shriver, *How Do You Do, and Why?*, 94–95.

If today's church does not recapture the sacrificial spirit of the early church, it will lose its authenticity, forfeit the loyalty of millions, and be dismissed as an irrelevant social club with no meaning for the twentieth century. Every day I meet young people whose disappointment with the church has turned into outright disgust.[42]

*[handwritten annotation: a "headlight" — not a "taillight."]*

Thus, teacher Shriver implored students to help inspire and lead the church toward a new day, living as a "headlight" rather than as a "taillight."[43]

Meeting with international church leaders in the 1966 Geneva World Council of Churches Conference on Church and Society, Shriver engaged in conversations with many critics of the war in Vietnam. The next year, April 4, 1967, exactly one year before his death, Martin Luther King Jr. lifted a prophetic address heard around the world, in opposition to the war and linking it to the American Civil Rights Movement. He pictured the war as a tragic and misguided adventure that was drawing "men and skills and money like some demonic destructive suction tube."[44] He prophesied that "We were taking the black young men who had been crippled by our society and sending them eight thousand miles away to guarantee liberties in Southeast Asia which they had not found in southwest Georgia and East Harlem."[45] "*Somehow,*" King preached, "*this madness must cease.*"[46] Reinhold Niebuhr hailed King's controversial stance as "nonviolent resistance to evil" and as "a real contribution to our civil, moral and political life."[47]

The following month, Shriver, who had been drafted after WWII for brief service in the U.S. Army, chaired the committee that dealt with the Vietnam War at the Southern Presbyterian General Assembly meeting in Bristol, Tennessee. In his Foreword to Malcolm Calhoun's memoir, he recalled how meticulously Calhoun had supplied his committee "with painful data."[48] Shriver was the major author of the adopted resolution, "Vietnam: Some Questions for Christians." Among the questions were:

> If we believe that God is sovereign in human history, can we believe that our own nation needs restraining by other nations? Must we not also believe that others need restraining by us? What is God telling us through our fellow Christians around the

42. Shriver, *How Do You Do, and Why?*, 102.

43. Shriver, *How Do You Do, and Why?*, 99.

44. King, "Time to Break Silence," 233.

45. King, "Time to Break Silence," 233.

46. King, "Time to Break Silence," 238.

47. See Oates, *Let the Trumpet Sound*, 439.

48. Shriver, "Preface," xv.

world who criticize the American role in this war? Even if we believe that some wars are 'just,' what limits must we observe in visiting destruction on enemies? Do we have to grieve the death of one Vietnamese child as much as that of one American? Are we truly committed to the Gospel of Jesus Christ as good news to communists as well as capitalists, to the stranger as well as the friend? Are we truly reconciled to the One who is not the enemy of our enemies or even the enemy of his own enemies?[49]

Nearly one-half century later, Shriver recalled: "They were all difficult searching questions. They are as pertinent now as in 1967. They belong in our conversations about wars past and present."[50]

*E. T. Thompson*

III. *"The dead hand of the past"*

I represented Union Seminary, Virginia, as a page at that rather contentious General Assembly, which pitted ultra conservative PCUS personalities such as G. Aiken Taylor and Robert Strong in visceral opposition to progressive standouts, epitomized by Shriver and his career-long colleague Randy Taylor. As I saw it played out, their polar viewpoints on Bible, theology, ecclesiology, racial justice, war, the Delta Ministry, and other crucial matters relating to the church's role in the world amounted to "the dead hand of the past" over against a prophetic hope for a new day. As a younger member of A Fellowship of Concern, I was fortunate to attend its final meeting in 1968, held at a western North Carolina retreat center during my Hickory internship. The large gathering was filled with many who had attended the 1967 General Assembly and who had become mentors and ministerial role models, such as Shriver, Taylor, John Lyles, Wellford Hobbie, George Telford, James Mays, John Anderson, and Ernest Trice Thompson. There, in what proved to be the final year of the historic Civil Rights Movement, the members declared that their institutional mission of extending financial and pastoral support to pastors in racial crisis had finished its helpful course, and voted to discontinue as an organization.

Returning to Union Seminary in Richmond, the fall of 1968, I enrolled in a Senior Social Ethics Seminar taught by Don Shriver, which proved personally to be the most significant course I have taken. The times, which were violent and tumultuous, demanded the course. Commander of the American Nazi Party, George Lincoln Rockwell, had been assassinated in Alexandria, Virginia, in late August 1967. Turbulence had occurred in one

49. Shriver, "Readers' Outlook," 4.
50. Shriver, "Readers' Outlook," 4.

hundred American cities following Dr. King's murder in Memphis, April 4, 1968. Robert F. Kennedy had perished in Los Angeles, on June 5, 1968. That same spring, Rebecca Thompson and I had witnessed student convulsions in Paris, brought forth by anti-Vietnam War hostility, environmental concerns, university chaos, and massive strikes. Furthermore, our ethics professor had just returned from the Democratic Party National Convention in Chicago, August 26–29. Outside the Convention, especially in Grant Park, twenty-three thousand members of the Chicago Police Department and the Illinois National Guard, using tear gas, mace, and billy clubs, had collided on national television with ten thousand civilian demonstrators, many of whom were students attending a convention that had been planned by the National Mobilization Committee to End the War in Vietnam.

Shriver's pedagogy was captivating. As our instructor, he also saw himself as a research colleague. That is, he distributed to our seminar papers he had written about the Convention as examples of the reflective papers on critical issues he expected us to produce, particularly those impacting the impending U.S. presidential election. He had come to the Convention as one of two Democrat delegates from North Carolina committed to the presidential candidacy of Senator Eugene McCarthy of Minnesota. Race and war were front and center. During the Convention floor debates on the Credentials Committee report, a young black delegate had remarked to Shriver bitterly: "Poor people look at this Convention on television and say: 'This is not my world. And the decisions these people make are not my decisions.'"[51]

In a paper titled "Memo to a Young McCarthyite from an Older One," our riveting professor affirmed McCarthy's "conviction that world peace demanded some drastic changes in this nation's policy in Vietnam."[52] Shriver depicted the Convention's rejection of the minority plank against the war as an act of aggression against our future. He upheld McCarthy's judgment that the war had become "increasingly senseless," and he applauded our student generation as those who had "learned to cherish personal experience and personal relationships as the indispensable kernel of a worthwhile existence."[53] We had "learned to test the worth of any political order by its impact on the lives of persons," said Shriver.[54] By becoming politically involved against the war, we had made it clear that in this world every person's "'thing' is interwoven with that of his neighbor," and "that the value of every

51. Shriver, "Justice and Compromise at Chicago," 1.
52. Shriver, "Memo to a Young McCarthyite," 7.
53. Shriver, "Memo to a Young McCarthyite," 4, 9.
54. Shriver, "Memo to a Young McCarthyite," 4.

single person registers in the decision-making of the society as a whole."[55]
We truly resonated with and were nurtured by his serious affirmations,
for we were convinced that opposition to the Vietnam War had become
a significant part of Dr. King's legacy at the near-end of the Civil Rights
Movement. The war's pronounced racism was also for us a burning matter, as a disproportionate number of young blacks and poor whites were
being sacrificed on a hubristic political altar. We further believed that an
abhorrent just-beneath-the-surface feature of U.S. foreign policy relating to
Southeast Asia was that Asian life was considered to be cheap life.

By Shriver's design, our class research projects were group-centered
rather than individual-centered. As he freely shared his own current research and commentaries, he insisted that we, too, would draw and share
from everyone's research and written reflections, often working in teams.
My own major shared research included papers on "George Wallace and the
'Law and Order' Issue"; reflections as a Democratic Party precinct worker
in the 1968 presidential election; and a collaborative term paper, "The Right
Finds George Wallace," which included interviews, required by professor
Shriver, with Wallace party workers and leaders. Two of our seminar par-
ticipants brought helpful political reflections from their involvements in
Union's Church and Society Intern Program, which Shriver directed. Gerald
"Rusty" Butler served in the Washington, D.C. office of Wisconsin Sena-
tor William Proxmire, and Joseph Condro with Illinois Senator Charles H.
Percy. The following year, Charles N. Davidson Jr. interned with Wisconsin
Senator Gaylord Nelson.

Our church and society mentor also insisted that ethics has intimately
to do with action. He said that in America, our power to reason and our
power to act are intimately associated. He looked at thinking without doing
as potentially fruitless. Directing us to T.V. Smith's *The Ethics of Compromise*, he described politics as the "art of the possible," and amused us with
an ironic truth: although politicians are expected to compromise, they are
frequently criticized for doing so.[56] In his shared paper, "Justice and Compromise at Chicago. . .," he instructed us with Smith's prudent advice that,
above all others, the politician should be "unafraid of ambiguity."[57] Indeed,
the politician "has to start with the ambiguous; for he begins with individuals or groups at each others' throats . . . "[58] With Smith, Shriver taught us
that when astute political leaders turn ambiguity into compromise, "each

55. Shriver, "Memo to a Young McCarthyite," 5.

56. Thompson, Seminar Notes. See Smith, *The Ethics of Compromise*.

57. Shriver, "Justice and Compromise at Chicago," 11.

58. Shriver, "Justice and Compromise at Chicago," 11.

party to a conflict gives up something dear, but not invaluable, in order to get something which is truly invaluable."[59]

Shriver grounded us in his teacher H. Richard Niebuhr's *Christ and Culture* and in Reinhold Niebuhr's *Moral Man and Immoral Society*, two of the most important American treatments of Christian ethics to this day. Because most of us were preparing for parish ministry, we dearly appreciated knowing that the brothers Niebuhr and Don Shriver had grounded their illustrious academic careers in parish ministry. Shriver had served as pastor of Linwood Presbyterian Church, Gastonia, North Carolina, 1956–1959, where he had joined a picket line on behalf of a labor union. He currently served as minister to students at North Carolina State University, and as Director of its Program on Science and Society and Urban Policy in the Raleigh, Chapel Hill, and Durham Research Triangle region. Shriver's abilities in integrating the classic disciplines of theological education with contemporary events, issues, and pastoral ministry seemed exceptional. His multiple vocational involvements fed us with measures of hope and possibility for our own vocational journeys and creative possibilities. *Social Ethics*

A key aspect of his Social Ethics Seminar for future pastors was Shriver's crucial question, "What can you do to cultivate ethical reflection in congregations?" His advice hovered over me for thirty years of parish ministry. Never stop asking questions about ethical matters, he said. Ask questions, which will dig into the specific challenges facing church and society. Don't have the answers in your back pocket, he warned. Point to the church as the place where questions can be asked, which can't be asked elsewhere. Use case studies as a strategy for getting people to reflect on decision-making and commitments. He urged us to serve as caring conduits for reflection on current community crises, and to try to address crises, if possible, before they occur. Thus, we were required to ponder a prophetic sermon by Robert H. Walkup, preached at First Presbyterian Church, Starkville, Mississippi, 1962, and published in *The Unsilent South*. Walkup's sermon on the segregation issue had been steeped in pastoral relations developed over a period of years. In his typical spirit of authentic humility, Shriver also told us to establish and cultivate the "right to be wrong." The spirit of liberty, he counseled, is the spirit that is not overly sure of its rightness. We are founded in the forgiveness and grace of God, he reminded us, and therefore we don't have to be right. Such an attitude will release people to think, he promised.

Girding us for our future work as Southern Presbyterian pastors, Shriver provided rich written reflections about changes that had occurred in the denomination's social witness during the Civil Rights Movement.

*Cultivate the "right to be wrong."*

59. Shriver, "Justice and Compromise at Chicago," 11.

*"Unafraid of ambiguity"*

Historian Shriver's starting point was gleaned from the ever-trustworthy mind of James McBride Dabbs, who had said, not unlike William Faulkner: "We are historical creatures. We carry the past into the future, and it carries us."[60] Yes, Shriver echoed. The "best 'use' of history" is "to look at history with a realistic eye in order to eye the future yet more realistically . . . "[61] Whereas the dominant motto of our ecclesial past had been "The Unchanging Witness of the Southern Church to an Unsocial Gospel," theological and ecclesiological issues had surfaced in the civil rights period that placed four liberating questions on center stage.[62]

First, he asked, "Are there any social questions without moral and spiritual dimensions?"[63] No, he concluded. In the 1950s and 1960s, a new generation of church leaders had convincingly shown the relation of the Gospel to culture and the church to society in a way radically different from the segregationist past that had been hidebound by the doctrine of the spirituality of the church. With Dr. King as their bold inspirer, he and colleagues had declared: "nothing human is immune to the re-forming power of the Word of God."[64]

Second, he asked, "What is the usefulness of social conflict for the achievement of a new order of social justice?"[65] From the Montgomery bus boycott onward, Dr. King and followers in black congregations had usefully embodied and employed what Reinhold Niebuhr had prophetically called creative coercion. Demonstrations of all kinds had forced Southern whites and, indeed, an entire nation to come to realistic grips with social conflict's creative capacity to bring about social justice. Creative conflict had led to successes that would have been unlikely apart from its infusion into the social order. Dr. King and the Old Testament prophets had given the Civil Rights Movement an operating philosophy poignantly described by Don Shriver. "Demonstrate visibly against injustice, call the evil of discrimination by name and stand out against it, and perhaps enough white people will get the message to change things. Use . . . conflict with the system to get conscientious people to change the system."[66] Our conflict with the present

60. Shriver, "Thirty-Five Years of Change," 1.

61. Shriver, "Thirty-Five Years of Change," 1.

62. Shriver, "Thirty-Five Years of Change," 2.

63. Shriver, "Thirty-Five Years of Change," 8.

64. Shriver, "Thirty-Five Years of Change," 9.

65. Shriver, "Thirty-Five Years of Change," 9.

66. Shriver, "Thirty-Five Years of Change," 10.

social order can be a valuable instrument in producing "a more just future social order," Shriver testified.[67]

Third, he asked, "What alliances with non-church institutions are appropriate to the church's ministry in Southern society?"[68] Shriver pointed to the NAACP, the federal food stamps program, day nursery programs, low-income housing programs, and urban coalitions seeking economic improvements for the poor as helpful allies that the church should cultivate for cooperative engagements. When possible, the church would be pragmatically wise to align also with forward-looking business leaders who were accommodating their enterprises with efforts for justice and mercy. Whenever ethically possible, the church should encourage new and fruitful alliances with the university, the voluntary association, the government, and the corporation.

Fourth, he asked: "Can wisdom from the past become a true servant of the future?"[69] Black citizens had rightly protested against a future that would repeat the sins of the past. Will the Southern Church foster wise decision-making in helping to build a different South, heretofore unimagined? Will the church help communities seek industrial growth for the benefit of both the rich and the poor? Will the church work against society's nagging temptation to lower taxes at the expense of educational equality? Will the church envision itself as an aesthetic instrument of protection against urban blight? Will the church assist a highly competitive society in clinging also to the time-honored virtue of neighborliness? Will the church help a nation of achievers in reclaiming our biblical memory "that we are creatures of grace and forgiveness?"[70] If the church was unwilling to do so, Shriver cautioned, religion in the South was in danger of becoming the non-reforming protector of those "who are afraid of change and who use religion to justify and to fuel their fear."[71]

Perhaps my most vivid memory of Don Shriver's Social Ethics Seminar is the abiding picture of one who challenged us to yearn for a faith that equipped us for change instead of a faith that protected us from change— one who demanded, in his own dynamic words, a "rethinking of . . . romanticized versions of the Southern past; rethinking and restudying the social pertinence of the Bible; rethinking the individualism of our creeds, the moralism of our ethics, the abstractness of our preaching, and the club-like

67. Shriver, "Thirty-Five Years of Change," 10.
68. Shriver, "Thirty-Five Years of Change," 11.
69. Shriver, "Thirty-Five Years of Change," 12.
70. Shriver, "Thirty-Five Years of Change," 13.
71. Shriver, "Thirty-Five Years of Change," 13.

nature of our church activities."[72] And to our rethinking he commended huge doses of relentless experimentation.

Our response to his remarkable teaching and leadership was to elect him to serve as our commencement speaker for our graduating Class of 1969.

## BIBLIOGRAPHY

Calhoun, Malcolm. *With Staff in Hand*. Laurinburg, NC: St. Andrews College Press, 1996.

King Jr., Martin Luther. "A Time to Break Silence." In *Testament of Hope: The Essential Writings and Speeches of Martin Luther King, Jr.*, edited by James N. Washington, 231–44. New York: HarperSanFrancisco, 1986, 1991.

———. "The Church on the Frontier of Racial Tension." Unpublished speech, Montreat Conference Center, Montreat, North Carolina, August 21, 1965.

———. "Letter from Birmingham City Jail." In *Testament of Hope: The Essential Writings and Speeches of Martin Luther King, Jr.*, edited by James N. Washington, 289–302. New York: HarperSanFrancisco, 1986, 1991.

———. Letter to A Fellowship of Concern, February 9, 1968. The Archive: The Martin Luther King Jr. Center for Nonviolent Social Change, formerly Archives of Martin Luther King, Jr., Atlanta, Georgia.

Oates, Stephen B. *Let the Trumpet Sound*. New York: Harper & Row, 1982.

Pritchett, Carl R. "The March on Washington." In *The Unsilent South: Prophetic Preaching in Racial Crisis*, edited by Donald W. Shriver Jr., 99–108. Richmond: John Knox, 1965.

Roper, John Herbert. "Introduction." In *With Staff in Hand*, by Malcolm Calhoun, viii–xiii. Laurinburg, NC: St. Andrews College Press, 1996.

Shriver, Donald W., Jr. "The Churches and the Future of Racism." *Theology Today* 38 (1981) 152–59.

———. Letter to Dean K. Thompson, March 10, 2015.

———. *How Do You Do, and Why? An Introduction to Christian Ethics*. Richmond: Covenant Life Curriculum, 1966.

———. *How Do You Do, and Why? Leaders' Guide*. Richmond: Covenant Life Curriculum, 1966.

———. Interview Film by Carolyn Crowder. *At the River Oral History Project: Profiles in Quiet Courage*, July 11, 2016.

———. "Justice and Compromise at Chicago: The Case of North Carolina." Unpublished paper, 1968.

———. "Looking Around: Are Presbyterians Losing Traditions of Social Justice?" *Presbyterian Outlook* 7, no. 190 (March 3, 2008) 23–25.

———. "Memo to a Young McCarthyite from an Older One." Unpublished paper, 1968.

———. *On Second Thought: Essays Out of My Life*. New York: Seabury, 2010.

———. "Preface." In *With Staff in Hand*, by Malcolm Calhoun, xiv–xvi. Laurinburg, NC: St. Andrews College Press, 1966.

———. "Readers' Outlook.'" *Presbyterian Outlook* 196, no. 20 (September 29, 2014) 4.

72. Shriver, "Thirty-Five Years of Change," 13.

———. "Social Ethics." Seminar, Union Theological Seminary in Virginia, Richmond, VA, fall 1968.

———. "Thirty-Five Years of Change in the Southern Church's Witness." Unpublished Paper, 1968.

———. "Two Saints: A Grateful Memory." *Presbyterian Outlook* 194, no. 26 (December 24, 2012) 17.

———, ed. *The Unsilent South: Prophetic Preaching in Racial Crisis.* Richmond: John Knox, 1965.

Smith, T. V. *The Ethics of Compromise.* Boston: The Starr King, 1956.

Thompson, Dean K. "Conflict and Change (1914–1945)." In *Virginia Presbyterians in American Life: Hanover Presbytery (1775–1980),* edited by Robert P. Davis and Patricia Aldridge, 157–215. Richmond: Hanover Presbytery, 1982.

———. "Ernest Trice Thompson: Gentle Presbyterian Prophet." Part 1 of 2. *Presbyterian Outlook* 175, no. 21 (May 31, 1993) 7–9, 16.

———. Seminar Notes. "Social Ethics." Seminar, Union Theological Seminary in Virginia, Donald W. Shriver Jr., Instructor, Richmond, VA, Fall, 1968.

———. "SFTS Celebrates J. Randolph Taylor's Presidency." *Chimes,* Special Edition, San Francisco Theological Seminary (May 1994).

Thompson, Ernest Trice. "Foreword." In *The Unsilent South: Prophetic Preaching in Racial Crisis,* edited by Donald W. Shriver Jr., 9–10. Richmond: John Knox, 1965.

# Union Presidency:
# Faculty Perspectives

# 2

## Hanging in There for a Good Cause
### Donald Shriver's Presidency at Union Theological Seminary

*Gary Dorrien*

Every friend of Don Shriver's has heard his puckish, rueful, and somehow lighthearted summary of his sixteen-year presidency at Union Theological Seminary: "My chief qualification for being the president of Union Seminary was my immense capacity for absorbing hostility!" I heard it first during my first conversation with him, twenty years after I graduated from Union. I invited Don to speak at Kalamazoo College's baccalaureate service, he and Peggy Shriver got caught in slow traffic from Chicago to Kalamazoo, I improvised to a packed house until they burst through the door of Stetson Chapel, and afterwards we celebrated and decompressed at a local hotel bar. Don uncorked the "absorbing" summary after ascertaining that I had studied at Union for one year during his early presidency.

Ten years later, after I had joined the Union faculty and befriended Don and Peggy as neighbors, he told me the back-story of the summary quip. Shortly before Don retired as Union's president in 1991, a senior member of the seminary staff told him that he brought two precious gifts

*1946 — 1991*

27

to his work as Union's president: his capacity for absorbing hostility and his astonishing marriage. I cannot improve on this apt observation, and my knowledge of Don's presidency is mostly second-hand, resting mainly on treasured friendships with Peggy, him, and mutual friends. But Shriver's exemplary books on forgiveness and reconciliation did not flow only from the four debts he always cites: esteemed teachers and colleagues, his early career as a Southern Presbyterian minister in the civil rights movement, his international network of peacemakers, and Peggy. The books flowed from his resolute, caring, reconciling, hang-in-there stewardship of a famously contentious but creative and scrappy seminary.

Shriver was forty-seven years old and three years into his teaching position in ethics and society at Candler School of Theology when Union's board search committee reached out to him in the spring of 1975. He had never been a candidate for a seminary presidency or considered the possibility, and Peggy Shriver had landed a rewarding position at the Atlanta headquarters of the Presbyterian Church USA. Shriver had no connection to Union. His degrees were from Davidson College, Union Theological Seminary of Virginia, Yale Divinity School, and Harvard University. His mentors were H. Richard Niebuhr at Yale and James Luther Adams at Harvard—in the Union orbit, but not of it. He had served for three years as a Presbyterian pastor in Gastonia, North Carolina after graduating from Union-Virginia in 1956 and worked as a campus minister at North Carolina State University after graduating from Harvard in 1962. The job at NC State morphed into a dual role in ministry and teaching, where he directed social ethical studies supported by foundation grants. He published a book in 1972 on moral issues in American economic life, the same year that he moved to Candler, where he ran the Doctor of Ministry program. This record caught the attention of Union's search committee. Shriver was well aware that Union was said to be in a death spiral, because Union's inner turmoil and financial disarray were very publicly known. Union had fired its twelfth president, a liberal Episcopal bishop, in an ugly fashion that yielded months of bad publicity, and then offered the position to a candidate who turned it down after judging the school was ungovernable. In May the board offered it to Shriver, who surprised himself by accepting it, officially on July 10, necessitating a hurried move to New York.

It helped that Shriver admired Union's board search chair, John Coburn, an Episcopal rector in New York City soon to become the bishop of Massachusetts. Most important was that Peggy Shriver evoked her husband's Calvinist sense of calling by asking which of the three jobs in question—hers, his, and the Union presidency—mattered most in the long run of church history. Putting it that way settled the issue. Peggy Shriver came first to the conviction that the Union presidency was Shriver's calling. Afterward he relied on his and her belief in it throughout his Union presidency, while Peggy served as assistant general secretary for planning at the National Council of Churches. When friends and onlookers asked Shriver why-in-God's-name he took the job, he said he felt called to it. And what else? Certainly, he would say, there were other things, but all went into the calling. Accepting the Union presidency as his vocation was the sum of the whole thing; the call wasn't one factor among others. Many times during his first decade at Union, Shriver told himself that the only reason not to quit the position was that he was called to it.

Union's history as the quintessential liberal Protestant seminary became something to overcome after so-called "mainline Protestantism" began to collapse in the late 1960s. The old-line Protestant churches that fought off fundamentalism in the 1920s and came to be called "mainline" in the 1950s never outgrew their ethnic families of North European origin and failed even to replace themselves demographically. The ethnic and demographic factors alone doomed mainline denominations to breathtaking downfalls. No amount of anything else that didn't change these two factors—better theologies, charismatic ministers, programs on church growth, better hymns—would have averted the great plunge that occurred. Mainline Protestantism in the 1940s, fifties, and early sixties had immense cultural status, wealth, and ecumenical infrastructure. The National Council of Churches gathered in commanding assemblies that routinely got front page attention in the *New York Times,* and mainline denominations took for granted their custodial role as guardians of the nation's moral character. In 1960, 50 percent of U.S. Americans belonged to a mainline Protestant denomination. Then the long-coming demographic realities kicked in, necessitating steep downsizing in liberal Protestant institutions, carried out by children of the post-World War II heyday; today the mainline figure is 8 percent.

Union epitomized the trend, but Union's legendary history persuaded much of the faculty and many alums that Union should be great regardless of what happened to mainline Protestantism. Union's enrollments averaged slightly over seven hundred through the 1960s. In 1962–63 the seminary needed twenty-three months to settle on a presidential successor to Henry Pitney Van Dusen, selecting John C. Bennett, a shy, soft-spoken, highly respected, Union social ethicist and former collaborator with Reinhold Niebuhr. Bennett was mostly a caretaker of Union's long tradition of liberal evangelical presidencies under Van Dusen, Henry Sloane Coffin, Arthur C. McGiffert, and Francis Brown. But Bennett's outspoken pro-Zionism and strong advocacy of ecumenical relations with Roman Catholics broke the WASP-patrician mold at Union, very much in contrast with Van Dusen and Coffin, and Bennett went on to hire Union's first African American and female professors.

In 1967 Union had three prominent Roman Catholic scholars—Raymond E. Brown, Bernard Häring, and Hans Küng—on the visiting faculty. Increasingly the seminary described itself as ecumenical Christian, not liberal Protestant. Union worked out cooperative relationships with Jewish Theological Seminary and the Jesuit-run Woodstock College, and Bennett played a leading role in a prominent antiwar organization, Clergy and Laity Concerned About Vietnam (CALCAV). Based at Union, CALCAV was founded by Bennett, Martin Luther King Jr., Union theologian Robert McAfee Brown, Rabbi Abraham Joshua Heschel, and Jesuit activist Daniel Berrigan. For nearly two years, CALCAV beseeched King to throw himself into the antiwar movement. Bennett and Union were thus deeply involved in King's eventual attempt to fuse the civil rights and antiwar causes, until King was assassinated in April 1968. Two protest organizations at Columbia University, Students for a Democratic Society (SDS) and Students Afro-American Society (SAS), staged spectacular demonstrations at Columbia, occupying buildings. Protest wildfire spread to Union, confronting Bennett with a different kind of protest culture that treated Union administrators as part of the problem. In the midst of campus drama and prolonged meetings that yielded an assembly governance structure at Union, a faculty position for the founder of black liberation theology, James Cone, and demands for black economic development funds, Union damaged its reputation by botching its search for Bennett's successor.

A board search committee began meeting in March 1968, eventually adding two professors and two students. In March 1969 it selected Wesleyan University provost John Maguire as the new Union president. Maguire had a strong personality and a background in civil rights activism, having co-written, with Vincent Harding, the historic Riverside Speech of April 1967 in which King lambasted the Vietnam War. A faction of the Union faculty led by church historian Cyril Richardson vehemently opposed Maguire's appointment, charging that his activist background, assertiveness, youth, and lay status made him too tough a character to lead such a refined group as themselves. They protested that young faculty upstarts were trying to scuttle the seminary's patrician WASP ethos.

Maguire reluctantly declined the Union presidency and went on to a distinguished career as president of Claremont Graduate University. Union reaped the grapevine beating it deserved for the Maguire fiasco, just as it roiled internally over challenges to the seminary's self-image as a progressive institution. Union had never been as progressive or prophetic as it claimed to be. It lacked a single African American faculty member until religious historian Laurence N. Jones became Dean of Students in 1965 and religious historian C. Eric Lincoln joined the faculty in 1967. In 1970 the seminary named one of its board members, J. Brooke Mosley, as president. Mosley was the Episcopal bishop of Delaware, not a scholar, and had no background in theological education. But he radiated the personable churchy manner that senior faculty demanded, and they already knew him.

Nearly everything went badly for Mosley, except that Union never failed to attract outstanding students. His arrival coincided with the great enrollment falloff of the 1970s, which worsened year by year: 676, 628, 535, 469, and 456. The loss of income from a sharply reduced market, the recession of the same years, and diminished giving from Union's donors forced the seminary to drain its endowment to cover deficits. In 1970 the inclusive faculty list numbered fifty-five professors, counting visiting professors. Four years later the comparable figure was thirty-five. Union got a bad press detailing its downfall. The fact that the seminary fell from so high up added drama and *schadenfreude* to the story. The *New York Times* showed up at Union's commencement in 1971, producing a story about once-mighty Union floundering in financial disarray and low morale. The seminary treasurer was quoted as saying that Union would not survive if it did not gain access to government funds for higher education. The board chair said Union had to find new sources of funds because the seminary's elite donors disliked Union's left-wing turn and their children preferred secular causes. Several professors told the *Times* that Union should become a research institute with a faculty, a library, and no students. Administrators were called out and Mosley was described as "a good process man" who probably lacked a vision of Union's future but who optimistically regarded the financial crisis as an opportunity to find one.[1]

Mosley lost his optimism and the faculty in very short order. He struggled with the unwieldy assembly structure, never acquired the requisite competence or authority to lead the faculty, and ran up frightening deficits, peaking at $500,000 in his last year, in a budget of $4 million. Union historian Robert Handy, a participant in the tense faculty meetings, later recalled that some of his colleagues treated Mosley "ungraciously, talking behind his back both at the seminary and beyond."[2] Union took another grapevine beating laced with insider barbs. Bennett, having supported Mosley in the early going, provided for Handy the quotable explanation of what happened. Bennett said Mosley's lack of experience in theological education

1. Fiske, "Union Seminary," 41.
2. Handy, *History of Union Theological Seminary*, 305.

was probably too much to overcome, and he—Bennett—would not have been able to overcome the financial straits that Mosely inherited.

In 1974 the board terminated Mosley, supposedly with a year left to run, but a press release announced his firing and Mosley lost his chance to make a non-humiliating exit. Faculty social ethicist Roger Shinn filled in as acting president in the academic year 1974–75. Shinn cut the deficit in half, as mandated by the board, raised tuition, made attrition cuts, did the early legwork on the sale of Reed House, and established Union's first real faculty table of organization: six in Bible, four in history, seven in theology, and nine in practical theology, plus the visiting Luce and Fosdick professors. Shinn's competence steered Union through a wrenching transition. He was the same kind of social ethicist as Shriver, on whom Shriver depended for years to come: empirical, judicious, temperamentally moderate, grounded in the church, committed to urban ministry and ecumenical internationalism, and determined to save Union Seminary. Shinn's successor in the Reinhold Niebuhr chair, Larry Rasmussen, had similar qualities, on which Shriver similarly relied after Rasmussen joined the faculty in 1983.

When Shriver arrived in the late summer of 1975, the recession had whittled Union's endowment to $20 million—scary, but not teetering-on-bankruptcy. Union had recently lost major scholars to retirement, notably theologian Paul Lehmann, church historian Cyril Richardson, and biblical scholars James Muilenburg, John Knox, and James D. Smart, plus theologian Daniel Day Williams to a tragic early death. Ominously, it also lost a stream of others to transfer, notably biblical scholar Reginald Fuller to Virginia Theological Seminary, religious historian C. Eric Lincoln to Fisk University, religious educationist C. Ellis Nelson to the presidency of Louisville Presbyterian Theological Seminary, and sociologist of religion Robert Lynn to the Lilly Endowment. In addition, popular New Testament scholar Walter Wink was denied tenure in the spring of 1974, which roiled the Union community. Wink was a victim of Old Guard conventions at Union. Shriver felt the urgent necessity of stemming the flow of faculty losses and replenishing the faculty. Union still had a strong faculty core when Shriver arrived, headed by biblical scholars Raymond E. Brown, J. Louis Martyn, and James Sanders, church historians Robert Handy and David Lotz, practical theologians Robert Seaver, Sidney Skirvin, and Ann B. Ulanov, and theologians James Cone, Tom Driver, Beverly Harrison, and Roger Shinn.

Shriver assumed a faculty position in social ethics, in studied contrast to Mosley. He plunged immediately into replenishing the faculty, welcoming ecumenical theologian Robert McAfee Brown to his third appointment on the Union faculty, plus two young black scholars who made immense contributions to the Union community, homiletics professor James A.

Forbes and religious historian James W. Washington. Building maintenance had been deferred for years, but Union's buildings were constructed for the ages, so more deferring occurred. Shinn had already found the easy savings, so only painful savings remained for Shriver, which compounded the larger problem that the seminary culture was fractious at every level.

Social critic Garry Wills observed in *Bare Ruined Choirs* that the chief rivalry at Union pitted the faculty innovators against the faculty mandarins. Shriver saw what he meant, and tried to bridge the divide. It helped that several mandarins retired just before he got there. It hurt that the leading peacemaker on the faculty, Williams, died unexpectedly in December 1973 from surgical complications following an injury. Many surmised that the bitter acrimony on the faculty weakened Williams to the point of making him mortally vulnerable. Shriver reasoned that his training in an inherently interdisciplinary field, social ethics, suited him to mediate Union's fractious relations. What mattered was to nurture the institutional strength of Union as a whole and not let personal criticism defeat him. Shriver later recalled that the latter part was the hardest part of the job: "Becoming the object of hostility from many directions was a new experience for me. Like most southerners, I was shy of conflict, and like most pastors I wanted everyone to like me . . . I had to learn not to take personally every hostile communication that came my way."[3]

Union had dropped the assembly governance structure only two years before Shriver arrived, so many students remembered what it felt like to co-manage the school and resented losing their leverage. It took Shriver several months to absorb that many Union students had come to seminary through the antiwar movement and were determined to keep the 1960s going, halfway through the succeeding decade—their own decade, which they disliked. It felt to him that every person at Union brimmed with moral certainty about what should be done and what he did wrong. He alone, it seemed, felt unsure of himself much of the time. He did not see everything in terms of absolute moral imperatives, unlike almost everyone at Union. Shriver puzzled at how Union got like this. He had a rueful question on this theme that summarized the issue: "What ever happened to the spirit of Reinhold Niebuhr around here?" Shriver felt confident that he would have managed at the old Union that exalted Niebuhr, the theologian of ambiguity and conflicted moral responsibility. Whether he could make it at the new Union was an everyday uncertainty for him.

He eliminated longtime staff positions to close the budget deficit and was stunned by the ferocity of the backlash against him. Union got its first

3. Shriver, "President as Pilgrim," 120.

labor union as a consequence, and Shriver surprised many by welcoming it; being president did not change his mind about the importance of trade unions. At his inaugural address in February 1976, a latecomer because his appointment was late and hurried, Shriver posed three questions for the seminary to think about: What would it mean for Union to remain a center of excellence with no pretension of being preeminent? How might Union's diminished financial condition in a city facing a similar crisis offer an opportunity for Union to reclaim its Christian ethical mission? And how does the love of truth serve the truth of love? Shriver said he did not have the answers; he asked the Union community to join him in searching for them. Later he said that only the backing of the board got him through his first year at Union, as his inner commitment to being there dissolved under the battering.

It was all worth it because Union abounded with passionate faculty and students who made the place exciting, challenging, creative, justice-oriented, and forward-looking. Union had always been contentious, and now it was more contentious than ever. The difference was a byproduct of breaking the rule of the Old Guard. The breakthrough to a new Union began with Cone's appointment in 1969 and Harrison's promotion the same year to a dual position as assistant professor of social ethics and acting dean of students. It continued with the appointments of three brilliant teachers and scholars: German feminist theologian Dorothee Sölle in 1975, religious philosopher Cornel West in 1977, and feminist biblical scholar Phyllis Trible in 1978. In addition, Union restored its strength in traditional dogmatics and church history, respectively, by hiring young theologian Christopher Morse in 1974 and luring Richard A. Norris from General Theological Seminary in 1977—the same year it brought Latin American liberation theology founder Gustavo Gutierrez to the campus as the Luce Professor, his first appointment in North America. In addition to Morse's canonical courses on Calvin, Schleiermacher, and Barth, he provided expertise on the theologies of Dietrich Bonhoeffer and Jürgen Moltmann. These appointments restored and refashioned Union's claim to cutting edge importance in theology. If one wanted to study liberation theologies, no other school came close. That was already my feeling, in December 1976, regretting that I had not gone to Union, when a tragedy in my family propelled me to transfer from Harvard to Union.

Thus I witnessed, to the extent that a student could, a feminist watershed in theological education—Harrison's promotion controversy. Harrison had earned a master's degree at Union in 1956, studying under Niebuhr, Bennett, and Robert McAfee Brown. She returned to Union in 1963 to study for a PhD in social ethics and felt acutely the downfall of Niebuhr's preeminence and Union's. Union in the 1950s had seemed powerful, important, and self-confident to her. A decade later, her teachers seemed defensive and dispirited; even her mentors, Bennett and Shinn, seemed to be caught in the grip of a malaise that shrank from strong convictions. The Union to which she returned had no idea what came after Niebuhr and neo-orthodoxy. In 1966 Bennett named Harrison as assistant dean of students and instructor in Christian ethics, looking past that she was still a doctoral student. Three years later Harrison received a dual appointment as acting dean of students and assistant professor, still lacking a doctorate. Harrison was not a feminist when she joined the administration and did not know that a first wave of feminism had already occurred in American history, in the nineteenth century. She caught the second wave during her early years in the Union administration, realizing that she judged female students with sexist condescension. This realization, prompted by Betty Friedan's feminist classic *The Feminine Mystique,* led Harrison to become a powerful proponent of feminist social ethics.

Harrison was a mainstay of the faculty during a difficult period at Union, chairing its long-range planning committee and establishing a women's counseling team and women's center. In 1973 she was granted tenure, a year before she finished her doctoral dissertation on H. Richard Niebuhr's moral theology, which set off faculty muttering. She helped to launch a new organization, the Feminist Ethics Consultation, to support other feminist scholars in religious ethics, giving higher priority to solidarity work than to her own scholarship, which led to a seminary controversy over her faculty standing. In 1978 Union's committee of tenured faculty voted not to recommend Harrison for promotion to full professor. Her colleagues stressed that she had no book publications and earned tenure before she held a doctorate or published a book. They also stressed that nobody ever made an exception for them. It didn't matter that she was a stellar teacher and advisor, and a leading figure in social ethics, and that women's career trajectories of that generation were different from male scholars. In addition, some resented that the Union board bypassed the faculty in 1973 to award the Paul Tillich chair to Driver.

I was one of the pro-Harrison demonstrators at Union's tense Commencement of 1978 and struggled to fathom the opposition of teachers I admired. I had read Mary Daly's *Beyond God the Father* twice during my first week at Harvard Divinity School, enthralled at the book's feminist ferocity and its scathing Nietzschean humor. It astonished me that nobody at Harvard taught feminist theology. How could this tremendously important departure in theology be ignored? To me, Union seemed far ahead of Harvard because Union had Harrison, Sölle, West, and Cone. Moreover, in classes at Union we speculated about how black theology might change when black women began to enroll at seminaries. Nothing like that discussion occurred at Harvard in my two years there, but Union was a place that anticipated womanist theology before it was created—at Union, by Katie Cannon and Delores Williams. Many schools tried to hold on to the old liberal Protestantism after it collapsed; some had no choice but to try. At Union, only Handy and Lotz put the old liberal Protestantism at the center of their scholarship and teaching, as Handy was an expert on the American Social Gospel and Lotz was an expert on Ritschlian liberal theology. Union was committed to finding out where it needed to go, although it battled fractiously over what that meant. It had a president who radiated a Southern version of the old genteel liberal Protestantism, but who did not convey an anxiety to recover it.

The Harrison controversy dragged on for months after I graduated. The faculty studied the issue a second time and voted again to say no. Harrison had some support on the faculty, but not enough, and Shriver failed to nudge anyone to yes. Finally Shriver and the board overrode the faculty, voting in February 1979 to promote Harrison to full professor, which enraged many professors and left bitter feelings on both sides for years. The bitter feelings abated only slightly after Harrison's book on the ethics of abortion, *Our Right to Choose* (1983), became the gold standard Christian feminist text on this subject. To Shriver, the pro-Harrison arguments were persuasive and the controversy was sadly ridiculous. How could Harrison's colleagues fail to respect her immense importance to Union and to feminist theology? And how could an issue so small—a promotion for someone already tenured—be worth all the turmoil they caused? Later he recalled, "In the midst of the Harrison crisis, I remember gritting my teeth and saying to myself, 'It will take more than the difference between an associate and a full professorship to get me to quit this place.'"[4]

Shriver took warranted satisfaction that Union became a bastion of liberation, feminist, and womanist theology on his watch, and that Union rediscovered how to worship joyfully and creatively, mostly under the inspiration of worship professor Janet Walton. Nearly every search committee process contributed to campus tensions, but the same faculty made the appointment selections that changed Union. Robert Brown left the faculty again in 1979, lamenting that his teaching responsibilities at Union conflicted with his work in the global ecumenical movement, and that Union did not support his wife, Sydney Brown, as codirector of the ecumenical center at Union. Shriver deeply regretted losing Robert and Sydney Brown

4. Shriver, "President as Pilgrim," 123.

to Pacific School of Religion, as their ecumenical network, especially in Latin America, was unparalleled. But Union recovered by appointing Kosuke Koyama to Brown's position in ecumenics and world Christianity. A native of Japan, Koyama had an extensive background in World Council of Churches programs on faith and order, church and society, and world mission and evangelism. He was also theologically creative, already known for his book *Waterbuffalo Theology* (1974) before he came to Union.

The inflation of the late 1970s battered many seminaries and mortally wounded some of them. Shriver raised $6 million in the late seventies to boost the endowment, which turned out to be less than the endowment losses caused by inflation. That taught him two mordant lessons: Don't enjoy whatever fundraising success you achieve, because it will be wiped out anyway. And stop believing that raising more money will solve the budget crisis. Shriver made one of his best moves at Union before he got there, securing a commitment from the board for $600,000 for educational research. He realized that Union needed to think strategically about its mission and to acquire a knowledge base about the careers of its graduates. Malcolm Warford's research in this area helped Shriver prioritize what had to be saved when Shriver carried out the brutally painful budget cuts of 1981 that kept Union in business.

The headline cuts eliminated many staff positions and six faculty positions, which an enraged faculty reduced to four and a half positions. Union reeled from these cuts for five years while Shriver knew from Warford's research that he had bought only five years of relief. An external study by Cambridge Associates confirmed, in 1985, that the five-year estimate was right: Union was unviable and dying. This time Shriver asked the Union community to decide which of the terrible options it was least unwilling to accept. Move the school somewhere else, maybe to New Jersey? Give up either the Master of Divinity program or the PhD program? Settle for the research institute, which would at least save the jobs of a few professors? Sell the residential buildings? Or sell Union's air rights for real estate development?

Shriver convened Union gatherings at which the answer was vehemently no, no, no to every proposal. Nothing came close to being the least bad option. The Union community hated every option passionately and would not countenance a prolonged discussion of any of them. I say this with profound gratitude to the Union faculty and students of that time, because they averted the worst possibilities, even though they were wrong about all-are-equally-unacceptable. The research institute option was absolutely unacceptable, notwithstanding that it always had supporters. Giving up the master's program or the doctoral program was also absolutely unacceptable. After that, it all depended on how deeply one felt about not allowing Union to perish.

For many, then and now, it was better to let Union die than to sell residence halls or air rights, or move to New Jersey or the Bronx. Shriver mused ruefully that this supposedly radical seminary was actually deeply conservative when it came to internal change. It aspired to edgy radicalism in theory and politics while assuming a stable basis of support that did not exist. Thankfully, the intransigence of the Union community forced Shriver to make the lesser-evil decision and take responsibility for it, which he got right. He reached down for one more save-the-seminary campaign, making two decisions: He would not move the school away from Morningside Heights. And he would not give up the Master of Divinity program or PhD program. If Union rejected either given, he would know it was time to give up the Union presidency.

Most of the faculty agreed that Union needed to do what was necessary to survive as a degree-granting institution in Morningside Heights. That required more staff cuts and four years of painful proposals and counter-proposals, including four separate proposals by developers in 1987 to build a luxury condominium tower on top of Knox Hall. The previous year, Union racked up a $1.1 million deficit in its $8.6 million budget. Shriver floated the condo rescue tentatively, admitting he didn't like it. The Union community rallied forcefully against it, pleading with Shriver not to add moral bankruptcy to financial bankruptcy, and the air rights option was dropped again. It remained an off-limits idea at Union until 2014. I was a member of the strategic planning committee in 2009–10 that ruled out the condo option, came up with nothing that had any chance of saving the seminary, and thus paved the way to a last resort condo tower.

Meanwhile, in 1988, Union limped into its fateful decennial reaccreditation. Shriver tried to tell two accrediting teams that he was acutely aware of Union's financial crisis and on the verge of getting control of it. Scathing accreditation reports would not help Union to survive. Later he wished he had stalled the accreditation reviews for a year. The accrediting teams caught the fevered anxiety of Union students and faculty, and magnified it. Two harsh reviews forced Shriver to sell a huge residence hall when the market was low and before a new capital campaign had begun. Selling Van Dusen Hall required him to move eight professors and their families to another residence. Some were so bitterly hostile that Shriver counted this experience as the worst of his career. He had long accepted, by then, that a seminary president naturally loses friends every year, but nothing cut him like the way he was treated over the Van Dusen move. This sale bought ten years of survival for Union, with constant struggle over its budget, which

Shriver was too exhausted to wage. He grew tired of explaining to outsiders that scrappy independent Union had no university behind it and no denominational sponsor. By 1990, Shriver knew he would be passing the struggle to someone else, and that he would witness how it went, by retaining his faculty position. No Union president had ever finished with a stint of full-time teaching. Shriver retired as president in 1991, took an overdue sabbatical, and taught social ethics until 1996.

He knew what his greatest achievement had been and didn't care when people said it was modest or conservative: He helped Union to survive as a progressive seminary in Morningside Heights. Shriver keenly understood that many Union insiders and alums believed the school was too great to dissolve. They scoffed at his warnings about Union's financial peril, except to say that he must be doing a bad job. Shriver told himself that theological scholars are naturally averse to thinking about money. It was his job to allow them to be that way, and he was lucky to be helped by two extraordinary board chairs, Walter Burke and Thomas S. Johnson. Shriver cut special deals with Raymond Brown and James Cone to keep them at Union, telling envious faculty to swallow it. Losing Brown or Cone would have been disastrous for Union, diminishing the seminary in a fundamental way. Shriver prized the research he commissioned from Warford, employed it in the planning crisis of 1981, and regretted that Union afforded only five years of it. Warford's research showed that Union's strongest students loved New York City, held a firm sense of vocation before they got to seminary, and sustained some affiliation outside Union—usually a church congregation—that shielded them from over-identifying with Union as their home. Today, Union students still love New York City, but most come to Union as seekers with little or no religious background, and 70 percent of each Master of Divinity class embarks on a ministerial path while at seminary. Union has thus become a place that *creates* many ministers, unlike in Shriver's time—a boon for religious denominations that Shriver's persistence made possible. Today Union is thriving because it embraced multiplicity and cultural change instead of trying to preserve its past.

It wounded Shriver when observers didn't notice or later forgot that Union raised $20 million in capital gifts and $10 million in annual gifts on his watch, a record exceeded to that point only by the 1907 to 1912 era of presidents Charles Cuthbert Hall and Francis Brown, when two wealthy Union board members, manufacturer D. Willis James and banker John Crosby Brown, basically created Union's campus in Morningside Heights. Shriver reasoned that Union's "persistently cantankerous" personality had something to do with its longstanding intense polarities: churchly *and* academic, evangelical *and* liberal, pious *and* scholarly, respectable *and* radical, obsessed with New York City *and* with internationalism.[5] Shriver didn't say it to distance himself from Union or its history. Coffin and Van Dusen epitomized the "liberal evangelical" moniker they conferred on Union, and Shriver wholly identified with it. A seminary president, he would say, needs to buy into the school's history. But Shriver wearied of being asked how he planned to restore the glory days of Niebuhr and Paul Tillich. He replied that founding several kinds of liberation theology was glorious in its own way and that Niebuhr would have found fewer followers and more critics at the later Union.

Shriver's chief tormenter on the faculty once explained that Shriver was, after all, a Niebuhrian. Shriver wanted to reply that he would be thrilled not to have to be so Niebuhrian. It was the unceasing fractiousness of much of the faculty that forced him to think constantly about why individual immorality compounds in groups. Shriver treasured Niebuhr's analytical focus on power conflicts, H. Richard Niebuhr's emphasis on ethical responsibility, and Robert Bellah's sociology of religion. His theological hero, however, was Dietrich Bonhoeffer, whose *Letters and Papers from Prison* he absorbed during his early ministry at North Carolina State University. Bonhoeffer looked for God in the center of ordinary life and activity. To Shriver, no theologian compared to Bonhoeffer in teaching and showing how the Christian gospel should be lived, not merely confessed. In 1976 he welcomed Bonhoeffer's friend and biographer Eberhard Bethge to Union as a visiting professor, which deepened Shriver's fascination with Bonhoeffer. A bit of exploring revealed to Shriver that a rundown tutor's study was the chamber in which Bonhoeffer lived during his decisive three-week stay at Union in 1939. It became the Bonhoeffer Room at Union, and Shriver appreciated deeply that his friendship with Bethge linked him to Bonhoeffer.

Bonhoeffer was surely *the* theologian for Shriver, but he didn't know Bonhoeffer, a very different personality. Another kind of affinity impresses me—his personal similarity to his doctoral mentor, James Luther Adams. Students called him Professor Adams, friends called him Jim, and everyone else called him JLA. In 1981 JLA was eighty years old and Shriver sponsored a celebration for him at Union. He said that to study under JLA was to be "graciously assaulted by the booming, buzzing confusion of historic, human reality."[6] He stressed that JLA did not write very much; Shriver used the word "fugitive" to describe his essays in obscure journals. But that got Shriver rolling on a striking analogy. JLA wrote scattered essays, and Jesus didn't write anything. Jesus trusted his disciples to write things down, to the

5. Shriver, "President as Pilgrim," 133.
6. Shriver, "Truth Befriended."

extent that he may have thought about it, and JLA left it to his protégés to create books out of his essays. JLA, Shriver said, truly believed in incarnation—the Word becoming flesh.

That was what made him an unforgettable teacher. JLA's incarnational method fused the high ground of theology with the low ground of ordinary human relationships. His classroom was a place of hospitable community. JLA did not make learning painless; he made painful things possible: Exposing ignorance, testing ideas, and challenging students to reach higher. He was an apostle of reuniting the fragments of our humanity that pride, prejudice, oppression, and its sins have alienated. Shriver put it theologically. Truth, ultimately, bears a human likeness, is revealed in human shape, becoming our servant, colleague, teacher, friend. You might call it Unitarianism of the Second Person. But whatever you call it, it is something remarkable.

I have heard Shriver say, more than once, that JLA had the gift of friendship. He would know, because Don Shriver has the same gift in abundance. He will tell you that without the friendship and support of his predecessors, John Bennett and Roger Shinn, he might not have made it at Union. But Don Shriver has been the same kind of steadfast, good-spirited, sympathetic, and supportive friend to all three of his successors, Holland Hendrix, Joe Hough, and Serene Jones, and his peaceable spirit has thus graced more history at Union than nearly all his predecessors.

## BIBLIOGRAPHY

Fiske, Edward B. "Union Seminary Is Reconsidering Its Purpose." *New York Times,* May 18, 1971, 41.

Handy, Robert T. *A History of Union Theological Seminary in New York.* New York: Columbia University Press, 1987.

Shriver, Donald W., Jr. "The Heart's Love Uttered with the Mind's Conviction." *Union Seminary Quarterly Review* 32 (1976) 3–16.

———. "The President as Pilgrim." *Theological Education* 32, supplement 3 (Spring 1996) 115–51.

———. "Truth Befriended: James Luther Adams as Teacher." Unpublished speech, 1982. Donald Woods Shriver Jr. papers, 1946–2017. Series 1A, Box 8, Folder 9. Burke Library, Union Theological Seminary, New York, NY.

Wills, Garry. *Bare Ruined Choirs: Doubt, Prophecy, and Radical Religion.* New York: Doubleday, 1974.

# 3

# Managing Union in the Shriver Era

*Milton McCormick Gatch Jr.*

In 1978, Donald Shriver approached me about the possibility of becoming academic dean at Union Theological Seminary. It was a surprising suggestion that had come to Don from John B. Coburn, a Union alumnus and former board member who had chaired the committee that recruited Don as president of the faculty. I was at the time a professor of English in a public university, the University of Missouri-Columbia. I had a doctorate in church history and was a seminary graduate and ordained Episcopal priest. My field of study was the history of the church in Anglo-Saxon England—not a readily marketable specialty in American religious studies faculties—and (after several years as chaplain and faculty member of a small midwestern liberal arts college) I landed a post in an English department because my dissertation on theology in vernacular sermons from pre-Conquest England qualified me to teach Old English. I had published highly specialized papers and a book on eschatology in those ancient homilies, but also had a theological book, *Death: Meaning and Mortality in Christian Thought and Contemporary Culture.* John Coburn knew of my theological education and my abiding concern for the ministry of the church; and he was aware that

42

I'd had some administrative experience. I had served as chair of the English department at Missouri—harmonizing the conflicts, allaying the anxieties, and encouraging the development of secular professors—and had been delegated by my dean to take the reins of the music department, guiding the selection of a new chairperson and reorienting its faculty.

Unlikely candidate though I was, Don was sufficiently intrigued to open a conversation. A first visit to Union—which involved an evening with Richard Norris, an acquaintance from college years, now newly established as the early church historian at Union—was spent mostly with Don Shriver and his administrative staff, and it was a very congenial time. A second visit with my wife Georgie included much more interchange with faculty. At a faculty supper party in the president's apartment, my stock went up when Georgie was warmly greeted by Beverly Harrison and James Cone, both of whom she had known in her capacity as director of An Ecumenical Ministry in Higher Education in Columbia. It did not hurt that some remembered the late Daniel Day Williams' admiration for my book, *Death*. In due course, an offer of the academic deanship and a tenured professorship was made and accepted. Thus began a long and productive collaboration with Donald Shriver: we were two persons of different demeanor and background, who admired and respected each other and worked together extremely well.

As I understood it, my mission as dean was to help bring normalcy to Union while reaffirming its longstanding tradition of academic excellence coupled with prophetic leadership in the church for social and economic justice and for peace. In the 1960s and seventies this stalwart heritage had been transformed, enriched, and deeply challenged by opposition to the Vietnam War, support of the civil rights movement, and the emergence of feminism. (Sexual identity was soon to join the field.) Whereas Union's neighbor and academic partner, Columbia University, seemed shell-shocked and defensive after its tumultuous time of student unrest, Union had been in some ways rudderless. Students who had come to Union as a place of sanctuary from the draft and protest, sometimes showed little interest in completing their academic course and had no clear vocational goals. Students with strong academic motivation felt marginalized. The increasingly large ratios of the student body that were Black, female, or Latino often felt alien in the Gothic-revival quadrangle. Faculty were divided: there were those who hewed to more traditional methods and those who struck out in radically new ways.

Don Shriver's administration had begun to enrich the faculty with appointments of women, notably the Old Testament scholar Phyllis Trible; and Cornel West, James Forbes, and James Washington, young Black scholars, who had recently joined James Cone on the faculty. But, in the course of the previous two decades, the financial support of a small cadre of wealthy, re-ligiously liberal supporters in New York had faded away—some in reaction to the internal eruptions, but mainly because a younger generation did not have the same charitable commitments as their forebears, and because of the decline of mainline Protestantism. Don, strongly supported by his board chair Walter Burke, worked valiantly to put the institution back on its feet. Faculty appointments were a key. The restoration of James Chapel and the reconfiguration of the library—though some mourned the extreme changes in the shape and function of these two institutional anchors—were strong symbols of commitment both to heritage and to a renewed and strength-ened seminary in a new age. Nevertheless, the financial situation remained perilous; the students—who earlier had co-governed the institution—were restless and combative; the faculty was deeply divided, underpaid, and with very little supportive institutional infrastructure.

I arrived at Union at an unusually challenging moment. The immediate crisis concerned the promotion of Beverly Harrison from tenured associate professor to professor. The issue was that Harrison, nationally known and respected as a leader in feminist theology and ethics, had been appointed assistant professor before completing the doctorate and in due course pro-moted to associate and granted tenure. At this juncture, she was still without a major publication but on the calendar would be eligible for promotion to full professor. The faculty committee on tenure would not recommend the promotion, but Don's sense of justice—not uninfluenced by the strong student and public support for Harrison—led him to recommend her pro-motion to the board; and the board acceded to this recommendation in February of 1979.[1] This situation in the wider academic world would have been regarded as anomalous in the extreme, and it was so seen by many of the Union faculty, not merely the traditionalist wing, but also the African Americans, who apprehended that they would be held to the higher stan-dard. I recognized Beverly's stature and was certain that, once ink started flowing from her pen, it would be a constant stream. Nevertheless, I was deeply disturbed by the situation, although I did not gainsay the president. In consultation with faculty and with advice and support from Hays H. Rockwell, chair of the board's committee on educational policy, I set to work to encourage the establishment of better procedures.

By the April 1979 board meeting, a proposal with strong faculty sup-port was brought forward. The old tenure committee would be succeeded by a committee on appointments, constituted of all tenured members of

1. I have refreshed my memory of many events mentioned throughout this essay by reviewing "Minutes of the Board and Executive Committee, 1978–1990."

the faculty with the academic dean as chair. (The president, as a tenured professor, was a member.) Only this committee could recommend faculty appointments, tenure and promotion, although the final power of appointment remained in the board, which also retained exclusive authority to select and appoint the president. The board delayed action on this major shift of authority from administration and governing board to faculty until autumn when, with counsel present for advice, the arrangement was approved. This development constituted a major enhancement of the prerogatives of the seminary's faculty. A procedure for faculty grievance was also proposed. Reviewed by Columbia professor of law, Ruth Bader Ginsberg, it was approved by the board in April 1980.

Yet another issue at the time was the proportion of the faculty that could be tenured. The board ruled that the tenured members should not exceed two-thirds of the faculty so that there would be frequent and (it was hoped) orderly rotation in the faculty. The biblical field had firmly established that in the faculty table of organization there would be two tenured professors in both Old and New Testament and that a third post in each area would be untenured, which resulted in junior posts that rotated every three or six years. The other fields were not able to arrive at such a formula, so the matter was always an uneasy one. It was tested in 1980, when Christopher Morse came due for tenure review. He had published his dissertation the preceding year and was eligible, yet his promotion and tenure would have violated the prescribed ratio. Morse had good support in the theological field, and the more conservative faculty were also supportive of his role balancing to his more radical colleagues. The board was persuaded to approve a third three-year appointment as assistant professor with no presumption of tenure. (The situation was ludicrous, as Morse himself knew. He told me that his mother had said it was no matter: "Just call yourself 'Ass. Prof.' and nobody will know the difference.") Ultimately, Morse advanced to associate with tenure and a long and honored career at Union. The two-thirds tenure rule was always difficult (even impossible) to enforce. "Untenurable," as it were.

In April of 1979, my office presented the board with two papers concerning faculty issues, both developed by James A. Hayes, who from this time became an invaluable resource of the academic office and was to serve as recorder of the faculty. The first had to do with retirement age, which at Union, as many other institutions, had been "normally" at age sixty-five, with a possibility of extension for five further years. The laws were changing so that seventy was becoming normative. Ultimately, there could no longer be a legally required or stated retirement age, and it became nearly impossible to ask professors about their plans for retirement. James Cone died in 2018 months short of his eightieth birthday, still an active member of the faculty, and he was not alone teaching beyond the age of seventy. This development, although it allowed for the long career of a path-breaking scholar and teacher like Cone, made it even more difficult to maintain the desired ratio of tenured to untenured faculty and to bring in new voices and talents.

The second paper concerned faculty compensation. In the crises of the sixties and seventies, faculty compensation had lain fallow. In January 1978 there had been an across-the-board increase of $1,000 for all faculty and many staff. This adjustment—albeit a step in the right direction—was prejudicial against the more highly ranked professors and, even so, inadequate for the lower ranks. The compensation paper attempted to take into account that faculty compensation included housing (most, indeed, of a very high standard for New York City) but that retirement benefits were based on the cash salary without allowance for the housing benefits, which put faculty at an extreme disadvantage when they had to leave Union apartments at retirement and procure housing for themselves. It was a bleak picture that we struggled to remediate throughout the years, always against the very limited resources available to manage the institution in its aging plant. One result was an increase of the faculty retirement benefit to 40 percent of cash salary to reflect the value of the housing benefit. There was a point at which I suggested that, despite concern about the operating deficit, increases be budgeted and that they be awarded on a merit basis—an inegalitarian and, thus, unwelcome suggestion in the view of some faculty. Older named faculty chairs were revived, despite the fact that they were not adequately endowed, and Don found funding for several new endowed chairs.

There were also issues concerning student admissions, retention, and financial aid that needed to be regularized. Enrollment statistics had been by body count, without reference to fulltime enrollment. We moved to counting full-time equivalency, which rendered more realistic—not always encouraging—but realistic and useful statistics. Financial aid had been available for extended enrollment, and we needed to limit eligibility for aid and housing to a reasonable time for completing degrees. There was an effort to make tuition rates roughly comparable with those of the divinity schools at Harvard and Yale and the freestanding Princeton Seminary. While implementing some greater academic regularity on students, we also sought to give appropriate support and to adapt programs to their needs. Counseling resources and the office of Dean of Students were modestly enhanced. It was at the request of a single student that in 1980 we negotiated a joint four-year program combining Union's Master of Divinity with Columbia University's Master of Science in Social Work—a program that is still offered after a quarter century. We recognized that the number of doctoral students who could be supported had to be strictly limited, leading to tense but necessary negotiations among faculty when applications were reviewed.

The institutional research of Malcolm L. Warford produced valuable insights about Union students. Warford had conducted in-depth interviews with a group of students who had entered the seminary in 1976, two years before my arrival, following them through their three- or four-year course of studies.[2] He concluded that there were characteristics that predicted success at Union: church commitment combined with an emerging vocational vision, academic ability, and the ability to function in urban New York. Self-evident as these are, perhaps, they helped us to focus in the admission and advisement of students. Warford's criteria did not preclude the presence of "seekers"—persons who were still forming their religious identity and career goals—but it helped to define what kinds of seeking might bear fruit in the seminary community. The students whom Warford surveyed were remarkably diverse—from poor urban environs, single-parent homes, middle-class and privileged, just from college or after some years of secular work, male and female, racially diverse. Absent from Warford's survey was a clear voice from the gay community, which would shortly become a central concern at Union during the epidemic AIDS crisis of the 1980s, when a number of faculty and staff were deeply involved in the struggles and deaths of affected students and staff. Race, sexual orientation, and feminism were three factors that deeply affected and engaged everyone in the seminary, including those who would not be counted in those groups.

Warford's study showed that life at Union was far from easy for students. Indebtedness was rapidly becoming a major concern. Union students (like contemporaries in secular schools) tended to identify themselves with issues—racial, feminist, sexual—and to organize themselves in caucuses. These organizations gave mutual support and called attention to the concerns of their members. They also tended to isolate members of one group from another, so that (for example) when the Black caucus organized chapel services, the white feminists tended not to attend—and *vice versa*. Some—especially Black women, who were just breaking into ordained ministry—felt not only marginalized in their churches but also isolated in the student body; they sometimes intentionally cordoned themselves off from association with other students. Drinking and open sexuality were particularly disturbing to students from morally strict religious backgrounds.

One Black woman in Warford's group confessed as late as the early twenty-first century that she had only recently been able to recognize the

---

2. "Reports from the Office of Educational Research, 1976–1979."

commonality of women of all races and persuasions as sisters.[3] A white mainline southern male, who had been on the liberal fringes of racial and theological issues at home, found himself labeled hopelessly conservative at Union.[4] Hispanic students struggled socially and linguistically between their Anglo and Latino communities.[5] Some of them resisted being formed by the intellectual and social issues that were central at Union but nonetheless wanted the affirmation of a Union degree. As I have already noted, in the 1980s, the presence of gays and lesbians became more and more central to student life, both as separate caucuses and as a unified movement (LGBTQ). And students actively pressured the Board to divest of stocks that supported the armament industries and South-African Apartheid. (A large group of students and faculty—Shriver and Gatch, among them—demonstrated against Apartheid at the South African consulate, were arrested *en masse*, and had to appear in court.) It was a challenge to try to draw and hold together these centrifugal forces.

Warford returned to eight of his students in the first decade of the twenty-first century to review their careers in the interim. All were still involved in pastoral (if not parochial) ministry. None were charismatic, high-profile success-stories, but all had grown in self-understanding and—despite periods of struggle and doubt—remained committed to their callings. A number of the group had complained as students that Union failed to provide training in the skills of ministry, yet all of them had learned what they needed on the job and brought to the task the ability to think critically and theologically. In various ways, they experienced the vicissitudes of Protestant churches in the three-and-a-half decades since they left Union and remained resolute, if sometimes battered, in their callings. That seems to me a quite remarkable outcome.

All of the work of the seminary in the 1980s—the faculty not always fully cognizant of the severity of the challenges; the senior staff struggling with them daily—took place against the background of continuing, continuous financial exigency. If I thought when I came to Union that my work would chiefly involve working with faculty on academic issues and with the Dean of Students (at first Sidney Skirvin, later Jualynne Dodson, and Katherine Henderson) on student issues, it soon became apparent that larger institutional issues would always be central both within the Academic Office and in consort with Don Shriver's close and functional senior staff. I was

3. Warford and Huggins, *Spirit's Tether*, 174.
4. Warford and Huggins, *Spirit's Tether*, 109–11, 178–79.
5. Warford and Huggins, *Spirit's Tether*, 71–72, 105–6.

also called upon several times to serve as acting president when Don was on leave or touring internationally on behalf of the seminary.

An early challenge was presented in a report by a committee of board, faculty and students on "Educational Excellence in the Eighties," known as the "Wilson Report" after the chair John Wilson, an alumnus, trustee, and professor of religion at Princeton University.[6] The committee identified five components of Union's state of financial exigency: the high rate of national inflation, the need to increase faculty compensation, the seminary's "inelastic" income, deferred maintenance of the physical plant, and overstaffing. Some of the efforts to address these issues have already been discussed. But, in general, it can be said that, although few could gainsay the accuracy of the assessment, the systems simply required vastly more capital. Some steps were taken to reduce the size of the faculty and staff, but much more was needed. The Wilson report came to the fore during the recession of the early 1980s, which was sometimes characterized as "stagflation"—concurrent high inflation and low economic growth ("stagnation"). I read a paper at the Association of Theological Schools in 1981 entitled "Maintaining Academic Quality in Economic Gridlock," which reported on the Wilson report and the difficulties of implementation, concluding that seminaries should "assume the grim rather than the optimistic scenario," that they should concentrate on the institution's values, and that they should close if they did not see a way forward before their assents had been entirely wasted.[7]

In 1981 the first of several conversations looking toward the possibility of merger with the General Theological Seminary of the Episcopal Church took place. Each time, the conversations were initiated by Union. Beyond loose arrangements for cross-registration of students and mutual library access, the discussions came to naught, largely because of the hubris of two venerable institutions, each with a strong sense of its identity and an unwillingness to abandon its neighborhood, its architectural identity, and its academic heritage.

Finally, in 1985, the Board engaged an advisory firm, Cambridge Associates, to consult on fiscal structuring. Their stringent report, aimed at achieving financial equilibrium, required further cuts, chiefly of staff, and a wholesale reevaluation of the mission of the seminary. In February of 1986, Don assigned me the additional title of provost, giving me responsibility for the internal management of the school, freeing him to work on development. The Cambridge Associates report led to the termination of one staff member, a genial and beloved doorkeeper, whose dismissal brought

6. A copy of the report is included in "Board of Trustees Minutes, April 28, 1981."

7. Gatch, "Maintaining Academic Quality," 98.

outraged outbursts from students. (He was shortly hired by a member of the board to a similar position in a commercial building.) But more serious were consideration by the entire seminary community of proposals for restructuring. The possibilities included moving from the city, reducing the academic programs, eliminating degree programs and becoming a theological think-tank, and restructuring the physical plant. All of these were unpalatable to faculty, students, and staff, but ultimately Don and the board decided to concentrate on the last. The possibility of constructing a high-rise apartment building on the site of Knox Hall was considered, and there was a presentation of proposals by several prominent architectural firms. The whole place was on edge and in turmoil. My wife, setting the table for Christmas dinner in our Knox Hall apartment, shed a tear, thinking that the very room might not be there another Christmas.

Ultimately, it was decided to sell Van Dusen Hall, which housed faculty, students and some staff. This caused more distress, particularly from faculty who would have to move. A point system was established based on rank and years of service, which would allow professors with more points to bump those with fewer from their residences. The instincts of some holders of high points were hardly charitable. In addition to this turmoil, there was a commotion over who would buy the Van Dusen building. A contract for a market price was negotiated with the Jewish Theological Seminary of America, across Broadway at 122nd Street from Union's campus. We were happy to have cemented that relationship, which Don had lovingly nurtured. But the land for Van Dusen had been bought from International House, whose building was adjacent, and few remembered that I-House (as it was known informally) had retained a right of first refusal should Union ever want to dispose of the property. To our astonishment, I-House met Jewish Seminary's price and trumped the deal. I remember attending the closing and arranging for a bank to remain open so that we could deposit the check after five o'clock. In the wake of the sale, a principal residence for students Hastings Hall was renovated, and its ground floor was devoted to hotel-like accommodation. The sale of Van Dusen was the beginning of a series of moves in subsequent administrations that has considerably reduced the size of Union's campus; the exercise of its right of first refusal by I-House foreshadowed the fate of McGiffert Hall in more recent years; and our exploration of development possibilities in the seminary quadrangle foreshadowed twenty-first century strategies.

One last piece of evidence of the struggle to maintain Union and bring it forward was the accreditation by the Association of Theological Schools in the late 1980s. The task of assembling the materials for the accreditation team was an arduous one, especially given the turmoil around the effort to achieve fiscal equilibrium. The team was suspicious of the situation. Their dubiety was reinforced by expressions of discontent within the institution. They questioned whether the enlarged role I had been assigned was appropriate, and—above all—they were doubtful that our fiscal restructuring would succeed. We passed academically, but there was a stern notation requiring a revisit to consider our financial stability.

In 1989, it was announced that I would leave the Academic Office and, after a sabbatical, assume leadership of the Burke Library. There I spent a happy time until the spring after my sixty-fifth birthday, managing a great library. Funds were scarce, so we were unable to keep pace with current acquisitions. I spent much of my time there arranging and funding an exhibition of the library's founding collection, the library of the German priest, theologian, and biblical translator, Leander van Ess, to proclaim publicly the distinction of the library's beginnings and impress on Union the importance of its library. The exhibit opened in New York and, over the next year-and-a-half, traveled to bibliographical venues in Mainz and Paderborn in Germany and to Toronto, and Dallas in North America. Thanks to Don Shriver's work to establish a shared Bonhoeffer Chair at Union and the Humboldt University in Berlin and to my research on the library of Leander van Ess, my last semester before retirement was spent in Berlin teaching a course on the documents of indulgences in the Middle Ages. I taught in German, and it was the hardest work I've done, but perhaps the most satisfying.

Managing Union in the Shriver years, then, was a long battle to keep the ship afloat and to put it on course for the future. Don and I sometimes have thought that the nature of our struggle and the extent of our successes has often not been acknowledged or remembered. We look back and acknowledge that we did not bring Union into perdurable financial equilibrium, but we restored some stability for students and faculty and brought the seminary to a fiscal condition that could last into the twenty-first century.

I often remember a visit to my office by Louise Richardson, the widow of one of Union's most distinguished historical scholars, Cyril C. Richardson. Mrs. Richardson, a formidable woman, in all seasons wearing an overcoat and a broad-brimmed blue felt hat, often let us know what she thought was amiss at Union. (The preservation of a stained-glass window, which many thought deplorable, was one of her favorite causes.) On this occasion, she wanted to tell me that every so often, from the 1840s to the present, the seminary found itself in precarious financial condition, and she thought it should at long last be brought to stability. I pointed out to her that those unsettled moments usually coincided with turbulence in the economy of the United States and were related to the fact that Union was freestanding and without the financial support of a university or a denomination, albeit with collegial relations in the academic and ecclesiastical worlds—and with a strong (some would say contrarian) determination to be intellectually independent and socially active. It is a precarious path that Union has elected to follow, and it will always be the right trail on which to struggle uphill.

## BIBLIOGRAPHY

Gatch, Milton McCormick, Jr. "Maintaining Academic Quality in Economic Gridlock." *Theological Education* 19 (1982) 89–98.
Union Theological Seminary. "Minutes of the Board of Trustees and the Executive Committee of the Board, 1978–1990." Union Theological Seminary Archives. Burke Library, Union Theological Seminary, New York, NY.
———. "Reports from the Office of Educational Research, 1976–1979." Union Theological Seminary Archives. Burke Library, Union Theological Seminary, New York, NY.
Warford, Malcolm L., and Kenneth Huggins. *The Spirit's Tether: Eight Lives in Ministry.* Herndon, VA: Alban, 2011.

# 4

# Discovering a Not-So-United Union Theological Seminary

*Larry Rasmussen*

Don Shriver saved Union Theological Seminary. That should serve as tribute enough. But more than that, he navigated changes that put in place a vibrant future Union, markedly different from the institution he joined in 1975.

My recollections begin well into Don's presidency. I joined the faculty in 1986, and while Union had been my "North Star" for theological and social ethics since graduate years in the mid-1960s, I had been content to skim the alumni news and take in the occasional conference. Neither insider contacts nor campus struggles were on my screen. So I arrived rather naïve in the fall of 1986.

Union had always been fractious; that I had long known. It was the downside of its ongoing creativity and the strong-minded convictions and commitments of students and faculty. To discover that "Union" still didn't mean "united" didn't take me by surprise.

But I was not prepared for the roiling financial *angst* and the straight-up opposition by faculty to solutions—invariably deep and costly—brought

53

forward by Don and the board. Even though the 1985 Cambridge Associates report said Union was "unviable and dying," every considered future was rejected without qualification—moving the seminary to the Bronx or New Jersey, building high-end apartments in and above the Quad, cutting the master's or PhD program, becoming a research institution, etc.[1] "Just say 'no,'" seemed the temperament, an ironic parallel to the later Republican Party stance vis-à-vis President Obama's agenda. But Don listened, knew the constraints, and searched for a workable, if reluctant, compromise. With no less than accreditation in the balance because of the shaky finances, the resolution was to sell Van Dusen Hall. Even that would stave off woes for but a season.

No doubt the diminished morale affecting the liberal Protestantism of Union's identity played an indirect role. A much-cited *Christianity & Crisis* feature story captured it well with a walk around the block. Union, the National Council of Churches and denominational offices in the Interchurch Center, and the Riverside Church all bespoke mainline decline. Deferred maintenance ruled, and the proud were humbled.

Still, financial migraines didn't stop another Union. To call it the Phoenix rising from its ashes would be unwarranted hyperbole. But it's not unwarranted to say that Don (and Peggy) Shriver led the way and put in place Union's future. The faculty appointments of Don's presidency, as well as the changing student body, tallied not only as progressive and grounded in cutting-edge research and publication (the continuities). The campus community became diverse, ecumenical, liberationist, and just plain interesting in unprecedented ways and degree. Moreover, worship and the arts in a changed and pliable James Chapel, also accomplished under Don's leadership, gave vitality to campus spiritualities the likes of which Union had not known and would not have imagined.

In short, and despite the troubles that landed in the President's office, any visitor to Union would never have suspected that "crisis" was the prevailing mood. Because it wasn't. Instead, the legendary vitality, charged exchange, and serious, contending ideas on full display in the classroom, were wrapped in the new forays of a deeper, broader, and more diverse Union. This was Don's doing, as much as any one person can take credit for (and he wouldn't). He had saved Union for another day, from a financial dead end and for its continuing mission.

---

1. The language is Gary Dorrien's summary in his account of the Shriver presidency in this volume, Dorrien, "Hanging in There for a Good Cause."

# BIBLIOGRAPHY

Dorrien, Gary. "Hanging in There for a Good Cause: Donald Shriver's Presidency at Union Theological Seminary." In *Christian Ethics in Conversation: A Festschrift in Honor of Donald W. Shriver Jr., 13th President of Union Theological Seminary in the City of New York*, edited by Isaac B. Sharp and Christian T. Iosso. Eugene, OR: Cascade, 2020.

# 5

# Donald Shriver

## Exemplar of Prophetic Leadership

*Cornel West*

Donald Shriver was the most prophetic seminary president in late twentieth-century America. His visionary and courageous efforts to preserve Union Theological Seminary as "an ecumenical school in the heart of New York City as a center of excellence which made no pretensions of pre-eminence" warrants not only attention—but also applause.[1] Union Theological Seminary was the preeminent institution for theological education during the golden age of liberal Protestant Christianity in elite America. From the inauguration of President Henry Sloane Coffin on November 4, 1926, to the departures of Professors Paul Tillich in 1955 and Reinhold Niebuhr in 1960, Union was the great center for theological education.

The genius of Donald Shriver was to wed the best of the "liberal evangelicalism" of Coffin, the unclassifiable creativity of Tillich and Niebuhr, to the emerging liberation theologies of James Cone, Beverly Harrison, and others at Union. Shriver's inaugural address on February 11, 1976, "The Heart's Love Uttered with the Mind's Conviction," is a gem—a minor classic

1. Shriver, "Heart's Love Uttered," 11.

in the annals of theological education in a time of financial austerity and spiritual sterility. Shriver prophesies that in the midst of this moment of "limited growth, limited power, limited virtue," Union Theological Seminary could still pursue "the service of the love of truth to the truth of love."[2] This gallant pursuit is driven by "the conviction that everything is of value to God gets nourished best in a community of people who demonstrate daily their value to each other."[3]

I experienced this sense of being valued the moment I stepped into President Shriver's office in the spring of 1977. As a fiery twenty-three-year-old Philosopher—in love of the pursuit of truth and grasped by the truth of God's love in Jesus Christ—I thrived on the integrity and sincerity of Donald Shriver. The mode of his way and the manner of his style convinced me he valued me as a human being, fellow scholar, and child of God. In White Supremacist America, this is no easy task. And for a White Southerner and Black Southerner (by way of California), this is a remarkable reality. And for the next forty-two years, our relationship has deepened, including our monthly lunches with Peggy Shriver, Mac Gatch, and Georgina Gatch in recent years. In fact, Donald Shriver is one of the most genuine human beings and sincere Christians I have known. My decision to teach at Union was providential.

Donald Shriver's invitation to me to join the Union Theological Seminary faculty—even after the soft opposition of the Black student group who were upset by my love of the works of Ivan Turgenev and Anton Chekhov over those of Richard Wright and Ralph Ellison—reflected his deep conviction to make Union the center for Black theological education in America and in the world. And he achieved his prophetic goal. Never before and never again has there been a group of such high quality Black scholars and high quality Black Christians in one seminary with such impact and influence here and abroad. Donald Shriver's support for James Cone—the world historical figure and founder of Black Liberation Theology—was monumental. Shriver's warm embrace of James Forbes—one of the few great preachers and teacher of preachers (and later to be Senior Minister of the historic Riverside Church)—was pioneering. Shriver's strong affirmation of James Washington—the greatest historian of the Black Church of his generation and my best friend in the world—was undeniable. Shriver's encouragement of Samuel Roberts—a fine sociologist of Black religion—was crucial. And Shriver's pioneering hiring of Jualynne Dodson—a superb Dean and later Professor—was groundbreaking. And there would be others to come. This

2. Shriver, "Heart's Love Uttered," 12, 13.
3. Shriver, "Heart's Love Uttered," 14.

Golden Age of Black Theological education at Union as well as the country and world was the result of the prophetic leadership of Donald Shriver.

Is it ironic that Donald Shriver—this son of the White South—would convene such a group of Black scholars and Christians in late twentieth century New York City? Is it a mere coincidence that that this White forty-eight-year-old Christian President of ecumenical Union Theological Seminary would gather descendants of U.S. Black slaves to be major intellectual shakers and movers of our understanding of what it means to be thinking and loving human beings in the world? I think not. Donald Shriver was simply being true to the best of his own calling and Union's own vocation. He remained deeply committed to other professors like Raymond Brown—the great Catholic in our midst then—and Ann Ulanov—the grand Jungian Christian among us then. Yet when the real history of the prophetic Christian education in late twentieth-century America is written, the name Donald Shriver, with his brilliant and poetic wife Peggy, will be at the center as institutional leader, prolific scholar, and humble follower of Jesus Christ!

## BIBLIOGRAPHY

Shriver, Donald W., Jr. "The Heart's Love Uttered with the Mind's Conviction." *Union Seminary Quarterly Review* 32 (1976) 3–16.

# 6

## An Unpredicted Challenge

*Janet Walton*

Don Shriver described his coming to Union as a "time of openness to new possibilities, to an expanded self and to a lot of risk."[1] What he could not have anticipated was how much the chapel would test these expectations within all the years of his presidency.

In the late seventies when Don arrived he found himself in the center of tremendous energy generated from insights around race, gender, class, global conflicts, and the impact of unrelenting poverty in our city and world. Faculty members and students alike were eager for more analysis of these problems and much more persistent action. Women, with the faculty leadership of Beverly Harrison, Mary Pellauer, and Linda Clark, were calling attention to the devaluing effects of patriarchal power. New faculty members James Cone, James Washington, Jim Forbes, and Cornel West were leading the community to a multifaceted awareness of the evils of racism. Tom F.

1. Except where noted, all quotations cited herein are taken from unpublished interviews conducted in preparation for "Practicing for Life," a video developed by Troy Messenger and Janet Walton on the history of worship in James Chapel. Shriver, interview by Messenger and Walton, 2013–14.

Driver and Robert E. Seaver, both involved in the theater in New York City, were urging the community to see that the collective, interactive patterns of theater performances were models for ways of worshiping that could engage the participation of every person.

Worship, once a week, led most often by faculty members, was coordinated by Jim Forbes and Linda Clark. Too few members of the faculty and student body regularly attended. Occasionally, there were services that pointed to something that could change these patterns. An early example was a service where Professors Linda Clark, Bob Seaver, and Letty Russell unscrewed and removed all the pews for one of the weekly services. It was a painstaking effort to demonstrate how a different arrangement of the people, in a circle, rather than one person high up in the pulpit and looking down on everyone else, would not only change how we worshiped, but could, in turn, affect how we related to each other day by day.

Then, one day, in the midst of a service a sound began to emanate from the organ. It would not stop. A cipher, that is, a pipe, was stuck open. The organist, Linda Clark, walked down to the congregation and said, "Look! It plays by itself." That was the final groan for the organ. It needed major repairs that would involve major adjustments to the physical structure of the chapel. After consultation with the board and the faculty, Don Shriver made a decision about worship in James Chapel early in his presidency that few other leaders would have had the courage to carry out.

The chair of the Seminary board, Rosie Havemeyer, joined Don to lead a community discussion about what was next. In his words:

> The time was not right for a form of worship service, which was formal and somewhat rigid. We had pews as in most churches; we had an architectural setup which was pulpit centered, and although that suited my own Protestant dispositions, it was in conflict with an increasing sense in the churches, Protestant and Catholic, that worship is something that belongs to the people, which is symbolized more by a circle than by parallel lines of seats.[2]

Rosie Havemeyer was convinced that the crisis with the organ was an invitation to the entire community to assess the whole worship program, which, for her, too, did not meet the possibilities that worship could offer. Her support was critical. Money was tight. The renovation would require allocation of funds that were not anticipated in the budget. Mrs. Havemeyer took responsibility for raising what was needed from the board.

2. Shriver, interview by Messenger and Walton, 2013–14.

Faculty members were divided about a radical change. For some, the space, as it was, hindered possibilities. In organist Linda Clark's words, the chapel was "cramped with inchoate energy."[3] The leaders of the services were always trying to work around the structure. Historian Bob Handy felt that both historic and contemporary liturgies did not fit comfortably in the chapel as it was then configured. For Carolyn Bilderback, professor of dance, the pews inhibited significant body movement.

In spite of enthusiasm for re-ordering the chapel a large number of faculty and alumni/ae wanted to keep it as it had always been. They contended that the chapel had been built for a particular arrangement of pews and pulpit that suited worship. They worried, in fact, were terrified, about what might happen with structural changes, both aesthetically and liturgically. Their memories were dependent on the arrangement of the space. In spite of Union's reputation as an innovator and change agent in worlds of theology and social justice, the thought of taking away the long accepted ways of worshiping was to betray its rich traditions.

The resistance was overcome when members of the Board of Directors insisted that this was a change whose time had come. Why keep it as it is, when by the lack of attendance, the community was saying loud and clear that it was not a space and time that nourished their spirituality, grounded their faith, or related to a ways of living needed now and for the future?

Shriver understood well the implications of the decision to renovate the chapel:

> It was a renovation of a space that meant destroying some things in order to create other things, one that required the leaders of worship to design it for the purposes of the worship. But perhaps the most important innovation was clearing out the space not to make it empty but to require the leaders to decide how to fill it.[4]

Shriver had another idea, too. He envisioned a door built between the chapel and the refectory to join worship and eating. "We're renovating spirit and not just bricks and mortar."[5]

Architect Philip Ives was chosen to design the renovated chapel in collaboration with a committee made up of faculty, students, and members of the Board. Expectations and controversy continued to be a part of the conversations as the pews and the dark wood were removed, a slate floor was added, and the new Holtcamp pipe organ was installed in a central position

---

3. Clark, interview by Messenger and Walton, 2013–14.
4. Shriver, interview by Messenger and Walton, 2013–14.
5. Shriver, interview by Messenger and Walton, 2013–14.

at the south end of the former chancel. Some called this modification "the worship of the organ." Further the walling off of the "Great Commission" window, which was necessary, evoked strong responses and remains a problem for many alums to this day. The community watched the transformation with a mixture of anticipation, unease and excitement. What if . . .

## THE DEDICATION OF THE CHAPEL

The photos of the dedication liturgy show Don Shriver in front of the new wooden altar table with people on every side, north, south, east, west. This image conveyed what was true. As president, he was central to the renovation process and to the possibilities it expressed. With a conviction that regular participation in worship was crucial to seminary education, Don looked in every direction and invited each person to be a part of this new moment in Union's history. In fact, because he stood in our midst his vision seemed to flow from within the Union community and not something handed down from a hierarchical realm.

The dedication of the chapel extended throughout the entire semester. There were organ concerts that gave voice to the new tracker-action organ. Diverse worship services took advantage of the totally flexible space. And there was something more. An important addition to the musical life of Union during the dedication became a part of its regular life. Bob Seaver invited Bettye Franks Forbes to organize what came to be called the Ebony Ecumenical Ensemble. Under her direction, a choir of faculty, staff, students, and people from the community gave their first concert in the new chapel. The program brought the repertoire of African American religious experiences, including traditional and contemporary spirituals, anthems, hymns and gospel music, to the Union community and to a wider public audience. From then on, the EEE rehearsed at Union and gave a concert every year.

## DAY BY DAY

I began my work as the Coordinator of Worship at Union Seminary in the fall of 1981. Don invited me to guide the use of the chapel in a wide variety of ways. In addition to worship, we gathered there for lectures, performances, community meetings, and art exhibits. It was a time for experimentation. Don was present for everything, daily worship, and all the events. He listened to critiques from near and far. Some of them were his, too. He did not cut off any exploration, prematurely. Instead he waited and watched, giving space and time to see what would happen. There were a number of kinds of feedback. Professor Bob Handy volunteered to collect daily responses. Every day, he stood in the back of the chapel at the end of a service. He listened to anyone who wanted to speak. A newly created ritual committee met frequently to share what we saw and heard, and every month, too, there was a community gathering for feedback.

Shriver envisioned two objectives for our worship: that our services would reflect the differences of backgrounds and traditions among us and that worship would be the center of our theological education. To that end, we worshiped four times a week instead of only once as in the past. Every Thursday we agreed to have a communion service in order to learn from each other's denominational experiences and also to explore emerging forms across our differences. There was no template to guide what we were doing. Given our priorities as a Christian institution, there was an understanding that we would read, listen, and interpret scripture keeping in mind the needs of this community and the world around us. In Peggy Shriver's words, "The daily chapel became a teaching center for worship. That was for me an exciting new experience."[6]

## WHAT HAPPENED?

Don Shriver set a tone of responsibility and presence. He expected people to plan worship with care and respect. He took his turn, too, leading services and participating in them. He was there, every day! Neither Don nor anyone else could have predicted the breadth and depth of experiences this new chapel would make possible. To create worship services became the community project of faculty, students, administrative and facilities staffs. All of us, together. We brought to each other the legacies of traditions and a yearning for what we needed now. We learned from one another, sometimes not easily, but every day and every year. Here are some comments from members of the community:

> The space became a player in how the community would interact with each other: you felt a sense of responsibility for one another.[7] —Professor Linda Clark

> The renovation itself accentuated the identification of a leader with the congregation so that a hierarchy and a patriarchy were dealt a severe discipline by this new space.[8] —President Don Shriver

6. Shriver, interview by Messenger and Walton, 2013–14.
7. Clark, interview by Messenger and Walton, 2013–14.
8. Shriver, interview by Messenger and Walton, 2013–14.

I was afraid when we took the pews out that we'd become a kind of circus without substance. One of the reassuring and comforting experiences of worshiping in the chapel was that it was always theologically solid. Even when we would do the most creative kinds of worship, it was always grounded.[9] —Alumna Katie Cannon

Each person would bring part of their old tradition and then bend it, twist it, and stretch it a little bit.[10] —Alumna Lisa Hill

The renovated chapel services kept the seminary alive, put in place Union to come. In the midst of financial migraines, a changing student body, and commitments to ecumenism and liberation theology, worship and the arts enabled a changed and pliable chapel the likes of which Union had not known and would not have imagined, from what was always the same and highly predictable to rich with diversity.[11] —Professor Larry Rasmussen

Even anger and venting could be part of the theological process as we expressed it in worship.[12] —Alumnus Seth Pickens

In this space you had to listen to the community, to exegete and study the community. You had to approach the biblical text in a dialogue, to find the heart of what the biblical word is all about.[13] —Alumna and Director of worship Susan Blain

In my theology it's a dead end to be a Christian for yourself. In this space you're in the presence of others, and that being in the presence of others is in fact the essence of what being a Christian requires.[14] —Tom F. Driver

The space became more hospitable, in short, and hospitality to worship is part of the whole meaning of being a church.[15] —Don Shriver

The architect Philip Ives also designed three pieces of furniture for the chapel: a table, a pulpit, and a cross. The use of these central symbols hints

---

9. Cannon, interview by Messenger and Walton, 2013–14.

10. Hill, interview by Messenger and Walton, 2013–14.

11. Rasmussen, interview by Messenger and Walton, 2013–14.

12. Pickens, interview by Messenger and Walton, 2013–14.

13. Blain, interview by Messenger and Walton, 2013–14.

14. Driver, interview by Messenger and Walton, 2013–14.

15. Shriver, interview by Messenger and Walton, 2013–14.

at the imagination and commitment of the seminary community to our use of the space and everything in it.

The table became a pivotal object for the community's worship. It is used not only for communion but it marks a space for gathering close to each other to experience many expressions of life and death, death and life. On it we will find bread, wine, or juice for communion, and also ashes, a book of remembrance, or other kinds of food; around it we speak our prayers and receive blessings to send us forth for every kind of action. The table is our place to collect and distribute food. Once a month, there is soup, salad, and bread. One table becomes many tables. Everyone picks up food cooked by members of the community and brings it to small tables for eating, singing, listening, and praying in smaller conversational groups.

Unlike the table, which is still in use today, the pulpit had a very short life. It was too big. Don felt that it obscured the readers and preachers. Another artist took it apart and rebuilt it with smaller dimensions. Though beautiful, it, too, engulfed the leaders. Finally, we agreed on something much smaller built from the initial wood. Most often, a lectern is the best place from which our leaders speak. It can be moved easily and is at the right height. Preaching closer to us is not viewed as someone telling us what we don't know but rather prodding our intellects to imagine and do more.

The most controversial piece was the cross. It is twelve feet tall and made of wood. Anticipating the need for flexibility throughout the chapel, Philip Ives provided three different places to store and use it. Most people had a strong opinion about it. Some complained of its size and weight and its meanings around redemptive suffering, the need to suffer death as Jesus did. Others, borrowing from orthodox traditions, felt that it was just right for decorating with flowers and carrying it in a procession. Another leader tried nailing the communion bread to the cross. "The bread nailed to the cross was really way out," said Jim Forbes, "but it proved to have a deepening of the sense of the Eucharist when you had that literal sense of the bread broken for you on the cross."[16] Some wanted smaller crosses that called attention to the pain of workers whose hands and feet were swollen from overworking; women wanted to see female bodies on the cross, some that expressed the beauty of female bodies and some that conveyed the violence done to them. The cross invited diverse interpretations and fabrications.

Most people agreed that chairs instead of pews presented the most fundamental change in our attitudes about worship in James Chapel. We looked at each other. The arrangement of the chairs became the first call to our worship. As people walked in they saw the structure for our engagement

16. Forbes, interview by Messenger and Walton, 2013–14.

that day. Maybe it was a circle, maybe a labyrinth, maybe the chairs were upside down, maybe along a winding path, maybe in small circles, or there might be no chairs at all. In that first glimpse the community felt anticipation and the care of the planners. Words read by Professor Bob Seaver during a service of mourning for a member of our community who had died of AIDS express well the journeys of life that the flexibility of the space invites: "I go where I have never been, not imagined before, and find a new grace."[17]

Examples of what the renovated chapel has made possible are endless. Something happens there every day, year after year. I have chosen three stories.

## Bringing the Streets into James Chapel

"As I started into the chapel, I thought, where is everybody? I looked more closely and I saw that everyone was sitting on packing boxes on the floor."[18] Union students Geoff and Ginger Worden had started a program called "Bridges" in the financial district. They went every Friday night to get to know the people who live on the streets. As part of a course they were taking they were required to plan a service for the community. For a short time, they invited us to consider what it feels like to be homeless, to sit and live on the city's streets. "Those boxes became the image for that whole worship service and I've carried it in my head for years."[19] *Peggy Shriver*

## 175th Anniversary of Celebration of the Founding of Union Theological Seminary

The celebration of the 175th anniversary of the founding of Union Seminary called us to focus on a vision for the future, the long and hard struggles it will require, and a readiness to accept what evolves. Jim Forbes, the preacher, collaborated with aerialist, Sarah Novotny.[20] He chose to speak about an interpretation of the Hebrew phrase *Lech l'cha*, meaning to go forth. As Forbes spoke, walking among us, Sarah Novotny climbed up and down a rope, climbing high, moving back to the start, even almost falling. To go ahead requires risks; we depend on each other for support. In Forbes' words:

17. Found on a program for an AIDS service.
18. Shriver, interview by Messenger and Walton, 2013–14.
19. Shriver, interview by Messenger and Walton, 2013–14.
20. Sarah Novotny, aerial artist and teacher at Streb Lab for Action Mechanics.

I was not, first of all, the centerpiece. I was the prompter through the word for people to create a worship experience while the worship is going on. What I was actually doing was bringing about transitions, calling attention to the aerialist who was above . . . worship was engaging the living presence of God in a live and active community and it had the principle of co-construction.[21]

## Silent Tears

The third example took place at the end of the second semester in 2018. The plan for the renovated chapel called for white walls that would be used for art exhibits. The most recent exhibit, "Silent Tears," was a multimedia exhibition of photographs based on "stories of women with a disability who have been subjected to violence and women who have acquired their disability because of violence."[22] Their stories are most often untold, even silenced. Images were mounted on the walls and suspended from the ceiling throughout the whole chapel. The photographs were very large. However, it was not easy to see the faces of the women. It required pausing for a while to look attentively through streams of water, a woman's tears. Worship in James Chapel intends to ask something of each person and the whole community. This art exhibit represented the mission of Union to address the problems and challenges of our world by "making religion real in life," (President Francis Brown) especially for those who are silenced.[23]

President Don Shriver bet on the community when he said yes to the renovation of James Chapel. He did not know if a space could make the change he so longed for, that is, community worship at the heart of theological education. "I wanted a space in which we could be more free to improvise and that blossomed."[24]

And so it was and is and so it will be.

## BIBLIOGRAPHY

Blain, Susan. Interview by Troy Messenger and Janet Walton, 2013–14.

Brown, Francis. "The Inaugural Address: Theology as the Servant of Religion." In *The Laying of the Corner-Stone of the New Buildings of the Union Theological Seminary and the Inauguration of the Reverend Professor Francis Brown as President of the*

21. Forbes, interview by Messenger and Walton, 2013–14.

22. "Silent Tears."

23. Brown, "Inaugural Address," 51.

24. Shriver, interview by Messenger and Walton, 2013–14.

*Faculty, November Seventeenth, 1908*, edited by Union Theological Seminary, 30–51. New York: Irving, 1908.

Cannon, Katie. Interview by Troy Messenger and Janet Walton, 2013–14.

Clark, Linda. Interview by Troy Messenger and Janet Walton, 2013–14.

Driver, Tom F. Interview by Troy Messenger and Janet Walton, 2013–14.

Forbes, James A., Jr. Interview by Troy Messenger and Janet Walton, 2013–14.

Hill, Lisa. Interview by Troy Messenger and Janet Walton, 2013–14.

Pickens, Seth. Interview by Troy Messenger and Janet Walton, 2013–14.

Rasmussen, Larry. Interview by Troy Messenger and Janet Walton, 2013–14.

Shriver, Donald W., Jr. Interview by Troy Messenger and Janet Walton, 2013–14.

Shriver, Peggy L. Interview by Troy Messenger and Janet Walton, 2013–14.

"Silent Tears: Disability, Violence, and Resilience of Women Survivors Globally." Brochure for the exhibition by Belinda Mason, shown at Union Theological Seminary, New York, NY, April 24–May 16, 2018.

Walton, Janet and Troy Messenger. "James Chapel Worship–Practicing for Life." Produced by Nicholas Blair A. Media LLC, 2016. Posted March 11, 2016. https://www.youtube.com/watch?v=gopCGZS43Uw.

# 7

# Divine Aesthetics

*James A. Forbes Jr.*

In the spring of 1976, Don and Peggy Shriver welcomed the Forbes Family to the Union Theological Seminary community. Linda Clark and I were invited to share leadership in teaching, preaching, and worship. An interesting aspect of our appointment was that I was from the black Pentecostal tradition and Linda was a white Episcopalian. This coupling and interdenominational mixture was not unusual at the Union Seminary Don Shriver was to preside over for nearly a score of years. Union had committed itself to being a truly inclusive diverse community of scholars and learners. Diversity was to characterize the makeup of the faculty, administration, student body, and the board of trustees. This was a genuine effort to be the beloved community and to embody the unity to which we had been called as Christians. To ensure faithfulness to this high ideal of qualitative inclusiveness, the seminary encouraged multiple caucuses to be both vigilant and vocal in holding the wider community to walk the walk and not just to talk the talk.

It was not easy to move beyond ingrained patterns of European dominance and white control to enable the whole community to achieve a solid sense of shared ownership of the theological enterprise. Nevertheless, with

Don Shriver's steady hand and unwavering commitment to justice and mutual respect, we made progress amidst the agonizing traumas of transition toward a more perfect unity in the body of Christ.

This essay provides an opportunity to express gratitude to the Shrivers for their friendship and support across the years. Out of my teaching and preaching experience on Broadway, Claremont Avenue, and Riverside Drive I have come to a most important theological insight, which I am delighted to include in this festschrift in President Shriver's honor. The insight emerged from events connected with the renovation of James Memorial Chapel at Union, a proposal to update the sound system in the nave of The Riverside Church, and the discussion regarding the architectural design of the Interchurch Center, popularly referred to as "The God Box." In each of these situations the convening problematic was related to what I choose to call "Divine Aesthetics." There was no course in the curriculum with that name but perhaps there should have been. So many of the problems we face have to do with how we define the good, the true, and the beautiful. How we assign worth, value, and recognition. Whom we respect, protect, honor, and adore. What we promote or demote and why. Whence the source of our standards, what principles inform our system of awards or justify our punishments.   _aesthetics_

People of faith who worship God claim to derive their sentiments, their sensibilities, and their delight from the nature of the God they serve. We tend to forget the words of the prophet Isaiah: God's ways and thoughts are not the same as ours. When we attach idolatrous worth to the things that conform to our taste, we may be at serious variance from what brings pleasure and delight to the heart of God. If we want to do God's will, we would do well to sharpen our understanding of divine aesthetics. Several intense conflicts in my time on Morningside Heights forced me to pay more attention to the necessity to see things more through the eyes and the heart of God.

Children are given early instructions in aesthetics when they are taught not to trust first impressions or to rely upon surface observations alone. "Remember you can't judge a book by looking at the cover." "A beautiful red apple may have a worm in it." "Beauty is skin deep but ugly is to the bone." They learn that beauty is as beauty does. What may be good to your appetite may not be good for your health. What may seem pleasurable at one moment may turn out to have disastrous consequences later on. Such are early indications that cursory observations may be misleading. The state of North Carolina has as its motto "Esse Quam Vederi"—to be rather than to seem.

In regard to issues of faith the plot thickens. The prophet Isaiah introduces us to the more profound dynamics of divine aesthetics. The beauty of the sanctuary and the carefully designed liturgy may be so ugly to God that it may be declared an abomination in the eyes of God. A basic understanding of the difference between our evaluation of the good, the true, and the beautiful and that of God is set forth in the words of Isaiah 55:8–9:

> For my thoughts are not your thoughts, nor are your ways my ways, says the Lord. For as the heavens are higher than the earth, so are my ways higher than your ways and my thoughts than your thoughts. (NKJV)

When Samuel saw that the most likely of Jesse's sons was not chosen but rather the least likely, he gathered that God "does not see as mortals see; they look on the outward appearance, but the Lord looks on the heart." (1 Sam 16:7 NRSV)

As we continue to work our way through conflicts of race, class, ideology, and religion, we are required to measure our integrity by standards informed by "divine aesthetics."

When I arrived at Union Seminary in 1958, it was my daily practice to worship in James Chapel. Its Scottish gothic divided chancel and neatly ordered cushioned pews made it feel like the "holy of holies." One felt the very presence of God just by entering that hallowed space. I had no difficulty therefore understanding the fierce resistance from many when the decision was made in 1979 to renovate the chapel space to remove the divided chancel, the stately organ with impressive ranks of pipe, the magisterial pulpit with its eagle wings lectern, and the beautiful paneled walls. The entire space was to be cleared, opening it to be configured according to the various traditions now calling the chapel its place of worship. The liturgical space would be staged to accommodate the symbolism and style of worship on an ad hoc basis. Staff and equipment would be made available to work with members of the alternating worship planning committees. No particular tradition could claim exclusive domain, all would be free to prepare the meeting space for the encounter with the divine presence. What a powerful theological question such newly acquired freedom placed before all of us. What kind of space best satisfies the divine taste?

We fully recognized the call to worship the Lord in the beauty of holiness. Yet we also acknowledged that beauty refers not only to architectural style, proportion, balance, harmonies, and artistic ornamentation, but also to the quality of relationships fostered by the temporal, spatial arrangements. As the seminary struggled to rise above the dominating proclivities of the past, it was abundantly clear that a structure of limited aesthetic delight could honor the longing in God's heart that the place of worship reflects the collective integrity of the whole community.

After a period of intense debate, the decision was made and the chapel was renovated. One of the last issues to be resolved was the question of musical instruments. Okay, we would replace the grand organ of James Chapel with a less imposing Holtcamp organ, but the suggestion was made to also purchase a Hammond organ, frequently used in black church worship. So vigorous was that debate that the President decided not to buy a Hammond organ, but rather to rent one if such were required for any particular event.

In 1989 I accepted the call to be the senior minister of the famed Riverside Church right across the street from the seminary. Words are inadequate to describe the beauty and majesty of the procession of nearly three hundred robed clergy representing a vast interfaith array of ministerial colleagues who had been assembled on June 1 of that year to launch Riverside into its interracial reconciliation and prophetic rededication to peace, justice, and compassion. I suspect there was even angelic representation that evening as we entered one of the most wonderful worship spaces since Chartres Cathedral was dedicated in France in the thirteenth century. The music was ethereal and the Rev. Gardner C. Taylor bellowed forth words of hope for new and exciting happenings on Morningside Heights.

For a time, it seemed that all was right with the world. But, in the course of time, we were rudely awakened to how difficult it is to bring heaven down to earth and to sustain even approximations of it—for long. In a few months some members discovered what had been largely overlooked, "Oh my God . . . He's black!" There was a difference in style between Coffin and Forbes. People started responding to the sermons with "Amen!" and "Hallelujah!" Was the music going to change? And why does it take so long for the spirit to get around to the point? How long will it be before we hit the tilt factor, turning Riverside into just another black church in Harlem? Let me report that Riverside is still an interracial, interdenominational, and international church. But all has not been peace and joy down by The Riverside. What we continue to be has come at great price.

One of the challenges in the transition had to do with the sound system in the vaulted gothic space. The beauty of the space in terms of sight left something to be desired concerning sound. It was suggested that the quality of the sound might be improved if we mounted speakers on the columns of the nave—color coordinated, of course, to blend in with the gray interior of the church. But then it was brought to our attention that there was a formal prohibition from affixing anything to the walls of the church or even inscribing new information there. What good is it to fiercely maintain the visual beauty of a worship space if doing so inhibits the transmission of God's word? I thought, here that question is again: "What kind of space best satisfies the divine taste?"

Most frequently, "taste" means "my taste." My "taste" is usually better than the taste of "the others." In the heat of culture change we rarely stop to think of "the taste of God." This is because there is the blurring of the line between mine and the divine. We seek to offer God our very best and our very best understanding is derived from the cultural milieu in which we were socialized and therefore "aestheticized."

We need to take time to discern the finer points of the divine aesthetic. Serious reflection on the consequences of a divine critique of our aesthetics, customs, habits, and desires could revolutionize our whole way of life. It will provide much needed wisdom as we work against Dr. King's triple evils: racism, materialism (greed), and militarism (violence).

I am happy to report that over a thirty-year period of agonizing controversy and conflict, the Riverside Church has been blessed with spiritual instructions in the area of divine aesthetics. We may not yet be ready for the final exam but we are making a passing grade on the questions of tradition vs. innovation, black, brown, Asian, and white, gay and straight and transgendered, congregational polity vs. more authoritarian and hierarchical governance. And by the way, we are facing the challenge of enjoying the vaulted sense of the holy in a gothic space and, with the aid of modern technology, we are better able to hear and see the choirs and the preachers in the sanctuary and even to stream the prophetic word around the world. Nobody complains about the speaker on the columns or the TV monitors around the wall.    *1989-2007*

On June 1, 2007, I retired from my post as senior minister of Riverside Church. Shortly thereafter I founded the Healing of the Nations Foundation. After several temporary locations I settled into a beautiful suite of offices in the Interchurch Center across the street from both Union Seminary and the Riverside Church. Outside of the offices of Paula M. Mayo, the Executive Director of the Center, are large photographs associated with the construction of the building and the cornerstone laying. I recall being in the large crowd assembled in the Riverside Park to observe the cornerstone laying by General Dwight W. Eisenhower, then the President of Columbia University. This took place on October 12, 1958. I was in my freshman student year at the seminary. As I stood with the crowd observing the ceremony from the shade of Riverside Park, I was struck by the utter absence of ornamentation or stylistic distinction of the building. It was like a big box. What led to the choice of that design for a building that was to house the major denominations of the church and also serve the social agencies of the community? It will be no surprise to anyone that some form of our perennial question had been considered in the final choice of the architectural design. From Paula Mayo, I learned that it was Mr. John D. Rockefeller's desire to provide a building that could be for all the denominations. No one denomination was to view the building as representing its tradition. There was to be equality in the sense of shared claim to the space. It was to be a place where there was a family reunion to do the Lord's work. Among the various proposals submitted, the one that won out had the distinction that no one could call it uniquely her or his own. It would be theirs together. If it looks like a box, so be it. Might even that kind of bland space satisfy the divine taste?

In 2018 we commemorate the martyrdom of Dr. Martin Luther King Jr. He gave his life in pursuit of the dream of our becoming the beloved community. What will the beloved community look like? How will it be designed in terms of social, economic, and political power? What will the racial, class, gender, ideological, immigration, trade, or tax policies be? How will resources be produced, managed, distributed, consumed, and accounted for? How will the powerful and the vulnerable be held accountable for the common good? How will the human community show responsibility to each other and to our cosmic neighbors? In his last sermon, Dr. King offers prophetic wisdom that speaks to the issue of divine aesthetics. In his final paragraph he offers seven words that may be instructive to those of us who are charged with helping to mold the beloved community. A beginning point will be to join our prophet in his mantra: "I just want to do God's will."[1] To place the divine aesthetic above our will, our way, our preference, our prerogative, will help pave the way to the beloved community.

Then Dr. King prophesied that we will get to the Promised Land. Of course, his use of "we" held special resonance for blacks, poor people, the downtrodden, and the outcast, but he always reminded us of the inescapable mutuality and the single garment of destiny that requires "we" to be understood as radically inclusive. His was an African sensibility that says, "I am because we are." The divine aesthetic considers us as one humanity. Divided humanity is illusional and reflects an intrusion of an evil, alienating spirit that locks us into concupiscence, narcissism, selfishness, and greed.

Perhaps this is why Dr. King's final speech was delivered at Mason Temple Church of God in Christ—a denomination whose historic emphasis has been on the power and presence of the Holy Spirit. It is as if the Lord was saying to Martin:

> You have brought the movement as far as you could. Even though you're in the midst of planning the Poor People's Campaign, there will not be much progress until the gross despiritualization of this nation has been acknowledged and addressed. In order to see the vision of the beloved community and to discern

1. King, "Mountaintop."

the value by which to build it, there must be a revitalization of
values, meaning, purpose, and mission. The Spirit holds the key
to the divine aesthetic. The Spirit holds the key to community.
Re-spiritualization will prepare the nation to begin to build toward the beloved community and the realization of the dream.

As I am completing this essay, our nation has paused to observe a
weekend of national mourning—the deaths of Aretha Franklin and Senator
John McCain. Their memorial events were held in quite different settings.
One in the Greater Grace Temple in Detroit, and the other at the Washington Cathedral in the District of Columbia. One lasted for eight hours and
the other for two and a half hours. One was characterized by solemn ritual
of the Episcopal tradition and the other the free church spontaneity of the
black religious experience. Are we prepared to declare which of the two was
more acceptable to God? Or is it more likely that the divine aesthetic would
be more focused on the truth, the beauty, and the integrity manifested in
either place? And on the basis of that aesthetic, perhaps God could smile
with delight on both events.

Of all that I learned on Morningside Heights from my days as a student, professor, or pastor, I have been enrolled in an unofficial course on
how to become one people under God. The guardians of the old status
quo as well as the newly engrafted constituents all had their principles to
protect, interests to promote, and objectives to advance. Intense conflicts
were inevitable and, at times, warring parties felt that they were merely
championing the very mandates of God in upholding non-negotiables in
the fray. Because we were a covenant community committed to rational justifications for the claims we held, dialogue about foundational convictions
was always a non-negotiable requirement if we were to stay at the table of
sisterly and brotherly love. All the various factions had to seek to live up to
the high level of Dr. King's seven words of prophetic faithfulness. But what
is God's will in times of change from old verities to uncharted pathways?
Although we did not register for the course, we found ourselves engaged in
the community-wide team-taught seminar on divine aesthetics. What in the
eyes of God is true, good, beautiful, just, kind, and worthy of the categorical
imperative to embrace perspectives we could genuinely offer as worthy of
universal affirmation? The one aspect that may be fundamental to the divine
aesthetic is: the divine aesthetic flows from the nature of the heart of God.
Among the many attributes of God, I think of God as ultimate relationality;
what is most beautiful to God is when all of God's creation, without exception, relates intimately and harmoniously with itself, with others, and with
God. If I want to honor the commitment I made to Dr. King the day of his

death—"Martin, you shall not have died in vain"—I apply the test of this divine aesthetic.

In matters relating to environmental responsibility, international relations, reproductive rights, tax and trade policy, gender justice, sexual orientation, immigration policy, incarceration practices, personal behavior, and care for the poor, I quote the words of King: "I just want to do God's will." And in seeking to discern the will of God, I pose this question—what quality of relationality will result from the action I take? And I hope to hear the God of creation say concerning the steps I take, "Now, that's good."

## BIBLIOGRAPHY

King, Martin Luther, Jr. "I've Been to the Mountaintop." Address Delivered at Bishop Charles Mason Temple, Memphis, Tennessee, April 3, 1968.

# 8

# Striving for Women

*Phyllis Trible*

## INTRODUCTION

Although Donald Shriver and I did not meet until the third year of his presidency at Union Theological Seminary (1978), links between us originated at birth. We are both Virginians, he born in Norfolk and I, a few years later, in Richmond. Growing up in that "mother of all states," we carry in our psyches its proud and scandalous histories. From Jamestown (1607) and the coming of slaves (1619), from Pocahontas to Thomas Jefferson, from the Declaration of Independence to the declaration of the Civil War, from bloody battlefields and the defeat at Appomattox, from Reconstruction to racial separation (Jim Crow)—all these and other memories mark "true" Virginians to this day.[1] From the beginning, then, Donald Shriver and I connected, though we knew it not. More was to come.

---

1. Reflecting recently on our Virginia roots, Don Shriver and I separately came upon an engaging article by Drew Gilpin Faust (retired President of Harvard University): Faust, "Carry Me Back," 52–61. Intriguing parallels and contrasts among the three of us surfaced. (a) We come from three distinct areas of the state: Shriver from the east

Completing high school in Virginia, each of us chose to attend college in North Carolina. Don, a Southern Presbyterian, went to Davidson College near Charlotte (at that time strictly a men's institution), and I, a Southern Baptist, went to Meredith College in Raleigh (a women's institution to this day). Upon finishing, we—again unknown to each other—chose to pursue graduate work in theological institutions: Don first at Union Theological Seminary in Richmond (now named Union Presbyterian Seminary) and then at Harvard Divinity School and I at Union Theological Seminary in New York.

## WOMEN ON THE UNION FACULTY

These unknown links, from birth to adulthood, lay in our backgrounds when first Don and I met, at Union Seminary in New York in 1978. The purpose was to discuss my joining the faculty in the field of Old Testament (so then designated). As I reflected on the offer, certain memories of my own student days at Union (mid-1950s to early 1960s) surfaced. The memories included the only two full-time, tenured faculty women in the 1950s and sixties. With neither of them did I study but in some deeper ways I identified. Dr. Mary Ely Lyman, holding a PhD from the University of Chicago in New Testament as well as being the author of several scholarly books, held the telling title Jesup Professor of English Bible. In other words, she was not allowed to teach basic required courses, only supplements in English. Dr. Mary A. Tully, a Canadian with an EdD from Teacher's College, Columbia University, taught courses in Religious Education (considered a lesser discipline in the curriculum) and did student counseling on the side. Never the author of a book, she was kept at the rank of Associate Professor. In those days, faculty appointments at Union fit the mold of patriarchy in seminaries as in the culture at large.[2]

Across years changes respecting women entered the theological scene. In 1963 the second wave of feminism in America arrived with the publication of Betty Friedan's *The Feminine Mystique*. Soon thereafter came Mary Daly's *The Church and the Second Sex* (1968).[3] It called for an exodus from

---

(Tidewater); Trible from the center (Piedmont); Faust from the northwest (Shenandoah Valley). (b) We were born in three sequential decades: the 1920s, 30s, and 40s. (c) As adults, we each chose careers in academe. (d) We worked in major cities of the Northeast, namely New York and Boston/Cambridge in an era when feminism was making its mark in higher education. (e) Each of us continues to carry devotion with criticism for our native state.

2. For a comprehensive study, see Handy, *A History of Union Theological Seminary*.

3. Daly, *The Church and the Second Sex*.

patriarchal religion (though later she repudiated the book as reformist rather than revolutionary). Reverberations from such books formed part of the background for faculty women during the presidency of Donald Shriver. When he arrived at Union (1975), the Seminary had four white women (three Protestant and one Jewish) of varying ranks on its full-time faculty of approximately twenty-six members—plus a few female and male part-time lecturers.[4] The four were Beverly Harrison, Dorothee Soelle (Visiting Professor from Germany), Ann Belford Ulanov, and Marcia Weinstein. By the time Shriver retired from the Seminary (1996), it had eight full-time faculty women (six with named chairs) out of a total of approximately twenty-four members (excluding adjuncts). The eight represented different races, ethnicities, religious orientations, and educational backgrounds.[5] Listed alphabetically with their highest ranks, they included:

- Mary C. Boys: Skinner and McAlpin Professor of Practical Theology
- Ada María Díaz-Stevens: Associate Professor of Church and Society
- Beverly Wildung Harrison: Carolyn Williams Beaird Professor of Christian Ethics
- Edwina Hunter: Joe R. Engle Professor of Preaching
- Phyllis Trible: Baldwin Professor of Sacred Literature
- Ann Ulanov: Christiane Brooks Johnson Memorial Professor of Psychiatry and Religion
- Janet Walton: Professor of Worship and the Arts
- Delores Williams: Paul Tillich Professor of Theology and Culture

Of these eight women, Harrison, Hunter, and Díaz-Stevens are now deceased. The others are retired and scattered here and there, with some close to Union.

---

4. Data given throughout this article about numbers and identities of faculty come from my perusals of select sources that are available in the Office of Development and Alumni Affairs at the Seminary. See *Directory 1975–1976*; also *Catalog for 1995–1997*. Although the data are reliable, I do not vouch for complete accuracy in transmission. Occasionally, exegesis proved difficult; e.g., how to rank a woman (or man) who was not technically a faculty appointee but nonetheless held faculty status.

5. For a special, perhaps unique, picture of women faculty (in the broad sense) in the 1980s, see Handy, *History of Union Theological Seminary*, 337. This picture includes tenured, non-tenured, and staff members: Jualynne Dodson, Dean of Seminary Life; Ann Ulanov, Psychiatry and Religion; Phyllis Trible, Sacred Literature; Janet Walton, Worship and the Arts; Beverly Harrison, Christian Ethics; Ardith Hayes, Professional Development; Dorothee Soelle, Theology.

During the years of Shriver's presidency, I would be asked at times by various people—faculty, students, friends, and the curious—"How do you women on the faculty get along?" (Was this kind of question also asked about and to the male faculty? I wonder.) The short answer remains a four-letter word: "fine." The longer answer adds the phrase, "but with differences." The year preceding my arrival, so I am told, a debate had ensued about the proposed promotion of Beverly Harrison to full professor before she had published a book. In time the promotion came to pass, with the support of the new president.

In my years at the Seminary, women faculty espoused varieties of "feminism" in varieties of ways. I recall different views and emphases under this label and, further, its extension and alteration with the arrival of "womanist" theology and the like. An example of differences appeared in how we women viewed the Bible. Some of us saw this foundational text as friend and challenger; others as enemy. Still others were just not that interested in the sacred word (for shame!). Again, some faculty feminists focused on social dimensions of faith. Some explored the depths of the psychological pilgrimage. Some embraced ecumenism, including Jewish and Christian relations. Some reached out to cover what we now call the LGBTQ community and some to stress ethnic and racial dimensions of faith. Though we did not vote as a unit at faculty meetings (nor did we sit in a group), we were all committed to the demise of patriarchy, sexism, racism and to the persistence of feminism, womanism, and the like; in other words, to the rule of justice and mercy for all. Personalities and pursuits differed. Throughout the years, whether vocal or silent, the support of Donald Shriver was present.

## STUDENT ENROLLMENT AND PARTICIPATION

As significant changes occurred within the faculty during the Shriver presidency, related developments happened within the student population. The increase and impact of women altered the daily academic life and social outreach of the Seminary. New courses appeared in the curriculum; new contexts and content appeared in traditional courses.

As I ponder the changes, I revert first to my own student days in the 1950s and sixties, again to the somewhat isolated faculty figures of Dr. Lyman and Dr. Tully. Next I recall the composition of my own entering class. Of approximately one hundred enrollees, no more than seven were females (including women in the Master of Religious Education program). Only four can I identify as BD students. (One remains a friend to this day.) At the time, that number was hailed as the largest enrollment of women to date! (One does not forget such "praise" from well-intended patriarchs.)

To jump from these memories to the beginnings of the Shriver era omits stories and points of view across decades. This jump we make. In 1975–76 student enrollment at Union consisted of 192 men and 127 women, a difference of sixty-five.[6] In 1996–97, the year of Shriver's retirement, the figures were 124 men and 165 women, a difference of forty-one, with movement from a male to a female majority.

## CHANGES IN TEACHING

The stronger presence of women students affected research, lecturing, and discussions. Professors could no longer rely on staid ways of interpreting their disciplines. Even as the faculty continued to lecture and lead discussion, it also learned more excellent ways. In biblical studies, for example, we began to exegete neglected texts and characters, such as the daughter of Jephthah and the unnamed concubine in the book of Judges. Familiar texts and characters also received new meanings, such as the intelligence and perception of the Syrophoenician woman who called Jesus to account by using his own words to teach him (Mark 7:24–30; Matt 15:21–28). Similarly, focus on Mary Magdalene as the first disciple was heightened (John 20:1). Overall, patriarchal elements of Scripture and interpretations thereof came under sharp scrutiny.

Don Shriver remembers a conversation with Professor Raymond E. Brown, SS, who, after his retirement, taught courses at Roman Catholic seminaries. Shriver asked Brown what he missed most about no longer teaching at Union. The reply, "I miss the presence of women students in my classes." Female students mattered; they made a difference. The answer has made a difference for Shriver also. He has not forgotten.

Sharing this story recently with my friend and former colleague David Lotz, Washburn Professor of Church History Emeritus, I asked if he would reflect briefly on what difference the increased presence of women students made in his own teaching. A selection from his written reply, dated September 12, 2019, reads,

> The steady increasing number of women students during my thirty-three years of teaching at Union (1968–2001) prompted me, with some frequency, to review and revise my course offerings in Medieval and Reformation Church History. For

6. This information was provided by staff in the Office of Development and Alumni/ae Affairs at Union Theological Seminary.

example, whereas I once devoted several lectures to the thought of Bernard of Clairvaux and to Meister Eckhart, I now turned to a detailed analysis and exposition of primary texts by two medieval women visionaries: Hildegard of Bingen and Catherine of Siena. I was greatly aided in this venture by two of our women doctoral students who served for a period of years as teaching assistants . . . I remain grateful to so many women (and to the men, of course!) for their presence and spirited participation in my classes across many years; I still keenly miss them![7]

Another faculty member during Shriver's presidency (and after), was Janet Walton, Professor of Worship and the Arts. Reflecting on the difference the increasing number of women made to the life of the Seminary, she submits this statement:

Women at Union changed conversations in the classroom and within the faculty. New courses were designed that focused on women's experiences. Introductory courses in every field included resources by female authors. Women felt empowered to honor their particular questions. Men and women were challenged to enlarge the parameters of what constitutes being human.[8]

All in all, for students and faculty, a distinctive new era emerged at Union during Shriver's presidency. Women made the difference.

## CONCLUSION

When Don retired in 1996, he and Peggy chose to remain in Morningside Heights so as to participate, as appropriate, in the theological life of the Seminary as well as to enjoy other opportunities in the City. Two years later, in my own retirement, I too chose to stay in the area (with excursions to teach in North Carolina). Accordingly, links between Don and me, which first emerged with our births in Virginia, continue to this day. Again, the arrangement happened without our planning it. Further, as I review the list of faculty women during Don's tenure, I observe that three others still live in Manhattan, indeed at or near the Seminary: Mary Boys, recent Academic Dean and continuing faculty member; Ann Ulanov, with the Jungian Psychoanalytic Association; and Janet Walton, consultant in worship for several synagogues in New York. The "old order" endures even as the new takes

7. Lotz, Message to author, September 12, 2019.
8. Walton, Letter to author, July 2019.

its place. Accordingly, we remember with gratitude the striving for women at Union Theological Seminary during the presidency of Donald Shriver.

## BIBLIOGRAPHY

Daly, Mary. *The Church and the Second Sex: With a New Feminist Postchristian Introduction by the Author*. New York: Harper & Row, 1975.

*Catalog for 1995–1997*. Union Theological Seminary in Association with Auburn Theological Seminary, New York City.

*Directory 1975–1976*. Union Theological Seminary, New York City.

Faust, Drew Gilpin. "Carry Me Back: Race, History, and Memories of a Virginia Girlhood." *The Atlantic*, August 2019, 52–61.

Handy, Robert T. *A History of Union Theological Seminary in New York*. New York: Columbia University Press, 1987.

Lotz, David. Message to Phyllis Trible, September 12, 2019.

Walton, Janet. Letter to Phyllis Trible, July 2019.

# Union Presidency: Friends and Family, Neighbors and Colleagues

# 9

# Conversations with Don Shriver

*Robert Pollack*

## I. DON AND PEGGY SHRIVER

Don and Peggy have been friends to Amy and me from the very first time we met in the early 1990s, when Don was the chancellor of Union Theological Seminary and I had just stepped down from a seven-year stint as the twelfth Dean of Columbia College. Don was in the midst of his ongoing work to bring about justice with mercy for members of a number of marginalized groups of people, and I was coming to terms with the experiences I had been through as the first Jewish Dean of an Ivy League College. I cannot point to any single event, but I feel strongly the tug of memory of many conversations with Don in which the subject always was how to say and write what one meant, at a time when I was working on my first book, *Signs of Life: The Language and Meaning of DNA*, and Don was beginning to plan his groundbreaking book *Honest Patriots*.

The noun conversation means the informal exchange of ideas by spoken words.[1] The word comes from a Middle English word that carried the

1. Wikipedia, s.v. "Conversation."

87

meanings of "living among, familiarity, intimacy," via Old French from Latin *conversatio*(n), from the verb *conversari*.[2] In short, conversation is more than an exchange of words, it is a safe exchange among people familiar with each other and capable of intimate confidences. I did not know it then, but I know it now: Don taught me the deep human necessity of safe and clear sharing of ideas; the centrality, that is, of simple conversation.

Well, so what? On the face of it, this is fairly banal. After all, don't we all converse, all the time? I am afraid not. We do talk to each other, and we do listen. But talking and listening are only necessary, though not sufficient components of conversation. Conversation can occur only among equals, two or more people who respect the others sufficiently to assure that differences will be tolerated and explored, rather than being the tinder for an explosion of condescension, insult, or worse.

## II. THE EVANESCENCE OF CONVERSATION

Here's one example, from that time when Don and I met. When I had been chosen as Dean of the College, I had taken it upon myself to meet a promise that would cost a lot of money: to assure that admission to Columbia College would be held totally apart from any consideration of an applicant's financial situation. For that, alumni would have to give me sufficient funds each year to assure scholarships would be available as needed for anyone who had been admitted, so that they could attend classes, live on campus, and engage in the life of the College. That policy I then coupled to one that meant the world to me: I was given the gift of breaking a 240-year precedent by opening admission to Columbia College to women for the first time since 1754 when the college—then King's College—was founded. Putting these two policy changes together meant that I was committing the College to increasing its diversity in a very serious way.[3]

The case I made to alumni who had the capacity to help fund these policies was simple: I needed funds to do my job in the only right way. I quickly received a number of gifts that outpaced my ability or need to spend them in the year they arrived. The consequence was what you would expect: my immediate superiors in the University administration informed me that, as I had an excess of funds for financial aid, they would be taking those funds for financial aid in other schools of the arts and Sciences. When I objected I was told, "There are those who get asked, there are those who get

2. Oxford University Press, "conversation."
3. Van Gelder, "Study of Life," 11.

told, and there are those who decide. We decide, you get told." Now how could I object to that?

Burning with shame at having my promises to my fellow alumni over-ruled, I arranged to be called by a trustee who had recently made a very large commitment to undergraduate life on campus. He told me I could not do anything about the decision; I needed to see that I was not in a conversation with my superiors, but rather in a position of absolute dependency. But, he said, he was not. So, in a conversation that changed my life, he shared with me his plan.

He created an "Alumni Fund Endowment" to hold the funds I raised for scholarships in the University endowment. He promised to add to it sufficient funds each year to assure that I would be able to spend the full yield of it each year. Within a few years we had raised and endowed $40 million, and that yielded enough each year to meet the policy and assure economic as well as gender and ethnic diversities. That elegant solution only lasted a few years, though, because the year after I stepped down as Dean, my successor was asked by his superiors to allow them to administer financial aid for the College as part of a move toward administrative efficiency, and this allowed the same superior officers of Administration to decapitalize the entire Alumni Fund endowment.

This was not a bad thing: the administrators in charge of financial aid continued to provide sufficient funds for a need-blind policy, albeit with an increasing debt-load for families who were eligible for student loans. The difference before and after was in whether the Dean of the College was permitted to engage in a specific example of conversation with his, or her, alumni. I narrate this story at length to illustrate both the power and the evanescence of real conversation in a world where talking and listening are so rarely carried out between equals, and where instead talking and listening are simply giving and getting of orders.


## III. THE BIOLOGY OF CONVERSATION

In 2014 Amy and I put together a book, *The Course of Nature*, that presented forty-four of her drawings on Natural Selection, with my short summaries opposite each drawing.[4] In chapter 9, "Becoming Human," Amy presented the attached drawing (Figure 1) and I wrote this in response:

> Darwin counted our unique mental capacities among the re-wards of natural selection for us as a species. So, on a foundation

4. Pollack and Pollack, *Course of Nature*.

of neural circuitry we have built temples in our mind, often with a personification, like Athena, of a wisdom we hope we may attain. What a great success natural selection has found in us!

Or, perhaps not. Our mental worlds are no longer subject to natural selection. In fact, they never were; that's the reason for our spectacularly disproportionate success at proliferating. We have broken out of natural selection's slow sieve of mutation; we can simply have an idea, and choose to act on it. No need to wait for natural selection's positive feedback loop to select for a DNA variation that permits that new idea. Any brain can have any idea, anytime.

So, the joke of our imagination is on nature, but as a consequence it is on us as well. Our minds can encompass nature, but they can also go beyond nature, and imagine things that need not be possible in nature. When we do that, we may escape nature for a while, but in the end, these excrescences of the brain will be brought back into alignment with the facts of nature by the fact of species mortality. If there is one place for imagination to generate wisdom, that would be the place.[5]

That brings us right back to a life of conversation. Conversation allows us to travel away from nature together, and to return safely (Figure 2). That is why conversations with Don have been so important; they ranged as widely as our imaginations could carry us, but never at the cost of leaving one of us behind. There is a good reason why conversation enwraps its participants. Conversation with another emerges from a prior activity of each of our brains, which begins in infancy and, if we are lucky, never leaves us. As adults we experience this gift of conversation as a chat with oneself.[6] It seems reasonable to suggest that the very fact of our social lives, our ability and need to know and be known by others, begins with this ability of the human brain to converse with itself.

## IV. THE POLITICAL NECESSITY OF CONVERSATION

Some years after we met, Don arranged with his successor as President of Union Theological Seminary, Joe Hough, to have UTS send me as an emissary to a meeting in Berlin, in honor of Dietrich Bonhoeffer. I was honored, frightened, and amazed to find myself so much at home in this event. I had to give a talk, and even though I was invited to speak in English, I

5. Pollack and Pollack, *Course of Nature*, 101.
6. Fernyhough, "Talking to Ourselves," 74.

felt obligated to open and close the talk in German.[7] I met this obligation in the best possible way, by finding help from a German student at Jewish Theological Seminary, across Broadway from UTS.

I ended my talk with a reflection on the importance of telling the truth. In the context of this essay in honor of Don, I'll quote what I said then, and hope that you will agree that I was also articulating the importance of real conversation at times like the ones we have been in for the past few years, when it is ever easier to get either angry, or frightened, or both:

> It took only the first month of life under National Socialism for Bonhoeffer to decide to tell his fellow pastors it was time to be 'a spoke in the wheel.' By the rest of his short life, he teaches us today that only by telling the unwelcome truth early and often while we are free to do so, can we hope never to have to be 'spokes in the wheel' ourselves.[8]

Thank you so much, Don Shriver, for giving Amy and me the gift of your conversation. Since writing our book, Amy and I have understood your capacity for true, shared conversation to be a gift of love. (Figure 2)

---

7. Pollack, "Religious Obligation," 79.
8. Pollack, "Religious Obligation," 110n 45.

## FIGURE 1, ATHENA ARISING FROM
## A NEURAL NETWORK

In Greek mythology Athena, goddess of wisdom, was born from the forehead of
Zeus her father. The Romans then gave this history to their goddess of wisdom,
Minerva. It is not a great stretch of imagination to bring that myth into the
present, by acknowledging that networks of neurons in our heads create ideas,
some of them as powerful and unnatural as this story of the emergence of the
personification of wisdom from the mind of a God.

# FIGURE 2, THE INHERITED CAPACITY FOR LOVE

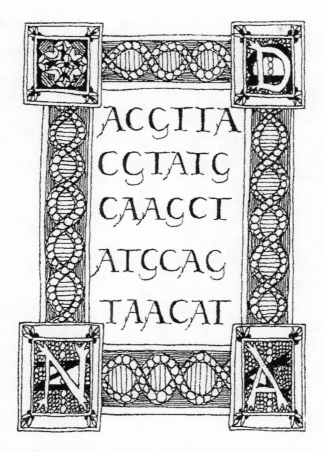

The philosophers speak of four kinds of love, each having its place in the life of a person. Eros, for desire; Agape, for unconditional love; Filia, for family and friendship; and Caritas, for love and kindness to the stranger . . . If there is one lesson we can take from our DNA sequences and the tapestry of our origins by natural selection, it is this: cynicism and despair are choices, but not ones encoded by our DNA. But these four kinds of love are encoded, and they can be expressed by any of us through our lifetimes. None of us could have begun without Eros. None of us could have survived the burden of our inherited late-maturing neural circuitry without Agape from someone who cared for us at a time when we were of no use nor value except for our lovability. None of us could begin to understand the world and our chance of happiness in it without Filia. None of us can be fully human without Caritas, both from us and to us.[9]

9. Pollack and Pollack, *Course of Nature*, 111.

## BIBLIOGRAPHY

Fernyhough, Charles. "Talking to Ourselves." *Scientific American* 317, no. 2 (2017) 74–79.

Oxford University Press. "conversation." *Lexico.com.* Oxford University Press, 2019. https://www.lexico.com/en/definition/conversation.

Pollack, Amy, and Robert Pollack. *The Course of Nature: A Book of Drawings on Natural Selection and Its Consequences.* Middletown, DE: Stony Creek, 2014.

Pollack, Robert. "The Religious Obligation to Ask Questions of Nature and the State: Bonhoeffer on the Protection and Dignity of Human Life, in the Context of DNA-Based Genetic Medicine Today." *Union Seminary Quarterly Review* 60 (2006) 78–110.

Van Gelder, Lawrence. "Study of Life Leads to Life as Dean." *New York Times*, October 2, 1983.

Wikipedia, s.v. "Conversation," last modified March 18, 2020, https://en.wikipedia.org/wiki/Conversation.

# 10

# Toward Atonement and Beyond

*Ismar Schorsch*

When I became Chancellor of Jewish Theological Seminary in 1986, Donald W. Shriver Jr. at the helm of Union Theological Seminary across the street in Manhattan awaited to befriend me. For years he had been a friend of my teacher and predecessor Gerson D. Cohen and he did not want those institutional ties to lapse. Our two seminaries had been interfacing and collaborating since the days of Reinhold Niebuhr and Abraham Joshua Heschel. The personal relationship of President and Chancellor bespoke the traffic of students crossing Broadway to take courses offered at Union or JTS, the team teaching of faculty members with mutual interests and disciplines and the social evenings of both faculties spent in conversation and study. Good leadership had turned proximity into a blessing.

Retirement did not bring our friendship to an end. Donald's two seminal works, *An Ethic for Enemies* (1995) and *Honest Patriots* (2005), drew us closer still by shifting our dialogue to German history. What I appreciate beyond measure in Donald's books is his resolute application of Christian ethics to the moral aberrations of the nation-state. His ethical values are quickly tested and grounded in the rough terrain of comparative history.

Since many a modern body politic is burdened with original sin, the question to be asked is to what extent has each mustered the willpower to confront that dark chapter of its past? To his credit, Donald does not spare his own in this discomforting and disputatious study. From both books present-day Germany emerges as an emblem of hope, a society which in fits and starts has faced down its past with unparalleled thoroughness and truthfulness.

I wish to confirm Donald's perspicacious analysis from my own vantage point as a historian of German-speaking Jewry in the modern period. While birth is destiny, I bring no memories of my early childhood in Hanover. My assessment of Germany's post-war trajectory is the product of study and experience that began in 1971–72 with an ambitious two-semester seminar given at the Seminary on the interwar years and the Final Solution. Accordingly, I will divide my comments between a survey of the national manifestations of Germany's quest for atonement and my personal experiences as a participant observer.

If I periodically slip into the religious language of atonement it is because the secular term of reparations is wholly inadequate. Nothing can restore the victims. Atonement is an exercise of self-cleansing, driven by remorse, candor, and self-incrimination. When done wholeheartedly it restores the possibility of a new relationship of at-one-ness between victim and assailant, precisely what is taking place in Germany today.

## II

My survey of the last seventy years is not chronological but rather a typological ordering of the diversity of manifestations of atonement. Often overlooked in the rush to judge is the singular fact that Germany is today a stable, functioning democracy firmly implanted in the West. Such an integration failed abysmally after the senseless carnage of the Great War which was hardly brought to a close by Versailles. Indeed, since Napoleon's humiliating occupation of Prussia, Germany fiercely distanced itself from the ethos and institutions of the West, including its rationalism, legal codes, emerging forms of self-government, and suspicion of religion in politics. The termination of that deep cultural rift by a wise occupation enabled America to forge a democratic Germany into a bulwark against Communism and a domestic scene conducive to an eventual confrontation with Germany's multiple acts of genocide. The stern leadership of Konrad Adenauer was essential to moving toward the achievement of both aspirations.

Thus the earliest manifestation of a spirit of atonement was the Luxembourg Agreement in 1952 between Israel and West Germany, which assured the nascent Jewish state of $822 million in money and materials over twelve years, enabling it to finance a decade of massive immigration. Nor was that to be the final instance of German reparations. Negotiations between the Jewish Material Claims (Conference) and the German Ministry of Finance continued annually and since 2009 produced another $9 billion in benefits to fifty-five thousand Holocaust survivors worldwide. Underscoring the significance of that initial agreement was the fact that in 1952 West Germany was still awash with former Nazis and their children and swarming with German immigrants expelled from their long-time homes in eastern Europe. Even Adenauer was halfhearted about the American de-Nazification program. Yet he understood that West Germany's only way into the comity of nations blocking the advance of the Soviet Union and its satellites was with a resounding gesture of contrition.

A second manifest expression of atonement was the creation of Holocaust memorials across Germany to ever remind its citizens of the inhumanity of their forbearers. Some are monumental in size and global in scope, while many others are modest and local. Their collective import is their ubiquitous dispersion, reflecting a state of mind unafraid to face an unvarnished history. Before their migration into Germany's urban centers in the nineteenth and twentieth centuries, its Jewish population was scattered and rooted in small towns and rural villages nestled throughout the German countryside. The state of Baden-Wuerttemberg in the southwest, for example, is pockmarked with poignant memorials commemorating the innumerable Jewish communities that once enriched the local landscape.

In the northern village of Sennfeld the former synagogue built in 1836 stands today as a well-cared-for Jewish museum. It escaped the torch of Nazi vandals on November 9, 1938, for fear of fire that might engulf adjacent buildings, but not their fury. Some twenty-five years ago a local Christian gymnasium teacher began to restore what remained of the once charming stone synagogue and its intimate sanctuary and stock it with relics of Jewish ritual and fragments of Jewish life that attest a continuous Jewish settlement from the middle of the fourteenth century. Assiduously he reconstituted the family histories of Jews who had once lived in and around Sennfeld and photographed and copied the tombstone inscriptions in the Jewish cemetery nearby. The father of this unpaid curator of Jewish memory was an early member of the Nazi party and a later prisoner of war, who never spoke to his son of his misguided past. Surely the selfless curatorial labor of his educated son took root in the arid silence of his guilt-ridden father.

In Burgdorf, a small town north of Hanover, I witnessed yet another singular memorial expression of atonement. Once home to a small Jewish community dating back some three hundred years and a synagogue built in

1811, its communal existence was extinguished on November 9, 1938, when its synagogue was pillaged and its contents destroyed. I spoke in the multipurpose room in the town hall in which the city fathers regularly convened on November 10, 2012. They had already refurbished the former synagogue as a civic cultural center with a large plaque identifying its previous history and begun to lay stumbling stones where Jews once resided. A Jewish community was no longer extant in Burgdorf. But what immediately struck me as a unique memorial was an earthen frieze that covered the front wall of the room. Inscribed in large white letters were the names of sixty-two individuals native to Burgdorf and murdered farther east, including an unnamed male child born in Riga in 1942. Dates of birth and death accompanied each person as well as the camp or ghetto in which they met their death. The brown earthen composition of the frieze was meant to lament the pitiful fact that neighbors did not rise to prevent their loss of the right to die and be buried where they had been born. Dedicated in 2008, this charged exhibit confronts city councilors each time they assemble to do their municipal business with a stern warning about the complicity of bystanders.

In May 1996 the German artist Gunter Demnig laid the first fifty of his famous *Stolpersteine* (stumbling stones) illegally in Berlin. By now there are well over sixty thousand of them across Germany, even in recalcitrant Munich. A small square brass plate placed in the pavement of a home in which a Jew and his family had once lived, the *Stolpersteine* relate the name, birthdate, the day of emigration or deportation, and the final location and date of death, if known. Each stone attests assiduous research, often done by local gymnasium students. Demnig's project is an inspired idea to turn a number into a name, a statistic into a human being. Decentralized, the project would have died aborning if it had not found receptive soil in the heart of countless German citizens who felt a national calling never to forget. The sudden sight of a *Stolperstein* is enough to arrest one's gait, to help one recall and imagine the individual who once had graced these premises.

My son lived for a time in the Schoeneberg neighborhood of Berlin, around the corner from the *Stolperstein* for Rabbi Leo Baeck, the brilliant leader of German Jewry in its darkest days and long before. We would never pass by without pausing to pay our respects. The significance of the remarkable *Stolperstein* saga is that the monumental memorials of Dachau and Bergen-Belsen, the Berlin Memorial and Wannsee, and many others have sunk deep into the consciousness of Germany's citizens to effect a quest for atonement truly national in scope.

Yet a third manifestation of atonement is the astounding presence of some 250,000 Jews in Germany today. Cities like Munich and Hanover are home once again to as many Jewish residents as before the war. Berlin may have as many as fifty thousand and the prominence on the city's skyscape of the majestic dome of the 1866 Moorish synagogue in the *Mitte* is eloquent testimony of their growing number. Other synagogues, both old and new, dot the expanse of the city. Across Germany there are some 105 functioning Jewish communities, with schools for the young and homes for the elderly, which increasingly draw their rabbinic and educational personnel from four bona fide graduate programs in Berlin and Heidelberg.

The dynamic eruption of this Jewish demography is the direct consequence of government policy. For years federal and state governments had been underwriting a large part of the construction and institutional costs of Jewish life without much impact on immigration. But with the collapse of the Soviet Union, Bonn and Berlin embarked on a low-key courtship of Russian Jews, to the dismay of Israel, and bore the heavy cost of their resettlement, despite the simultaneous burden of German reunification. The extension of such a red carpet to Soviet Jewish immigrants can only be understood against the backdrop of the Holocaust. Atonement also required the recreation of a replica of the Jewish community destroyed after 1933, even if it would take several generations of Soviet Jews to become appreciative of German Jews. In due time, the overt good will of German policy and the country's economic energy also attracted large numbers of enterprising young Jews from Israel and America.

A fourth remarkable achievement added still more resonance to the chords of atonement emanating from Germany. In the nineteenth century German Jewry had pioneered the development of critical Jewish scholarship as an alternative to tradition to understanding the history of Judaism. With young Jews streaming into German universities, the crucible of historical research, they gained the tools to found the field of Jewish studies, but not the recognition of their research as worthy of inclusion in the curriculum of the citadel of German scholarship. A Protestant ethos continued to govern the German university even at the pinnacle of its academic prowess, and fated the field of Jewish studies to retreat to the halls of German Jewry's three denominational seminaries with their faculties and rabbinical graduates as the field's primary practitioners. Though Jewish studies by the last quarter of the nineteenth century spread to eastern and western Europe and to the shores of the new world, even gaining a few university appointments in France, England, and the United States, the dominant language of publication till 1933 remained German.

It is that distinguished record which highlights the achievement of contemporary Germany. Some seventy-five years after the wasteland of the Third Reich, Germany is the third dominant center for the field of Jewish studies after Israel and the United States. Following the creation of the first

chair in Jewish Studies in 1964 at the Free University in West Berlin, German universities throughout Germany today sponsor Jewish chairs with
their cluster of attached researchers in many sub-fields of Judaica. Their
occupants have all spent time in Israel mastering Hebrew and other Jewish
languages, working on manuscripts and in Israeli archives, and collaborating with Israeli colleagues. Potsdam can even boast of hosting Germany's
first Jewish theological faculty, akin to its older Protestant and Catholic faculties and to its newer Islamic ones. Given that academic firepower and un-
diminished popular interest, Germany publishes some one thousand books
annually related to Jewish subjects, many of which are works of first-rate
scholarship. In short, one cannot be a scholar of Jewish studies today without a command of German, not to get at what was published before 1933,
but to read what is coming out now. And I would argue that this sustained
outburst of intellectual energy has everything to do with a convergence of
institutional funding and individual desire to make amends.

An important shift in attitude is the final manifestation of atonement
that has become noticeable of late in German life. Initiatives to commemorate, recover, or study what had been wiped out no longer seem prompted
solely by an impulse to redress a lost past to Jewish victims, but rather
spring from a desire to repossess for Germans what was once a part of their
own past. In their revocation of Jewish equality and integration, the Nazis
destroyed a vital chapter of German history, and not merely a legacy of a
despised minority. The empty bookcases of Israeli artist Micha Ullman's
searing 1995 memorial beneath the Bebelplatz of Humboldt University in
Berlin, which commemorates the Nazi bonfires of German books by Jewish
authors on May 10, 1933, were once filled with works of science, mathematics, literature, philosophy, and history that were inseparably linked to German culture. The flames left Germany itself grievously impoverished and
destined eventually to lose the war.

 I offer but one striking example of an act of restitution that goes far
beyond a feeling of atonement. In 2008, on the seventy-fifth anniversary of
the expulsion by the Nazis of Jewish civil servants from the German civil
service, the Goethe University in Frankfurt am Main mounted an exhibition dedicated to the Jewish mathematicians (men and women) who after
1933 could no longer continue in their academic posts. Put together by a
team of six mathematicians, the exhibit recounted in exquisite detail the
lives and works of some ninety-one German mathematicians of Jewish
birth who from 1780 to 1933 often made significant contributions to their
chosen field. Many converted to advance their careers, while those who refused languished for years on the periphery of the university world. Moritz
Abraham Stern born in 1829 earned his doctorate in Goettingen with Karl

Friedrich Gauss, Germany's premier mathematician, yet did not reach the rank of *Ordinarius* (full professor) in Goettingen till 1859, decades after his Christian peers. By 1933, after fifteen years of Weimar when it became easier for outsiders to become insiders, mathematicians born as Jews occupied twenty of the ninety-four chairs in German higher education reserved for mathematicians.

With a lot of signage and few photos other than portraits, the exhibit was not destined to be a blockbuster. Yet to compile the profiles of ninety-one mathematicians and read their works required an enormous amount of industry and the richly illustrated catalog composed that wealth of research into six thematic essays that contextualize the public and private lives of their subjects with authority, insight, and empathy. Nevertheless, though a riveting study of discrimination against Jewish mathematicians, I would contend that this exhibition was in fact an impressive instance of a German academic guild reappropriating an unheralded part of its own past. What could be more objective than mathematics, yet a sense of shame and anger at a pattern of pervasive injustice prompted a brave cluster of scientists to identify and unearth a chapter painful to their professional pride, a bitter lesson in the price that ideology always exacts from science.

## III

At this juncture I could end my discourse on the national scene in Germany, but I will try your patience a bit longer with a personal addendum that fully comports with my analysis at a distance. On this fraught subject my experience on the ground does not diverge from my vision of the landscape at thirty thousand feet. Though I was born in 1935 in Hanover where my father came in 1927 as the community's second young rabbi (*Ortsrabbiner* as opposed to *Landesrabbiner*) to reconnect its adolescent generation to the synagogue, my roots in Esslingen near Stuttgart run much deeper. The city had not only a small Jewish community with a modest synagogue, but also a Jewish orphanage and school founded in 1831, which in 1913 acquired a stately new building and surrounding farmland on a grand promontory overlooking Esslingen. No less than the King of Wuerttemberg himself attended the festive dedication. At the time, my grandfather Theodor Rothschild was the director (*Hausvater*) of the orphanage, having ascended to the post in 1899 when his father-in-law and director Leopold Stern died suddenly. Leopold had become director in 1873. Thus the directorship of this regionally important educational institution would be in the hands of my family from 1873 to 1939 when it was closed permanently by the Nazis.

My grandfather Theodor hailed from a half-Jewish village in the Swabian Alps. His five brothers were cattle dealers. But he came to Esslingen to study to become a teacher in its highly regarded Protestant teachers' seminary, after which he went to work in the city's Jewish orphanage. He was a man of the soil who knew the Latin names of its fauna and flora. As director he introduced agriculture and woodwork into the curriculum, freed the children of their uniforms, and had them take their meals with staff as members of a single family. He was not a gray eminence, but a father figure who cared deeply for his children. Each child was assigned his or her daily task. Theodor blended structure and informality with a soft touch. He was also an editor of Jewish educational texts that sold far beyond Esslingen, the last an anthology for dark days in 1936 named *Need and Hope (Not und Hoffnung)* after an epigram by Herder.

Theodor was a religious personality whose practice of Judaism abhorred affectation. The day began with prayer in chapel and grace always followed meals. On Shabbat morning, Theodor walked with his children down to the town's synagogue where he would conduct services for the community, for he functioned as its surrogate rabbi.

My father came to the orphanage in 1907 with his older brother from a family crippled by the mental illness of his mother. They lived in a hamlet in northern Baden quite far from the only synagogue accessible to them in a town several kilometers down the road. At a far greater remove in Wuerttemberg, the family of my father's mother could offer little support in the raising of her seven children, one of whom had died young, and under the burden she broke down to spend the rest of her days institutionalized till she died in 1937. On her tombstone my father noted laconically in the Hebrew inscription that she was ill most of the days of her life.

In Esslingen my father found a new home and a surrogate father. After finishing the *Volksschule* he attended the teachers' seminary like Theodor to graduate in 1919. A traumatic stint in the German army on the western front during the last year of the war convinced my father to consider taking up the rabbinate. To switch educational tracks in Germany, however, was no easy matter. Without the vaunted gymnasium diploma, he lacked the classical languages required for admission to any university. It took my father two years of solitary study to pass the state exam that would attest his having achieved the equivalence of nine years of Latin and seven years of Greek. With that hurdle behind him, he went on to earn his PhD at Tuebingen and his rabbinic ordination from the Breslau Jewish Theological Seminary, the forerunner of JTS. Throughout those arduous years, Esslingen was his base and in December 1926 he married Theodor's older daughter Fanny. Whenever possible my parents would come down to vacation in Esslingen and my older sister Hanna, born in 1929, cherished lifelong memories of our grandfather.

Hanna and I returned to Esslingen in July 1977. I was on my way into East Germany to do research in the Prussian archives that during the war had been moved from Berlin to Merseburg for safekeeping and suggested to my sister a roots trip into southwest Germany before I moved on alone. We arrived at the orphanage unannounced and when no one answered found the ornate front door with its pelican and zodiac symbolism unlocked. We entered on our own to find the premises devoid of any personnel. The orphanage still functioned as a Christian public school but clearly was not in session in July. But Hanna knew the contours of the building well and took me through its spacious rooms overcome with memory. As we climbed the elegant central staircase and scoured each floor, she identified the function of every space and filled it with people she loved. No staff intruded to distract us. Another absence, though, was distressing in the extreme. The building was utterly devoid of any signage that denoted its Jewish origins and former history. Not to embarrass the present, its Jewish past had been simply and totally erased. The willful amnesia drove home for us the still prevailing German refusal to come to terms with the country's unspeakable crimes, a posture of denial also writ large in the meager memorial and sparse signage at Dachau, which we had visited a few days before.

But things had begun to percolate in Esslingen. A brave local journalist wrote often of the distinguished Jewish past of the orphanage and called for renaming it after Theodor Rothschild, and an equally idealistic member of city hall took up the cause within the administration. By 1983 the city council adopted the proposal and in a dignified public ceremony affixed the name Theodor Rothschild Haus to the school on the promontory. The name change heralded the reputation of Theodor as a progressive Jewish educator, celebrated public speaker, and educational activist in the organizational network of Jewish educators in Stuttgart and beyond. A year later the city, like others in Germany, paid to bring back for a visit former Jewish residents of Esslingen, including those from elsewhere who had merely spent time in the orphanage.

Prior to *Reichspogromnacht* my grandfather had refused to apply in Stuttgart for an American visa out of fear that the Nazis would seize it as a pretext to shut down his beloved orphanage and boarding school. Theodor worried about the growing number of children in his care, many of whom no longer had functioning families to which to return. But on November 10, 1938, in broad daylight, Nazi vandals pillaged the facility, burned its books and papers, manhandled the faculty and staff, and threw the children out on the street. Theodor and his wife Ina rounded them up and walked them on foot to Stuttgart. By the summer of 1939 the orphanage was officially closed and Theodor's educational work moved to Stuttgart. The events convinced him to apply for an American visa immediately, but his high number never came close to being called and on August 22, 1942, he and Ina were deported to Theresienstadt, where he perished on July 10, 1944.

On the fiftieth anniversary of his death, Esslingen held a public commemoration on his playing field, the majestic lobby of the orphanage erected in 1913. Though the weather was hot and humid, the space was packed to standing room only. The director of the Stuttgart conservatory fittingly played a few piano sonatas by Victor Ullmann, who died in Theresienstadt in 1944. Both Hanna and I spoke, she movingly of chords of memory that so rarely vibrate within her. The honor added a living presence to the name that adorned the orphanage. Esslingen was manifesting its pride in its Jewish native son.

On that occasion I brought with me an heirloom of handwritten letters from Theodor to his daughters and their husbands in the United States. My aunt and uncle had emigrated at the end of July 1938 and my parents after the destruction of the Romanesque cathedral synagogue in Hanover on November 9 and a ten-day incarceration in Buchenwald by my father. Family in England had secured for us a visa from British Jewry's Chief Rabbi Joseph H. Hertz, who in 1894 had become the first rabbinic graduate of the newly founded Jewish Theological Seminary, of which I would in 1986 become the sixth Chancellor. Till America entered the war against Germany correspondence was still possible. To be sure the letters were rigorously self-censored, yet convey sadly how the lives of Theodor and Ina were shrinking remorselessly. Throughout Theodor reported on the decline of his visa application number.

Stirred by these letters, a devoted band of Esslingen members of Denk-Zeichen (an association committed to acts and memorials of reconciliation) set about to produce a collection of essays that would do justice to the charisma and character of Theodor. From the letters they garnered a grid of his extended family, a sense of his robust love for his native Wuerttemberg, and a taste of his irrepressible optimism. His writings and public lectures provided his educational philosophy and the testimony of former staff and children added insight into how he conducted the orphanage. The engagement of the authors is deep and their empathy palpable and they eventually produced a four-year labor of love. Published by the city of Esslingen, the book came out in 1998 under the title *Troestet Euch, uns geht es gut* (Take comfort, we're doing okay), a collage taken from the Prophet Isaiah (40:1) and a phrase used by Theodor to reassure his children in a letter the day after the orphanage had been plundered. The work reunited me with a grandfather I barely knew and showed me for the first time just how deeply he contributed to the shaping of my father. Though the book bears the sub-title *Theodor Rothschild, a Jewish Educator Between Respect and Contempt (ein juedischer Paedagoge zwischen Achtung und Aechtung)*, it is not a speci-men of parochial history, but rather a proud chapter of Swabian history. Its production culminates a quest for atonement in Esslingen that declaims the adoption of Theodor as a gifted local son, as much Swabian as Jewish. And this trajectory in one corner of Germany I submit mirrors the stages by which the country as a whole has overcome its discomfort in the face of the Holocaust to identify with and take pride in its Jewish past. Since the book I have been back to speak twice and don't believe it is a gross exaggeration to claim that in me Esslingen has come to cherish a spark of my grandfather and a touch of their revered Jewish educator.

The German Jewish prayer book in current use omits understandably the traditional Hebrew prayer for the welfare of the German state and its ruling government. Given Germany's persistent effort at acts of restitution, commemoration, contrition, atonement, and even expressions of German pride in the impact of its Jews, that omission is no longer warranted. Jews in Germany are no longer but "A Guest for the Night" in the language of Shmuel Yosef Agnon.[1]

## BIBLIOGRAPHY

Agnon, Schmuel Yosef. *A Guest for the Night*. Translated by Misha Louvish. New York: Schocken, 1968.

Feiner, Joseph, Elias Gut, and Theodor Rothschild, eds. *Not und Hoffnung: Gedichtsammlung für jüdische Schulen*. Leipzig: Engel, 1936.

Schroth, Claudia. *Tröstet Euch uns geht es gut: Theodor Rothschild: Ein jüdischer Pädagoge zwischen Achtung und* Ächtung. Plochingen: Herba-Druck, 1998.

1. Agnon, *A Guest for the Night*.

# 11

## Your Birthday Salute

*Hays Rockwell*

February 5, 2018

Dear Don,

A week ago today we were meant to be with you and Peggy to salute you on arriving at your tenth decade. A microbe in the genre of the current version of the flu that is upon our land kept us from being there, causing us great regret, and making us very sorry to miss what I feel sure was a splendid event.

What I most miss is the chance to have greeted and congratulated you in person and to have tried to tell you of my admiration for the life and ministry God has entrusted to you. A professor of theology with whom I was a colleague once preached a sermon about what it means to lead a Christian life. He said it takes a cool head and a warm heart. Some people, he said, have hearts so warm they bake their brains. Others have heads so cool their hearts are frozen. What's needed to live the life in Christ is a combination of heart and head that issues in fruitful Christian witness.

That seems to me an accurate characterization of Donald Shriver. You gave your whole self to the leadership of Union seminary. With your heart you gave encouragement to those elements in its life that required compassion, many instances of which are known only to you and the colleagues and friends who were encouraged by you to carry on with the works of God.

With your cool head you dealt with a sometimes-unruly faculty and a Board made up of gifted people, most of whom brought strong egos to the table. To all of this you got the temperature just right, a cool head and a warm heart.

It was a privilege to work with you in the years I served on that Board and to leave it with the gift of your friendship. It was old Martin Marty who said about friendship that it is a gift from God to give us a foretaste of our truest destiny.[1] I believe that and feel great gratitude for your friendship.

I am yours, in Christ,

Hays

## BIBLIOGRAPHY

Marty, Martin E. *Friendship*. Allen, TX: Argus, 1980.

1. Marty, *Friendship*, 226.

# 12

# Being Chair in a Time of Crisis

*Thomas S. Johnson*

My involvement with Union Theological Seminary was one of the greatest gifts of my life, for three main reasons. First, it was the result of my expressed mild frustration that despite a pretty successful business career up to that point I hadn't had the opportunity to have a role in helping any socially important work, as both of my parents had had when I was growing up in Racine, Wisconsin. This was likely due to my not having grown up in New York and thus not having early associations with New York institutions, as well as my being a commuter and therefore not having an easy way to get involved. When I expressed this concern to my friend at Chemical Bank, Doug Ades, I told him I was very happy with my family and with my work but felt there ought to be something more for me to do to contribute.

Doug asked me if I'd ever heard of Union, and I told him I had indeed and had a distant very positive impression of it, probably in part because one of my Trinity College classmates whom I admired greatly (and still do), Bill Polk, had gone there. He offered to introduce me to Don Shriver and Don asked me to become a non-Board member of Union's finance committee. (When you are a banker, no matter what the reasons might be for your becoming involved with a not-for-profit group, they always ask you to work on finance or audit!) This led to my ultimately going on the Board and then my period as chairman.

Second, I came to realize that Union was for me the realization of the preparation I'd been given by my family for a Christianity broader than my identification as a Catholic. Without in any way diminishing my being raised as a Catholic, my parents had brought my sisters and me up to have a sincere appreciation of the other denominations of the faith. My father was a convert to Catholicism, and he and my mother taught us that our Protestant relatives deserved our respect for their devotion to the same broad religious faith as ours. So my going to Trinity College, with a special orientation to the Episcopal Church, came naturally to me and didn't compromise my own identification as a Catholic. The respect shown to me by all the elements of Union, from the students to the faculty to the alumni, confirmed to me the greater unity of the Christian family and enriched my devotion to the greater Church.

Third, the people I was privileged to work with for Union enriched my life more than any other group with whom I have been associated other than my own family. Having the opportunity to know people like Roger Shinn, Jim Cone, Mac Gatch, Jim Forbes, Janet Walton, Keith Reinhard, three Havemeyers (!), Hays Rockwell, and so many others, inspired me immeasurably and made the job of presiding with the Board not nearly as difficult as it could have been during a stressful time for Union. These individuals, so devoted to Union's heroic mission of delivering the Christian message in an inclusive, courageous, even risky way, made for an atmosphere in which dealing with practical challenges was made easier than it would otherwise have been.

And this is before you get to Don Shriver. Don's insistent devotion to the Christian message, and particularly to the various dimensions of justice that have been the hallmark of Union's insistent role in the modern Church, inspired all who worked to ensure the Seminary would thrive and continue its work. His leadership, often demonstrated by his willingness, even eagerness, to listen to the ideas and concerns of others, made the role of the Chair not easy but more doable than it would have been without him. My ongoing association with him and with the other wonderful members of the Union family continues to enrich my life, and I am deeply grateful.

# 13

## The Fourth Child

*Lionel Shriver*

Throughout our upbringing, my parents took pains to emphasize to my two brothers and me that money wasn't important. We were not to measure ourselves or anyone else by income. We should consider how we wanted to spend our time more than how to spend our cash. In choosing both livelihoods and spouses, we should pursue our passions, even if that meant our prospects for building any kind of fortune might be scant (an encouragement I idiotically took to heart in declaring an impractical determination to become a writer from the age of seven). In those days, my father seemed to harbor a mild aversion to the world of business. However tiresomely necessary to enable us to buy a loaf of bread—A&P rye, preferably, with caraway—the realm of Mammon always seemed tainted.

Well, as of 1975, that whole lofty gestalt flew right out the window. My father took on the presidency of Union Theological Seminary, and all that mattered was money.

So total was our father's commitment to UTS fundraising that he almost seemed to think he *was* Union Seminary—in which case this aggressive, obsessive panhandling amounted to a form of personal avarice. But the formulation our family settled on was more paternal. Union Seminary was "the fourth child."

Make no mistake. If technically older than my father himself, this adopted sibling clamored for his attention with an unseemly mewling that would have got the rest of us sent to our rooms. It's always the nagging, unruly kid who draws more parental energy than the quiet, biddable ones, and UTS was no exception to this rule. Likewise it is the prodigal for whom the fatted calf is slain. My father's desperation to rescue his institutional ward at all costs echoed the sort of heroic dive into turgid waters you see other fathers make when one of their children is drowning, and alas all three of us corporeal kids could swim. So you couldn't blame us for being a little jealous. By any measure, the fourth child was my father's favorite.

Unlike many contributors to this volume, I am in no position to re-count the conflicts over the school's "mission" during board meetings, the fractious faculty's arguments over my father's insistence on keeping a lid on his own salary (the better to keep a lid on theirs), or visiting notables' wrangling over classical Biblical scholarship versus liberation theology. That's because I was in the kitchen.

Literally, in the kitchen. When my parents moved into 4E Knox Hall, I was in college. My father needed cut-rate catering, since one of the first line items he slashed to the bone was the entertainment budget. I needed pocket money. So throughout my undergraduate and graduate studies at Barnard and Columbia, I cooked in that capacious kitchen—with two ovens, eight burners, a stand-up freezer, and an expanse of broad black counters, whose scalloped aluminum edging I can still recall vividly down to the dents, though I haven't laid eyes on that room for nearly thirty years. I spent a lot of time in that kitchen, often with everyone else in bed, while I stirred up five gallons of Southern pork barbecue at four a.m. Yes, not only was the fatted calf slain for the favored prodigal son, but then I personally had to cook it.

We never formalized the arrangement, but over the years my father and I arrived at an understanding: I would cater UTS events in the apartment for below-market rates, and in exchange I could use the Knox Hall kitchen to cook for events elsewhere, often for the larger Columbia community. At the end of any UTS dinner, while my right-hand-man younger brother and I were still cleaning up, my father would launch into the kitchen and declare, "Now, don't you throw any of that cake away!" Since there was never any danger of my throwing the product of my labors in the trash, the ritual imperative decoded, "You'd better damned well leave us all the leftovers."

Catering is the hardest work I have ever done. In comparison, writing books is a walk in the park.

To support myself through the composition of my first novel, I continued to cater out of that kitchen until I was about twenty-eight. Both the faculty and the board were gratifyingly appreciative of my efforts. In fact, toward the end of my tenure as a seminary chef, one trustee took me aside to encourage me to drop this writing lark and just keep cooking. I think his career advice was meant to be a compliment. What the hell. Maybe it was. Lots of people can write a mean sentence. Fewer people can produce six trays of cannelloni with homemade pasta and an earthy hint of chicken livers; serve it on time, neither burnt nor soggy, and piping hot; and not make anyone sick.

I do feel I should declare myself. Despite my parentage, I am not a practicing Christian, nor have I been, well—ever, really. I'm leery of religion in general. So it would be unnatural of me to unduly venerate an institution dedicated to ministerial education and theological scholarship. I only care about UTS because it means a great deal to my father. Yet I can still appreciate the ferocity that Don Shriver brought to his presidency of that school. After all, it was up to my father what he wanted to dedicate his life to.

Because I was constantly arriving with cartloads of sundried olives, unbleached flour, and cage-free eggs, I was sometimes witness to the underside of James Hayes's admiration of my father's capacity to "absorb hostility." I especially remember the night after he'd received an anonymous letter of complaint about the way he dressed. This forerunner of the internet troll asserted haughtily that the president of UTS was under some obligation to represent the institution with sartorial class. She—my mother and I were certain the complainant was female—especially objected to his wearing "green suits." In point of fact, my father didn't own any green suits. Bit mysterious. Although "green suits" soon became a running family joke, the mockery must have smarted. I've been subject to similar digs online, and they introduce an element of insecurity and destructive self-consciousness that can last a surprisingly long time.

For in my latter career, I've also had a taste of what it feels like when people say mean things about both you personally and your work—often vicious, slanderous things. That experience makes me retroactively more sympathetic with the kind of heat my father had to take when making painful budgetary decisions that raised the hackles of the faculty and staff. I can certainly verify that religious people are no more gracious about sacrificing for the greater good (especially in regard to *housing*) than anyone else.

If I can't pretend to feel strongly about the UTS purpose, I am ardently attached to the UTS *architecture*. In fact, I whispered in my father's ear for decades about my view that an institution like Union Seminary may not be its buildings, but it isn't worth much without its buildings. A school is not just an idea, a mission, and a faculty, but also a place, which is one reason that internet tutelage doesn't inspire much brand loyalty. Ownership of the grand English Perpendicular Gothic structures bordered by Amsterdam, Broadway, W. 120th and W. 122nd Streets comes with a cultural responsibility. In the big aesthetic and historical picture, the preservation of the integrity of those structures matters, even to secular sorts like me. I was one of the many people horrified by the idea of selling the air rights for some ghastly luxury condo development.

For regardless of my indifference to theological education, given my family's intense involvement with the fate of UTS, I can never pass by that austere granite structure and feel nothing (although once that monster highrise goes up in the quadrangle, I'm bound mostly to feel rage). Maybe I owe my father gratitude for raising the funds that substantially delayed the construction of that atrocity, which will destroy UTS on an architectural level forever more. I'm convinced that his lack of interest in money while I was growing up was genuine. Money bored him. By mucking up to the neck in a quantity under-stimulating to his considerable intellect for sixteen long years, he paid with the heart of his career for many a previous administration's fiscal sins. However revered such sacrifices can grow after the fact, the New Testament suggests that at the time they're almost always thankless.

# Union Presidency:
# Student Perspectives

# 14

# From Union with Love,
# Freedom, and Peace

*David Kwang-sun Suh*

## "UNION SEMINARY? THAT'S A SCHOOL OF DEVILS!!!"

That was 1962, when I was accepted to begin my theological education at Union Theological Seminary in New York City. I just completed my Master of Arts degree work in philosophy at the University of Illinois. I made my decision to give up on my study in philosophy and go to a theology school to follow my father's ministry back in Korea. My Presbyterian minister martyr father was shot to death by the North Korean military firing squad during the Korean War (1950–53). He had long been accused of being an anti-communist and pro-American preacher by the pro-Soviet Communist regime of North Korea. Since my childhood, it was my father's long-standing and ardent wish for me to follow his hard life as a Christian preacher. I had been resisting his wish because the preacher's family has to suffer from chronic poverty. And on top of it, I blamed my preacher father for my mother's death at her youthful age of thirty-two from tuberculosis due to malnutrition and her fifth child birth in Manchuria (Northern China).

I wrote to my stepmother in Korea as soon as I received the admission letter from Union Theological Seminary. Her reply was a shock and surprise. She wrote me back to say that I should not go to Union! Her church pastor told her that Union Seminary is a wrong choice, condemning it as "a school of devils."

Upon hearing from my stepmother about the "reputation" of Union Seminary, I decided that I made the right choice to go to Union Seminary in New York City. As a matter of fact, my academic adviser in the Philosophy Department at the University of Illinois recommended me to apply to Union in spite of my ignorance about the school. Actually, Union was not initially on my list of theological schools to which I planned to apply for admission. When I reported back to my advisor with the letter of admission to Union, he was so happy for me and said: "David, congratulations! Union is right about choosing you! You are a Union type! You will be happy and successful at Union. I'll tell you, that is a great school. You will like it." I lost my chance to ask him about his exceptionally high opinion, even praise, on Union Seminary. Looking back on my life and work, I must say that he was right about Union.

## EXISTENTIAL QUESTIONS AND THEOLOGICAL ANSWERS

On the first day of Union, I kneeled down at the altar of the Seminary Chapel and opened my entire being to God: my family history, suffering from diseases, hunger, poverty, the war, killing, bloodshed, American bomber planes, Russian tanks, Japanese soldiers, Chinese Liberation Army, and my military service in the Republic of Korea (South Korean) Navy. On the altar, I surrendered myself to God, and decided to wait for God's response and ultimate answers. In my prayer, I asked for God's embrace to accept me as a humble servant of God.

When I entered Union, I was a thirty-one-year-old philosophy student with a BA from a small liberal arts college in the western USA, and an MA from a huge state university in the state of Illinois. Prior to my coming to America for college education, I was selected to study in a US Naval School for technical training, during my military service in the South Korean Navy in 1953. There, I was befriended by an American sailor who arranged my higher education in his home town, Billings, Montana, beginning in the winter of 1956. With the admission papers from Rocky Mountain College, I was honorably discharged from the five years of military service.

I brought to Union a huge bundle of existential questions: Why did that North Korean medical officer save my life from service on the battle-fields of the Korean War? If it was God's doing for my life, what would be the purpose of keeping me alive? What is the will of God in my life? On top of it, I needed some intelligent and intellectual answers to my questions, perhaps theological, that I had against my preacher father's fundamentalist theolo-gy—about the Bible as the word of God and about the strict, moralistic, and puritan life of discipline enforced by my father as an important part of being a Christian. In spite of my questions about my father's faith orientation, I have all along simply admired my father's almost stubborn anti-Japanese politics—his loyalty to God, his love for the country and people, and his passion for freedom, religious as well as political freedom, to the point that he had to give up his life. How can I understand his spirit of martyrdom, giving up his life for his loyalty to God? And I wanted to understand the entire intellectual basis of Christian faith and theology in conjunction with, or even against, the philosophical tradition of the Western world.

Like my other first year BD classmates, I was drawn to the big lecture hall for the class "Introduction to the Old Testament." The lecturer was Pro-fessor James Muilenburg. He had a red face with shiny white hair and he had a clear, loud voice when he spoke. He looked like one of the Old Testament prophets. More than anything else, he challenged me to change my "Sunday school knowledge" about the Bible. His lectures on Genesis covered only the first three chapters in a semester. But he covered the entire history of Old Testament Biblical criticism. And I was challenged to change my fundamen-talist prejudice about the Bible as the unquestionable words of God. I came to understand the Bible as the human quest and as about human beings and their history in the light of God and God's work in the world. I came to the conclusion that Union was not a school of devils, as my stepmother's church preacher said. I learned through Professor Muilenburg's lectures that Union was the most intellectually honest school, open to all kinds of philosophical and theological questions. I enjoyed all the classes in Biblical theologies, and the Church History classes, as well as the systematic theology classes given by Professors Daniel Day Williams and John Macquarrie.

## THEOLOGICAL FRIENDSHIP IN
## THE UNION COMMUNITY

My life at Union began with the meeting of my roommate at Hastings Hall. A tall, blond, and all-smiling man grabbed my hand tightly as he was introducing himself: "Hey, David, I am Timothy . . . Tim Light . . ." He was just too tall and too handsome for me. On top of it all, he was a Yale undergraduate who had just returned from Hong Kong where he taught English in a university there. As we were decorating our dormitory rooms, two rooms on the seventh floor of Hastings Hall, we put our reading tables side by side, and at the center of our individual desks, each of us displayed sizable picture frames of our respective fiancée's smiling photos. Tim left his fiancée, Joy, whom he met and fell in love with in Hong Kong. And I told Tim about my fiancée, Sunyong, whom I met and fell in love with in Illinois.

When I walked into the Union "Quad," I was the only BD (Bachelor of Divinity, now MDiv, Master of Divinity) student from Asia. There were some Japanese pastors there to do their STM (Master of Sacred Theology), and one or two PhD candidates from Japanese theological faculties. I was happy to welcome Rev. Park Hyung Kyu from Korea, an STM candidate. Since the time of a reception for the new international students to Union, Rev. Park and I became close friends.

During Rev. Park's stay at Union for his degree work, we had a kind of private tutor meeting almost every Sunday night at a nearby Italian pizza place, from which I would return to my dormitory around midnight. From the first year on, as a part of Practical Theology course, I was assigned to a "racially integrating" congregation in Jamaica. Rev. Park almost brainwashed me from my close-minded fundamentalist understanding of Christian faith and theology, and he tutored me about the history of missionary Christianity in Korea. His midnight conversations inspired me and moved me to make up my mind to return home to Korea and work there.


## INTERNSHIP AT EWHA WOMANS UNIVERSITY
## AND KOREAN STUDENTS' POLITICS

In the spring semester of the academic year of 1962, another VIP from Korea joined the two of us Korean students at Union. That was Dr. Helen Kim, President of Ewha Womans University, who was just fired by the military government of Park Jung Hee. Park fired all the Korean university presidents over the age of sixty. Dr. Helen Kim, a PhD from Columbia and the first ever Korean woman PhD in the early 1920s, was invited by a longtime friend of Union President Henry Pitney Van Dusen.

Toward the end of her stay at Union, she offered me an invitation to teach at Ewha Women's University. I decided to follow her advice and accept her kind invitation. Furthermore, she advised me to take up Union's internship program at the Ewha University chaplain's office and to teach in the Department of Christian Studies after finishing up my second year at Union. I was able to follow her practical advice to pursue the institutional internship of the Practical Theology Department and returned home to report to the Ewha University Chaplain's office in early May of 1964. My internship program was possible only because of the generosity of my roommate, Tim Light, who raised money for my travel expenses roundtrip.

Dr. Helen Kim and the Ewha community also came to bless our marriage—Sunyong and me—at our wedding ceremony, which took place at the historical Ewha's Emerson Chapel Hall on June 12, 1964.

I did do my utmost in sharing my philosophical and theological training with Ewha students. But beyond my teaching and caring, I learned more from Ewha students who organized themselves to speak against the Korean military government's reparatory treaty negotiations with Japan. The university students and religious and academic leaders opposed the military government's approach to Japan as unfair and humiliating, begging the Japanese for the money robbed from Korea in the thirty-six years of colonial occupation and earned from the Korean suffering during the Korean War. The Japanese have never given formal and official apologies for the Japanese crimes against the Korean people. I learned from the student demonstrations against the military government's pushing of the reparatory treaty negotiations with Japan, and about the politics of resistance of the collective intelligence of the academic and religious leaders in Korea at the time.

At this critical time, my wife and I had to return to Union to finish up my theological education. During my internship, I had found the potentiality for the gift of teaching within myself, and I promised my wife Sunyong and the Ewha administration that we would return to Korea after my completion of degree work in the United States.

## MARTIN LUTHER KING JR. AND POLITICAL THEOLOGY OF UNION AND KOREA

Upon my return to Union, I found that it had become entirely a different place than I left a year before. The place known as an academic theological center of liberal theology seemed to have become a theological base for political action. Union's student community joined Martin Luther King's march for the liberation of the oppressed black people against the white supremacy and the structural racial discrimination in the USA. Furthermore, the Union students were involved in the free speech movements of American academia and the anti-Vietnam War movements.

And this was the time when my classmates were reading Dietrich Bonhoeffer's *Letters and Papers from Prison*, the English translation of his letters from the Nazi prison. Bonhoeffer was a well-known German theologian, who plotted to assassinate Hitler with his brothers, but failed and was arrested, tried, and sentenced to death. He died on the gallows, only four weeks before the end of the Second World War after the death of Adolf Hitler. We mourned Bonhoeffer's death by martyrdom and my classmates were in tears as we discussed his letters. Bonhoeffer reminded me of my father's death by the firing squad of North Korean Communist soldiers on the riverbank of North Koran capital city of Pyongyang during the Korean War of 1950.

In the midst of this revolutionary spirit of the time, I was deeply moved by Professor Paul Lehmann's prophetic teaching on the "Politics of God": God is doing politics in the world, and the politics of God is to humanize human beings and human political communities. He also called for Christians to join the revolutionary politics of God. And we were fascinated by the American theologians' announcement that God is dead. We were reading Harvey Cox's most contemporary book, *The Secular City*, and the Union Chapel was full of his readers, gathered to listen to him lecture on the book. I rushed to the Union Book Store to purchase Jürgen Moltmann's most recent book, *The Theology of Hope*, which inspired me to study his political theology further. I was fortunate enough to meet Moltmann in person at the World Council of Church's mission conference in 1972 in Bangkok, Thailand on the theme of "Salvation Today." And our theological friendship has continued via our mutual visitations in Germany and in Korea until today.

## POLITICAL RESISTANCE AGAINST MILITARY DICTATORSHIP OF PARK JUNG HEE

Upon returning home to Korea, I joined a group of Union graduates to fight against the military dictatorship of General Park Jung Hee, who had already ruled South Korea for ten years with an iron fist in the name of economic development by exploiting the cheap labor of young women and the poor. In the early 1970s when Park pushed a new constitution that would guarantee his dictatorship for life, Christian leaders joined the University students' all-out demonstrations against the military regime of Park, demanding democracy and human rights for the laborers and demonstrating students. Rev. Park Hyung Kyu, my Union mentor, was leading the resistance movement against General Park's military dictatorship.

In order to put down the student demonstrations, General Park issued Emergency Decrees and arrested hundreds of student leaders and university professors, accusing them of being Communists opting for the enemy North Korean regime and brutally torturing and imprisoning some of them with unfair military trials. In the middle of the political struggle against the demonic military dictatorship, ecumenical partners from WCC (World Council of Churches) and CCA (Christian Conference of Asia) came to comfort us and encourage us in the theological and political struggle for human rights and democracy. My theological friend and political theologian, Jürgen Moltmann, came to give us courage and hope as well. And I was so very grateful to Union Black Liberation theologian James Cone, who came to Korea upon my personal invitation to encourage us, the freedom fighters, with his precious experience of the Black struggle for freedom with Martin Luther King Jr.

## DON SHRIVER, THE UNION PRESIDENT'S VISIT TO KOREA IN 1979

On one of the cold winter days of January 1979, I was waiting for Dr. Donald Shriver, his wife, Peggy, and their son Tom to walk out of the Kimpo International Airport. It was their first trip to Korea to visit with me and other graduates of Union Theological Seminary, and it was the first time I met Dr. Shriver, the new president of Union. I was assigned by the Korea Union Alumni Association to greet the Shriver family as a "tour guide."

Upon our arrival at the hotel, the Shrivers were greeted by a number of black-suited men who did not identify themselves. But I recognized them right away as KCIA agents who were assigned to follow the Shrivers around anywhere and everywhere they would go. Shriver looked so pleased by the reception, and right after his last handshake with the last man on the "reception line," he turned around to me and asked me, whispering, "Who are these young men?" With no answer, I led the visitors to the dinner table. At the dinner table in the hotel restaurant, I told the Shrivers that the men were the most fearful and brutal KCIA agents who have been assigned to watch the foreign VIPs from America and their hosts, including me.

The KCIA agents followed the Shrivers everywhere they went for visits, and I had to debrief them about the Shrivers' itinerary of visiting

Christian universities and distinguished Christian leaders who were Union graduates. I told the Shrivers that it had been most oppressive for the last ten years under the Emergency Decrees from No. 1 to No. 9, which Park Jung Hee's military Yushin government had imposed on the people. And I reported to Don and Peggy how the Korean University students, laborers, and Christian intellectuals, in solidarity with the ecumenical church leaders, had been struggling for human rights and democracy against the oppressive government.

## PRESIDENT PARK WAS SHOT TO DEATH BY HIS KCIA CHIEF

The year 1979 was said to be the most turbulent year for the aggressive, almost life or death, labor struggles. In support of the suffering workers, university students continued with heightened spirit to fight against the oppressive Emergency Decrees and the brutal riot police on and off campus all over the Korean city streets.

At one of their lavish drinking dinner parties, in the presence of President Park, his close staff members were arguing against each other about the military action to fire, shooting down all the demonstrating students and workers in the southern cities of Pusan and Masan. The indignant and angry Chief of KCIA, who was sitting right next to the President, stood up and shot the President point blank. President Park was dead on the spot. That brought the abrupt end of Park's eighteen years of ironfisted military dictatorship. That bloody end of the all-powerful Yushin regime came on the deep night of October 26, 1979.

## "A FIRED PROFESSOR . . ."

An Army General, Chun Doo Whan, one of the close followers who had been with deceased President Park's *coup d'état* in 1962 and who went to the Vietnam War, began gathering up his army followers to grab power. By a coup, he pushed out the Joint Chiefs of Staff from the control over three divisions of the Korean military and appointed himself as Chief of Military Intelligence and the head of KCIA. In spite of General Chun's plot, the victorious opposition leaders and students, as well as the citizens' networks, came out in the open to dismantle the Park Jung Hee's Yushin Constitution and to bring out an entirely new democratic form of government and constitutional reform with the new election of the National Assembly.

Betraying the popular wishes of the people for the new democratic government, the power hungry General Chun imposed the Martial Law nationwide, dissolved the interim government as of May 17, 1980, and oversaw the mass arrest of major political leaders such as Kim Dae Jung and Suh Nam Cong, a leading Korean Minjung theologian, as well as other dissident academic leaders.

I received a phone call from a man who identified himself as an agent from the Joint Military Investigation Center, which General Chun had opened to wipe out the "unclean and dangerous elements in society" after he grabbed the power. As Dean of the Liberal Arts and Sciences College of Ewha, I was conducting a meeting with natural science department heads discussing the new science building to be constructed with the financial support of EZE of Germany. The importance of the meeting, which I tried to explain to the man on the phone, was completely ignored. I was taken into the Center of the Military Investigation. Their reason for detaining me in the Investigation Center was to get my confession about my political crimes against the government, more particularly about my intention to overthrow the anti-communist government by agitating the students. They demanded that I write a political and theological confession. I thought it would be a God-given opportunity to reflect on my life and work, and perhaps to produce a piece of literary confession like Augustine and something like Bonhoeffer's letters from prison.

After about two-and-a-half weeks in prison, as I handed in my "political confession," a precocious autobiography, to the impatient interrogator, he ordered me to write a resignation paper to the President of Ewha Women's University. Almost immediately after I handed in my resignation paper, I was released. As I was walking into my home on one of the summer evenings at dusk, my wife Sunyong came out of the door and wept in tight embrace.

Toward the end of that hot and humid summer, political weatherwise, some thirty plus activist university Christian professors, all over the country, were forced out of their teaching posts. I was one among the six Ewha University faculty members who were purged from the lecture halls. One of them was Professor Hyun Yong Hak, a Christian Ethics professor and a senior Union graduate in the 1950s who had studied under Reinhold Niebuhr. Professor Hyun was invited to be the first Henry Luce Visiting Professor from Korea during the time of Shriver's presidency in 1982.

## AS AN ORDAINED MINISTER IN THE
## PRESBYTERIAN CHURCH OF KOREA (PCK)

I took my political purge from the university as a gift, an important gift for my "mid-term life," to be ordained as a minister of my father's Presbyterian denomination to keep my promise to follow his footsteps. I was ordained into the Presbyterian (conservative Jesus) Church of Korea in November 1982. And I was called to serve in a small church located in a newly built apartment complex town in the south of the Han River of Seoul.

As I tried to settle into my new work of church ministry, and as soon as my exit from the full time university teaching was made known to my friends around the world, invitation letters began flying in from all over the ecumenical world and academic communities outside Korea. I was fortunate to receive a generous research grant from the Maryknoll Institute in New York to write on a history of Korean Christianity. The product of my research was published in English with the title, *The Korean Minjung in Christ*, by the CCA (the Christian Council of Asia) in 1983.

Suddenly I had become an ecumenical celebrity and a political *persona non grata*, and in the meantime, I was invited to attend various international theological conferences and consultations from all over the world to present my stories about the Korean ecumenical Christian struggles for justice and democracy. I went to meet the Catholic friends of freedom fighters against the Marcos government in the Philippines, and attended the CCA's theological consultation on liberation theologies and "theo-praxis" in Asia. And I joined the EATWOT (Ecumenical Association of Third World Theologians), a progressive community of theologians from Catholic and Protestant communities from the so-called Third World countries and the Black American theologians such as Jim Cone from Union. I was commissioned to join the PTE, Program for Theological Education, a committee of WCC to bring together theologians and theological educators to share the ideas and practices of theological education around the globe.

At the PTE meetings, I met Don and Peggy Shriver, who came to join the WCC committee as an advisor and a mentor, along with other prominent world leaders in theological education. We were to meet in Geneva, Prague, in an Indonesian theological school, and in Ghana for consultation as well as Christian dialogue and fellowship. Wherever we met, Don Shriver and I organized an alumni meeting with the Union graduates in various programs, women and men, to share stories of theological struggles for the revolutionary changes, *metanoia* in our faith, and work for the liberation of the oppressed.

The Ewha Womans University community was excited and honored to hear about the nomination of Dr. Kim Okgill as the recipient of the Union Medal in 1983. She was an honorary president of the university and former Minister of Education during the interim government of Korea in 1980. The Union Medal was installed by President Shriver in lieu of honorary doctoral degrees. She was the most popular president among the students during her tenure from 1961 to 1979, especially during the time of students' political resistance against the Park Jung Hee's military dictatorship of eighteen years. She was always visible at the center of students' street political rallies, standing against the riot police, supposedly to protect the demonstrating female Ewha students from police brutality.

During my politically enforced "Sabbatical Years," I was invited to come to teach Korean Minjung Theology and history of Korean Christianity at the summer session of Claremont School of Theology by the personal invitation of Professor John Cobb in the summer of 1983. I spent following summers in San Francisco Theological Seminary to teach the active pastors from Korea pursuing the Doctor of Ministry degree. The DMin program was initiated jointly with the SFTS by Dr. Cyrus Moon and Dr. Yongbok Kim, the faculty members of Korean (Jesus) Presbyterian Seminary in Korea.

As I was leaving for San Francisco for the teaching assignment for the Korean DMin candidates in SFTS in the early summer of 1984, I received an official notice that all the dismissed activist professors, of some thirty, would be reinstated to their respective teaching positions. I returned to the Ewha campus after four years in academic exile.

## RETURN TO UNION AS A HENRY LUCE VISITING PROFESSOR OF WORLD CHRISTIANITY

Exactly twelve years after my reinstatement to my teaching position, I officially retired from Ewha in 1996 at the compulsory retirement age of sixty-five. With an official ceremony on my retirement from Ewha behind, I returned to Union as the honorable chair of Henry Luce Visiting Professor of World Christianity for the fall semester of 1996. With a deep appreciation for the most productive and rewarding life of teaching and theological involvement in the Union community, I was honored with the Unitas Citation of the Union Theological Seminary, granted to its alumni, on April 25, 1997, by President Holland Hendrix. In Union's seminar rooms, I had the privilege of meeting the students who were so eager to learn about Korean Minjung Theology, a contextual theology of liberation. I must add that one of the most rewarding gifts was Shriver's most recent book, *An Ethic for Enemies: Forgiveness in Politics* (1995). I asked Chang Yun Jae, a Korean PhD student studying under Shriver, to translate the book with me into Korean, and it was published by the University Press of Ewha University in 1997. The book has been used for the various seminars on the issue of personal and collective political forgiveness and reconciliation between Korea and Japan as well as between North and South Korean people.

During my stay in the Union quad, I was busy traveling around the world as part of my duty as the President of the World Alliance of YMCAs. I was honored to be inaugurated at the memorable occasion in 1994 of the service commemorating 150 years since the founding of London YMCA in 1844. The service was held in the Westminster Abbey with the graceful presence of Queen Elizabeth. I retired from the position in 1998 at the YMCA World Assembly in Frechen, Germany.

After Union, I was invited to teach Korean and Asian theologies at Drew University School of Theology for three years. And the United Board for Christian Higher Education in Asia pushed me out to Hong Kong to establish a new Asia Office as Vice President for Programs. Dr. James Laney, my Social Ethics professor when I was doing my PhD work at Vanderbilt, and the Board Chair, and my dear life-long friend and advisor, my Union classmate and roommate Tim Light, were the main promoters of the Hong Kong office of the United Board and my appointment. After the most rewarding work for and with Asian educators in Christian higher education for five years, I retired and returned home to Korea (2006) to live with my family and among my old-time friends and colleagues.

## THE LIFE OF GRACIOUS FREE GIFTS
## OF LIFE, LOVE, AND FREEDOM

As I was looking back on my eighty-eight years of life journey, I realized that my life was given by God as a precious free gift through the North Korean military medical doctor who sent me back home from the army drafting center, failing me from the physical examination. I believe that it was a gift of miracle to have met an American sailor, a school dropout, who provided my way to pursue American higher education, providing me with college admission and financial sponsors. Was this my martyr father's doing in heaven? I often wonder about the reason for his glorious martyrdom by the North Korean army firing squad: Was this a way of inheriting his ministry and mission to this unbelieving son? Dr. Helen Kim of Ewha came all the way to Union to meet me and invite me to teach at Ewha, a precious and unexpected gift to a wandering first year Union student. My wife Su-nyong showed up in my days of philosophical inquiry to become my life-long partner through the darkest nights of uncertainty and bright daylights of success and praise. And the gifts of numerous friends, colleagues, and teacher-mentors, especially among them Tim Light, Jim Laney, a UMC missionary to Korea and onetime US Ambassador to Korea, and Don Shriver, who have given me material as well as spiritual support throughout my life-long journey. For the overwhelming gifts given to me, I give thanks to God who led me to the life of love, freedom, and peace to work for God's Reign on the Earth. However, I ask myself, as I close this testimony, whether I led my life to have deserved so many gifts given freely to me from God, the Ground of my being, and from fellow human beings here on the earth and the heaven above.

## BIBLIOGRAPHY

Commission on Theological Concerns of the Christian Conference of Asia, ed. *Minjung Theology: People as the Subjects of History.* Singapore: CCA, 1981.

Cox, Harvey. *The Secular City.* New York: Macmillan, 1965.

Lehmann, Paul. *Ethics in a Christian Context.* New York: Harper & Row, 1963.

Marty, Martin E., ed. *Dietrich Bonhoeffer's Letters and Papers from Prison: A Biography.* Princeton: Princeton University Press, 2011.

Moltmann, Jürgen. *Theology of Hope.* New York: Harper & Row, 1967.

Shriver, Donald W., Jr. *An Ethic for Enemies: Forgiveness in Politics.* New York: Oxford University Press, 1995.

Suh, David Kwang-sun. "American Missionaries and a Hundred Years of Korean Protestantism." *International Review of Mission* 74 (1985) 5–18.

———. *The Korean Minjung in Christ.* Hong Kong: Christian Conference of Asia, 1991.

# 15

## Donald Shriver
### and the Connecting Roots of Interdisciplinary Teaching

*Roger Sharpe*

Early in the spring term of 1995, a mid-afternoon memorial service was to be held at the Cathedral of Saint John the Divine for James P. Grant, director of the United Nations Children's Emergency Fund (UNICEF). It was said that Jim Grant, who had launched a child survival revolution, "probably saved more lives than were destroyed by Hitler, Mao and Stalin combined."[1] The cathedral proper was closed for an advance team's bomb sweep by US Secret Service officers before hundreds of expected dignitaries would arrive, led by First Lady Hillary Rodham Clinton and United Nations Secretary General Boutros Boutros-Ghali. In my position as Seminarian at the Cathedral, a part-time appointment held three years while I was enrolled as a divinity student at Union, I was asked by Dean James Morton to accompany Father Theodore Hesburgh to the sacristy. Here we were to remain through the bomb sweep an hour before other eulogists and guests arrived for the service.

1. Kristof, "Good News," A-31.

Father Hesburgh, president of Notre Dame University for thirty-five years, was coming from a meeting of Harvard's Board of Visitors on which he served. Having attended the John F. Kennedy School of Government and the Harvard Graduate School of Education, while completing my doctoral dissertation on the politics of education, I knew something of Father Hesburgh's preeminence nationally in education. Among topics we discussed during our time together, Father Hesburgh asked me what I thought of my professors, both at Harvard and at Union. Most all of them I named were well known to him. In addition to Union's then president, Donald Shriver, whose scholarship and prophetic leadership in Christian ethics drew me to Union in midlife, I named two other professors: Baldwin Professor of Sacred Literature Phyllis Trible, who mentored a generation of scholars and clergy in feminist theology, and Jungian Barry Ulanov, for his survey of world literature on direction of the human spirit, a course he taught at Union in the Department of Religion and Psychiatry after retirement from the McIntosh Professorship of Literature at Barnard College. I told Father Hesburgh that I loved these professors at Harvard and at Union, loved walking into hallowed ground of their temples of learning. Through them, I was able to glimpse that kingdom of knowledge that lies on the other side of the needle, a kingdom that even a boy from North Carolina's tobacco fields might claim as his own. Father Hesburgh knew exactly what love of learning and its adherents were about.

Speaking of differences between people, in his essay "History," Ralph Waldo Emerson wrote,

> The difference between people is in their principle of association. Some people classify objects by color and size and other accidents of appearance; others by intrinsic likeness, or by the relation of cause and effect. The progress of the intellect consists in the clear vision of causes, which overlooks surface differences. To the poet, to the philosopher, to the saint, all things are friendly and sacred, all events profitable, all days holy, all persons divine. For the eye is fastened on the life, and slights the circumstance.[2]

That I can name Donald Shriver as one of my academic life's most significant professors comes easy. My first acquaintance with Union's president and his influence on my thinking, however, reaches back more than a half-century when a regional newspaper published his op-ed letter on matters of civil rights and race relations. Then serving as pastor, he encouraged people of the Christian faith to respond with compassion and neighborliness in

2. Emerson, "Essay I. History," 15.

the racial desegregation of the state's public schools and other institutions. Reverend Shriver spoke in a different voice clear to me in 1963, a tenth grader attending a racially segregated public Harmony High School in the Blue Ridge foothills. I was active in the 4-H Club, a cooperative extension and land-grant university program initiated in the 1920s as an outreach incentive to the nation's rural boys and girls. Although 4-H was segregated by race, too, I had begun to meet others in the organization's leadership, like Reverend Shriver, whose views differed from the prevailing views of our society. It was his influence among others, I am certain, that one summer day resulted in my standing up from hoeing a row of tobacco and announcing to my father, "There had to be a different way of making a living." I was determined to go out beyond Sandy Springs into the world and meet my neighbors in it!

Nightly news reports from Walter Cronkite chronicled the nation's racial unrest and ferment, upended by President John Kennedy's assassination that November 22 in Dallas, Texas. I was scheduled just a few days after President Kennedy's funeral to attend a national 4-H related team competition in Pittsburgh, Pennsylvania. Our chaperone, 4-H Agent Beaman Nance, had the foresight to drive three of us high school students by way of Arlington National Cemetery on our trip home so that we might walk by President Kennedy's grave still covered with fresh pine boughs, above which burned the Eternal Flame. I took pictures with an early Kodak movie camera of this graveside visit and was able to show the film to my family, who with me during the four-day weekend of President Kennedy's assassination and funeral ate our meals as we watched the television set, and wept together as did our nation. By early spring after President Kennedy's death, I accepted an invitation to speak to an all-black youth 4-H Club in Iredell County, perhaps the first time for any white high school student to do so in North Carolina. I clipped Donald Shriver's op-ed from that 1963 newspaper, which had encouraged this teenager during a time of national unrest to consider a different view on race relations, saved the clipping, and submitted it to him when I applied to attend Union for the academic year 1992–93!

There were other exchanges with Dr. Shriver's thinking long before my coming to Union that mattered with respect to my social consciousness. One included his introduction from his office as Union's President on a New York film that examined the 1971 Attica Prison riot and its significance on correctional reform in the United States. I showed this film in criminal justice classes I taught in institutions across North Carolina. Another involved one of Dr. Shriver's books (coauthored with two sociologists): *Spindles and Spires: Religion and Social Change in Gastonia*, published in 1976. Because I had introduced college and university students beforehand to Liston Pope's 1942 work, *Millhands and Preachers in Gastonia*, they were knowledgeable of the financial relationship between textile mill owners and local church ministers in 1929 at the time of the textile mill workers' strikes, when National Guardsmen were called in to quell rioting and violent confrontations with local law enforcement. I welcomed *Spindles and Spires*, a reexamination of that relationship between textile mill owners and clergy of local churches attended by textile mill workers. That book, based in part on Shriver's work in the late 1950s as a Presbyterian minister in Gastonia, North Carolina, greatly informed our perspectives on religion and society and enhanced the understanding of my students who sought to become change agents in society. In later years, I asked my professor how his particular interest in textile mill workers had come about. He told me that Liston Pope, Dean of the Yale Divinity School, had once been his professor!

Donald Shriver's tenure as President of Union Theological Seminary in New York City covered the years 1975–91. Throughout these years of his presidency, I checked in with him periodically in my own career as state senator, as a special assistant to the national director of the US Office for Civil Rights, as executive liaison to the White House for the nation's ninety-five thousand locally-elected school board members, and as an executive with a national constitutional liberties organization, People for the American Way. Professor Shriver's stepping down from the presidency and his subsequent sabbatical as Visiting Senior Scholar with Bishop Desmond Tutu at the Institute for Justice & Reconciliation in Cape Town, South Africa came to an end about the time I arrived at Union to commence my first year of divinity studies, fall term, 1992. It had not been lost on me, based on a realization from a night of writing years earlier, when I saw the sun rising over Harvard Yard, that many public advocates and reformers in American history had studied education, criminal justice, and theology in their careers. I was only catching up!

While many mentors prepared me for this transition to Union Theological Seminary, I must mention a few to demonstrate the variety of those who paved the way, some of them known to Professor Shriver. Among them were: Mississippi native Miriam Hollis Prichard, my first-year college Sunday School Teacher, a campus Baptist Student Union director and administrator coming to Raleigh from the Southern Baptist Seminary in Louisville, who first introduced me to the writings of Reinhold Niebuhr, Paul Tillich, and Dietrich Bonhoeffer; Dr. Anna Arnold Hedgeman, the only woman who served on the planning committee for Dr. Martin Luther King Jr.'s March on Washington, whom I met at the National Council of Churches (the "God Box") on a 1966 student trip to Union; Dr. Clarence Jordan, founder of Koinonia Farms in Americus, Georgia, who influenced the creation of Habitat for Humanity; Reverend Ron Rice whose intercity crisis control ministry in Winston-Salem received acclaim from the Reynolds Foundation as a national model for others; Reverend Will Campbell, the writer who headed the Committee of Southern Churchmen when Robert Kennedy was US Attorney General; the writer and poet, Wake Forest Professor Maya Angelou who once served on my board of directors at People for the American Way; Reverend Mahan Siler, a student of Thomas Merton in Louisville, who pastored Pullen Memorial Baptist Church in Raleigh and shepherded that prestigious congregation to affirm same-gender unions in 1990, years before others; Professor Phyllis Trible, mentioned earlier, whose writings on feminist theology had informed me in defense of the Equal Rights Amendment as fundamental rights of citizens when I served as North Carolina's youngest state senator; and South Carolina native Reverend Bob Clyde, a fourth generation Baptist minister and university chaplain, who sent me off to seminary with a line from Kierkegaard's sermon, "Purity of heart is to will one thing."[3]

Somewhere along the way in my educational journey I also had read with much interest volume thirty-nine of the Harvard Classics, *Famous Prefaces*. In doing so, I concluded that a reader of these prefaces and prologues was getting the best of an author's reflective mind once the whole of a written work was complete. It seemed to follow that studying under the guidance of noted theologian and ethicist Donald Shriver, at the conclusion of his tenure as President of Union Theological Seminary, I would also become a privileged beneficiary of his fresh reflective overview of all that he had learned, that is, the long view of his best thinking. The pace and scope of learning exceeded any expectations I may have held. Professor Shriver invited me to be his assistant, part-time, as a researcher for a manuscript on which he worked towards publication, and for graduate courses in ethics he would teach while I studied at Union. Three courses had developed curricula: "Ethics in Jewish and Christian Communities" with Rabbi Gordon Tucker, Dean, at the Jewish Theological Seminary; "The Church in the City" taught at Union for seminarians and perhaps the course best mirroring the role of the Seminary between Broadway and Riverside Drive in New York City and its boroughs; and "Leadership and Ethics in Business" with Professor James Kuhn at Columbia's School of Business and with whom Professor Shriver had coauthored *Beyond Success: Corporations and Their Critics in the Nineties* (1991). A fourth course, "Religion in the Media," was a new

---

3. Kierkegaard, *Purity of Heart.*

course developed in corroboration with Professor James Carey at Columbia's School of Journalism.

These courses co-taught by Professor Shriver included a mix of seminarians from Union and graduate students from other schools. Suffice it to say that the variety of subjects about which he could speak with knowledge and authority, understanding and clarity, both in facilitating discussions with professorial colleagues and graduate students, was phenomenal. In his teaching, I would observe our professor challenging us to expand our thinking on matters of justice, mutuality, and human kindness within our affairs and disciplines, to the end we might effectively raise questions before local decision-makers as well as parliaments and rulers of nations.

Donald Shriver's scholarship included the mastery of Union Professor Reinhold Niebhur's writings and those of his brother H. Richard Niebuhr, who taught at Yale. Our professor would often quote from memory a line from these nationally renowned prophetic voices, which added dimension and clarification to the topic at hand. Because the early 90s had not yet experienced universal computer and internet resources—I had to sign up at Columbia University's Butler Library for half-hour increment use of the search engine NEXUS—I easily utilized more than a dozen libraries in my role as Professor Shriver's research assistant. Union's own Burke Library, it's worth noting, held a collection of recordings of some of Professor Reinhold Niebuhr's lectures, and taking a cassette player I occasionally could steal away to Riverside Park and listen to him on these tapes.

When Dr. Shriver was appointed Senior Fellow at Columbia's School of Journalism my second year at Union, I was appointed his Research Associate, assigned a desk, and given wide access to the university's library holdings. The Freedom Forum of the Media Studies Center with which we were affiliated at the School of Journalism was funded generously by the Gannett Foundation (which also built the Newseum in Washington, DC, and publishes *USA Today*). Most of our shared time the next two years was focused on research for his seminal work, *An Ethic for Enemies: Forgiveness in Politics*, published by Oxford University Press in 1995. Its author poses the question on how nations, or ethnic groups, or races might learn to live side by side in peace after long and bitter struggles. The basic yet always unexpected solution lies in our capacity for forgiveness. Beyond what is usually reserved for personal religion and morality, Professor Shriver posits that we recognize the importance of forgiveness in secular, political arenas. He examines three case studies in modern American history to illustrate his argument on behalf of using forgiveness after political upheavals: our postwar dealings with Germany, with Japan, and our domestic issues with race relations.

After spring commencement in May 1995 and my graduation in midlife with a divinity degree, Donald Shiver invited me to lunch at a restaurant near the Seminary. My professor asked what I had learned that impressed me greatly in my studies. Among several topics we discussed, one most impressionable I told him, were the ancient stories of the Old Testament, and how these stories were passed down by oral tradition for centuries before being recorded. When I spoke of this oral tradition, I reached for a gift I had brought him, a photograph I had obtained from the Library of Congress. One of many ongoing discussions that had taken place between us during our three years working together at Union was about President Abraham Lincoln and his granting amnesty to confederate soldiers at the cessation of the Civil War. The wealthy merchant, William E. Dodge, a founder of Union Theological Seminary in 1836 and namesake of Donald Shriver's endowed chair in Applied Christianity at Union, was a voting delegate in 1860 to the Republican Convention that nominated Abraham Lincoln. Dodge was one of several businessmen who, for sake of the nation's economy, encouraged President Lincoln to move quickly in favor of reconciliation when the war was ended. My gift to Professor Shriver was the only known photograph of President Abraham Lincoln at the Dedication of the National Soldier's Cemetery.

It was there on those hallowed grounds our sixteenth President delivered the Gettysburg Address, November 19, 1863, speaking of a "government of the people, by the people, for the people" that should not perish from the earth.[4] Among several people seated on the platform with President Lincoln, there was a boy who sat near his father. As I passed the photograph to my esteemed professor, I knew that someday I would research the story of that boy. By interviewing his descendants, if any were to be located, I might gather his stories passed down through several generations about his being present at such a historic event.

Although Donald Shriver would write and publish other works in the years after my graduation, I am of the view that two of his greatest works, published a decade apart, are _An Ethic for Enemies_ and a book entitled _Honest Patriots: Loving a Country Enough to Remember Its Misdeeds_ (Oxford, 2005). While _An Ethic for Enemies_ speaks to forgiveness in political arenas, _Honest Patriots_ speaks to those whose misdeeds have caused harm to others and their need to repent for those misdeeds if real reconciliation is to take place. These two books should be paired for future scholars, practitioners, and multi-disciplinary students interested in public policies, politics, and ethics. Donald Shriver would take into account both books when he was

---

4. Lincoln, "The Gettysburg Address," 192.

a speaker to a public gathering of my family and neighbors in the restored two-room Joyner schoolhouse, used as the Sandy Springs Community Center, when he and Peggy Shriver visited me in the summer of 2005. They were making their way to Gastonia for him to keynote a daylong symposium sponsored by the North Carolina Humanities Council, which revisited the textile mill strikes and riots of 1929. In attending the Gastonia forum, I realized with a grateful heart, as I listened to my former professor speak, that prophetic voices like his and his professor at Yale, Liston Pope, had given voice to textile workers seeking justice by keeping alive their stories to the end that younger generations with ears to hear might work for a more just society. It is important to note that while Professor Shriver was nominated for the award twice, first in 2008 for his book *An Ethic for Enemies*, he was awarded the prestigious Grawemeyer Award for *Honest Patriots* in 2009.

I cannot close this essay without recalling for its reader a luncheon held in Hastings Refectory at Union Theological Seminary on January 29, 2018. What a grand day for celebration of Donald's ninetieth birthday, (December 20) for recognizing Donald and Peggy Shriver's contributions to the Seminary, and for providing an appropriate occasion that honored their very special announcement. Union's President Serene Jones presided at this joyful gathering of former and current trustees, faculty, and friends—a part of the oral tradition that must continue in education between disciplines and generations. I invited as my special guest Lincoln scholar Gabor Boritt, Donald Borock Professor of Political Science *emeritus* at Gettysburg College, founder of the Civil War Institute, and recipient of the Presidential Medal in Humanities, so that I might introduce my friend to the honorees and other invitees. Donald Shriver was honored both for his years of administration as President and for his scholarship in religion and society, as William E. Dodge Professor of Applied Christianity and as the author of thirteen books. He presented abbreviated remarks on his and Peggy's decision to fund the Dietrich Bonhoeffer Chair at Union Theological Seminary for a sum of one million dollars.

Speaking of his purchase of a paperback of Bonhoeffer's *Letters & Papers from Prison* in Harvard University's Divinity School bookstore, right after receiving his PhD in Religion and Society, Donald Shriver recognized the desire in any of us to be a fragment of stained glass that allows light to shine through on that sacred space where a beloved community of saints gather and to which every repentant is welcome. The body of his works will be prophetic for generations who come after us about religion and society, faith and politics, church and state.

## BIBLIOGRAPHY

Emerson, Ralph Waldo. "Essay I. History." In *Essays*, 5–40. New York: Hurst, 1885.

Kierkegaard, Søren. *Purity of Heart is to Will One Thing*. Translated by Douglas V. Steere. New York: Harper, 1938.

Kristof, Nicholas. "Good News: Karlo Will Live." *New York Times*, March 6, 2008, A-31.

Lincoln, Abraham. "The Gettysburg Address." In *Lincoln: Political Writings and Speeches*, edited by Terence Ball, 191–92. Cambridge: Cambridge University Press, 2013.

# 16

## Communitas, a Student Reflection

*Bill Crawford*

On April 1, 1980, twenty-four Union Theological Seminary students filed into the newly renovated James Chapel with its newly built and installed Holtkamp organ. They wore formal waistcoats borrowed from the historic collection of Riverside Church, which had been donned by the church ushers at Sunday worship when Harry Emerson Fosdick preached to John W. Rockefeller. The chapel was full of faculty, students, and even the president, Donald W. Shriver Jr., and his wife, Peggy Ann Leu Shriver. In advance, the event's professionally-done flyer written for the occasion promised a "Cantata and Organ Recital," assumedly another special event in the concert series that spring at UTS which marked the completion of the new James Chapel.

Because I had, in the month prior, organized the visit of South African journalist Donald Woods, biographer of the martyred Steve Biko, to the campus, and taken part in several pro-divestment protests myself, which included a recent sit-in and proclamation at a board meeting, my appearance as conductor may have also seemed appropriately serious. I strode in confidently. The room hushed. I took the podium and waved my baton. With that cue, kazoos, hidden in the waistcoats until that precise moment, popped out and the orchestra launched into the theme of the film *2001: A Space Odyssey*. This was followed by an "orchestra member" playing a child's tinny set of Muppet drums; noted as an "open Sesame moment." Then, to provide and substantiate something of an organ concert, a female doctoral student in a shimmering silver evening gown strode to the podium to present the first part of the heralded " . . . Organ Recital" entitled "The Duodenum," literally. Opening a page diagram from *Gray's Anatomy*, she located the organ and its contributions to the digestive trajectory, which she read from the text . . . and accordingly traced—with both cartographic and gymnastic finesse—against her bodice. A compelling performance!

President Shriver appeared to be beside himself with laughter, as were most of those in attendance (others seemed to be in a certain state of shock). In those particular moments at Union, around tensions over calls for divestment, budget pressures, and serious theological disagreements among the faculty, the community was united in a fun event, turning the creativity of its community to good humor. It was April Fool's Day, after all.

This actually speaks to one of the most directly applicable lessons I learned at Union, which despite its financial challenges at that time had received the enormous gift of the new organ. When I became the Senior Pastor of the Larchmont (NY) Presbyterian Church, the congregation was in the midst of just such a process of accepting a gift that was a musician's dream, but perhaps not that of the full membership. So at Union there is a somewhat implicit curriculum: we are driven by justice concerns, but we try to speak to them through cultural means and opportunities, with biblical and theological convictions. Holy paradoxes!

This appreciation of Donald Shriver's leadership of Union is not limited to his role as a fine, engaging professor; I had some advantages in understanding his service that others did not have. I came with an MSW and experience in community organizing and working with ex-offenders, and I had read *Spindles & Spires* as a student being taught the church's concern for the labor movement. I had been president myself—of the student government in a high school of four thousand—in a diverse part of Philadelphia. And I was old enough to have lost friends in Vietnam in 1968, the same year I was turning against that war that he also had opposed, as a professor and parent, coming from a similar pro-military context.

I came to Union in mid-year and lived in Van Dusen Hall. My next-door neighbors were Janet Walton, soon-to-become chapel director (appointed by Don Shriver), and Carter Heyward. With Robert and Sydney Brown, we formed an "Ice Cream Coalition." I was privileged to be part of a Wednesday morning study group that included students and professors, and I could see how broad their cultural and spiritual visions were. I was touched to hear Janet Walton and Bob Brown play cello and piano together. I had been introduced to James Cone's *Black Theology and Black Power* years before, as an undergrad (by then-conservative Presbyterian theologian Jack Rogers). I knew faculty and administrators were faithful human beings, and not parts of "blocs" or affinity groupings.

Thus I think I could see Donald Shriver as a kind of protagonist in our institutional dramas, and at times my heart ached for him. Gary Dorrien has it amazingly right from his later distance, in looking at the burden Don carried in dealing with the economic, cultural, and theological change of the period. The person he was, as much as the role he played, contributed to my formation . . . He earned his credible authority, and he did it as a straight, white man, and a Southerner. He played a role, but he did not play games.

Playing some roles for fun was something I did a bit of at Union: at cabaret venues as Mel Chizedek, "scriptural bartender" of the Rusty Canon; as the conspiratorial cofounder/writer of Balaam's Ass (a prelude to a rejuvenated iteration of the Union Dues); singing lead in the a cappella doowop sermonics with "The Recollections"; performing SNL-worthy sketches (I wished!) of John Calvin and Michael Servetus (the only heretic burned in sixteenth-century Geneva). By the time we got to the aforementioned "Cantata and Organ Recital," I think Don had grown to appreciate my "body of work" at Union. He welcomed and encouraged the sense of spirit and community. While I like to think that Dr. Shriver was quick to cite my theological acumen and scholarly contributions, he was all the more appreciative of the expressions and experiences that brought us together, of which I was so glad to be a part.

He was glad and grateful to be a part of it too. Looking back, he had some pointers for the Calvin-Servetus skit; he engaged the historicity, and I was bold to suggest a follow-up scenario/sequel, *a la* reconciliation, which we never got to. We smiled and registered our thanks for the "teaching possibilities." It was about the time that his work on *An Ethic for Enemies: Forgiveness in Politics* was underway. Years later, I saw him interviewed on PBS about *An Ethic for Enemies* by Bill Moyers who was inspired and in rapt attention to this consummate theologian, student, and teacher of forgiveness, and his thesis. Moyers cited Shriver's own doctoral thesis on forgiveness; Don noted gratitude to H. R. Niebuhr as a teacher of "the meaning of ethics focused on the mutualities of value and interests in the webs of history," along with his brother Reinhold and others.[1] I watched the program with deep appreciation for Don and the teachings of this fine book—which reads

---

1. Shriver, *Ethic for Enemies*, x.

like a life's work: teaching possibilities realized and teaching *possibility*, as Bill Moyers cited *An Ethic for Enemies* . . . "As the touchstone for the remnant of faithful looking for ways to make this world live more peaceably."[2]

Dr. Shriver's writing, during his Union tenure, also included: *Honest Patriots: Loving a Country Enough to Remember its Misdeeds*, for which he won the distinguished Grawemeyer Book Award—a distinction held by only three other Union faculty. Further, during his tenure at UTS, he held the distinction of holding faculty status at four additional graduate schools: Jewish Theological Seminary, Columbia University Schools . . . of Business, International Affairs, and Law. In so doing Don Shriver opened pathways in discourse, scholarship, ministry and community. A pathway—doorway literally—was opened when Don saw to it that the wall at the south end of the refectory was knocked down to construct the passageway from the chapel, thus making it easily possible for worshippers and chapel-attendees to gather for communal meals and events. (The recessional at the aforementioned Kazoo Cantata led attendees through that very same doorway!)

Union Theological Seminary in the City of New York is hardly a place of ecclesial accountability, denominational or otherwise. That might have been the case up until the days of Charles Augustus Briggs in the 1890s, if it ever had been so prior. Don Shriver came to see that firsthand. I am sure that every president in Union's history did, and has. Perhaps at times seeing more fragmentation than formation—it can be a "you're on your own kind of place"—wondering where is the union in Union, Don was left, and led, to hold Union together more by moral and ministerial than ecclesial or other organizational cues. I believe he did that with a passionate commitment to Christian faith, scholarship, and teaching . . . and the *oikoumene*/beloved community about us.

## BIBLIOGRAPHY

Shriver, Donald W., Jr. *An Ethic for Enemies: Forgiveness in Politics*. New York: Oxford University Press, 1995.

2. Shriver, *Ethic for Enemies*, book cover.

# Later Work:
# Local, National, and
# International Conversations

# 17

## Honest Patriot

*Robert W. Snyder*

On the morning of September 11, 2001, Don Shriver was at work in his country home in Chatham, New York, beginning to write a book about "moral assessments of the German, South African, and American past."[1] Then the jets struck and almost 3,000 people died. Soon, down in Manhattan, the air was thick with grief, anger, calls for war, cries for peace, and debates over dissent and patriotism. For the remainder of the fall, he said, he set aside writing to mourn the dead and ponder America's response to the attack.

Don's deliberations were informed by reading the *New York Times* (he's a regular reader and frequently writes letters to the editor). The *Times* of December 31, 2001, contained two especially helpful pieces: an editorial arguing that the enormous events of September 11 made old concerns seem small and an op-ed by Joyce Carol Oates arguing that awful events eventually fade in public and personal memory.[2]

---

1. Shriver, *Honest Patriots*, 3.

2. Shriver, *Honest Patriots*, 4. For the pieces in the December 31, 2001 *New York Times*, see "At Year's End," A10, and Oates, "Words Fail," A10.

For Don, whose previous book warned against the danger of "leftover debris of national pasts that continue to clog the relationships of diverse groups of humans around the world," certain forms of forgetting could be perilous.[3] On the same day that he read Oates' op-ed, he resumed writing his book, well aware that he faced a hard job. A point that Oates made stuck in his mind: "The future doesn't belong to those who only mourn, but to those who celebrate."[4] But what, given the United States' history of slavery and the conquest of Native Americans, is to be celebrated about the United States of America? And could criticism and celebration of a country ever be combined?    *Could celebration & criticism be combined?*

Four years later, Don delivered his answer in *Honest Patriots: Loving a Country Enough to Remember Its Misdeeds*, published by Oxford University Press. His answer was so important to him that he wrote it in italics. "What is celebratable about democracy in America? One answer is: *Those public moments and events when we mourn some features of our national past with new present awareness that we must never repeat such events in our future*."[5] The best patriots, he concluded, were "honest patriots," people who have revisited shameful aspects of their national past "not in a spirit of moralism but with explicit intention to confront a past for the sake of ridding the present and future of its lingering effects."[6] In 2008, *Honest Patriots* won the distinguished Louisville Grawemeyer Award for "highly significant contributions to religious and spiritual understanding."[7]

To read the book more than a decade after its publication is to encounter an engaging work on history, memory and public theology. In modest asides and acute first-hand observations, the book also illuminates defining trends in the author's life.

*Honest Patriots*, Don's fifteenth book, is something of an exercise in personal archaeology. In his introduction, he offers some autobiographical details and describes himself as "an American with a certain difference"—a Southerner, the inheritor of a history of regional hurt, healing, and racism.[8] *Honest Patriots* begins with chapters on Don's most visible international work, his examination of history and memory in Germany and South Africa. By starting his book overseas, he avoids any notion that he is an American going abroad to deliver answers from on high. Instead, he presents himself

3. Shriver, *Ethic for Enemies*, 4.
4. Oates, "Words Fail," A10, quoted in Shriver, *Honest Patriots*, 5.
5. Shriver, *Honest Patriots*, 5.
6. Shriver, *Honest Patriots*, 5.
7. See "Religion" at http://grawemeyer.org/religion/.
8. Shriver, *Honest Patriots*, 10.

1927-

as an eager and searching student. He then moves on to two chapters about African Americans, whom he once described as "my teachers in matters of justice, forbearance, empathy, and the dream of a political order in America hospitable to all sorts and conditions of human beings."[9] The book ends with the memory and history of Native Americans, including the history of the Mohicans of the Hudson Valley near Don's summer home in Chatham.[10]

*Honest Patriots* certainly explores "loving a country enough to remember its misdeeds," but it also might have been titled *Honest Patriot: The Education of Donald W. Shriver Jr.* Born in 1927, he grew up in Norfolk, Virginia, in a middle-class family. His father, unlike his mother, was college educated and had earned a law degree at the University of Virginia. The family had no Confederate or slave-owning ancestors, and the myth of the Lost Cause was not a presence in his house. (Although his father accepted the legal logic of secession.) On family excursions to the historic sites of the American Revolution, Don gained some appreciation for history; he got a glimpse of the world beyond Virginia in a visit to the 1939–40 World's Fair in New York City.

Family trips to Jamestown, where the Powhatans encountered the first English settlers, were reminders of the original inhabitants of his native state. But African Americans, defined by personal connections and great silences, were the largest presence in Don's life outside of his family—which employed Mary Oakes, an African American, as a housekeeper who traveled five miles a day by bus to work in that suburban household. As he observes in *Honest Patriots*:

> As I grew into adolescence, the unasked questions about our segregated city were legion: Why no black students in my high school when there was a black community directly across the street? Why an absence of blacks from the city council? From our large Methodist church? From homes in our neighborhood?[11]

Don's journey outward from this world began when he was drafted in postwar 1946. Although he was opposed to conscription and considered applying for status as a conscientious objector, his pastor persuaded him that there was value in sharing in his generation's broad experience of military service. In the Army, serving in the Signal Corps, he used his posting to Fort Monmouth, NJ, to make frequent weekend trips to New York City, where he enjoyed concerts and visits to art museums.

9. Shriver, *Ethic for Enemies*, xi.

10. Shriver, *Honest Patriots*, 223–30.

11. Shriver, *Honest Patriots*, 129.

After a year in the military, Don enrolled in Davidson College and majored in history, which he savored for its ability to impart lessons about human beings, social change, and the forces that influence human understanding of good and evil. While there were no African American students at Davidson, he did encounter impressive Presbyterian ministers and undertook participation in the Presbyterian youth movement and the ecumenical United Christian Youth Movement where he made contacts with African Americans that would shape the course of his life.

By his sophomore year, Don was a national officer in the Presbyterian youth fellowship. At a conference in the North Carolina mountains, where many of the participants were African Americans, he took communion from an African American minister, Lucius H. Pitts, for the first time in his life. At the end of the service, when Pitts said, "'Go in peace, brothers and sisters,'" he said that, "something changed in me. A fork in the road opened up. I was on my way into alliance with forces in American society already at work tearing down the political-institutional monstrosity of racial segregation."[12]  *Graduated Davidson 1951*

The road he traveled after that service was long and varied but consistently defined by a rich combination of scholarship, religious devotion and political engagement. He graduated from Davidson College in 1951 and in 1952 went to India to attend the Third World Conference of Christian Youth. Sitting on the deck of the HSS Queen Elizabeth, he read Reinhold Niebuhr's *Irony of American History*. In India he conversed with young people from around the world, met a communist for the first time, and was surprised to discover how much he felt and thought as an American. What that meant in ethical and historical terms prompted a lifetime of questioning.

Don's marriage to Iowan Peggy in 1953 provided him with a lifelong partner in religious, intellectual, artistic, and political matters. After study at Union Seminary in Richmond, Virginia in 1955 he became an ordained Presbyterian minister and immediately afterward he earned a master's in Christian ethics at Yale with study in ethics with H. Richard Niebuhr, Reinhold's brother. From 1956 to 1959, he then served as the pastor of a church in Gastonia, North Carolina, a textile town famed for a 1929 strike in which a worker and a police officer died. The local press and churches mobilized against the strike, and the strikers were defeated.[13]

In Gastonia, Don gained an insight that changed his career as a teacher. When he organized bible study sessions for his congregation, barely half of whom had graduated from high school, he found few takers; his

---

12. Shriver, *Honest Patriots*, 130.
13. Glass and Hill, "Gastonia Strike."

parishioners preferred church services that brought comfort. One church elder complained to Don, "I don't come to church to go to school again." Don was reminded that while schooling had been one of the enduring successes in his life, to many of his congregants it summoned up feelings of failure. He concluded that if he had experienced the pain and troubles of many of his congregants, he too might have embraced a religion of consolation.[14] With the three years in Gastonia he grasped that his future might involve more teaching than preaching. He left Gastonia to earn a PhD in the field of "Religion and Society" at Harvard University.

From 1962–1972, he served as a Presbyterian minister at North Carolina State University. With the help of foundation grants, he developed a series of adult education groups composed of faculty and professionals in the fields of science, business, and engineering. These efforts yielded in 1971 the formation of a new Division of University Studies that bridged departmental insulations with interdisciplinary courses taught by a faculty from across the university.

By his own description he was no radical in these years of the civil rights movement, but supported the local movement by service on the Mayor's Committee on Racial Relations, and he marched with Martin Luther King Jr. in Selma. (Don kept the news from his father, who disagreed with him on civil rights and thought the movement brought disorder and disruption.) He left NCSU in 1971 for Emory University to become a professor of ethics and to direct the doctor of ministry program at the Candler School of Theology.

Surprising to him, three years later a search committee for the new president of Union Seminary in New York visited him in Atlanta, and he found himself appointed to the position that would define his career. He would serve as president and professor of ethics at Union from 1975–1991.

In New York, Don took on heavy administrative responsibilities but continued to publish as a scholar. Among the first of his sixteen books, *Spindles and Spires: A Re-Study of Religion and Social Change in Gastonia*, was written with sociologists John R. Earle and Dean D. Knudsen and was published in 1976. The subtitle reveals much about the book: *Spindles and Spires* extended a line of research begun by Liston Pope, one of Don's professors at Yale, who in the book *Millhands and Preachers* argued that, in the Gastonia strike of 1929, ministers did not oppose the economic exploitation that fueled the uprising and afterwards helped perpetuate an unequal social order of Gastonia. In *Spindles and Spires*, Shriver and his coauthors found that Gastonia's churches were no longer central to the social order

14. Earle, Knudsen, and Shriver, *Spindles and Spires*, 17–18.

of an urbanizing and economically diversifying Gastonia, but they had the potential to contribute to social change in Gastonia if they had found the right mix of religion, conviction, and action.[15]

The blend of sociology, religious studies, and ethics that defined *Spindles and Spires* reflects the strong interdisciplinary strain in Don's career, a tendency that defined his work as a scholar and teacher at Union. Always invigorated by conversations across religious and professional boundaries, he taught courses with fellow professors at the Jewish Theological Seminary, the Columbia Business School, Law School, and Journalism School. He developed an especially close affinity for journalists, recognizing both the importance of their work and the fact that journalists, like ethicists and historians, take as their subject matter the entire human condition.

It was only natural that when the Gannett Center for Media Studies was established at Columbia University in 1985, Don welcomed it and embraced its mission of elevating the news media by identifying the ethical issues inherent to their craft and improving the education of journalists in company with theological students while improving the latter's understanding of the complexities of public affairs. As a fellow of the center, Don participated in its seminars and conferences. The director of the center, Everette E. Dennis, recalls him as "an intellectual spark plug."[16] This was the year (1993) when he researched and wrote his book *An Ethic for Enemies: Forgiveness in Politics.* In subsequent years he contributed articles to the Center's quarterly publication, *Media Studies Journal.* Later, when Dennis became the director of the American Academy in Berlin, Don was awarded a fellowship there and did the research that bore fruit in *Honest Patriots.* Dennis recalls that

> Don's contributions in the fellowship programs were far more than the books he produced, but in the ennobling influence he had on two institutions and their people. His kindness and personal attention to all around him were notable and appreciated by all. He elevated the programs by simply being there.[17]

For all his years as a scholar and teacher, Don knows that much learning takes place outside of classrooms. *Honest Patriots* is certainly a work of scholarship, but it is also journalistic in the best uses of the term. The book

---

15. Pope, *Millhands and Preachers*, 328–30, and Earle, Knudsen, and Shriver, *Spindles and Spires*, 341–47.

16. Dennis, Letter to author, November 10, 2018.

17. On the history of the Gannett Center for Media Studies, see Dennis and Stebenne, "Requiem for a Think Tank," 11–35. Everette E. Dennis' reminiscences of Don as fellow at the Gannett Center for Media Studies and the American Academy in Berlin are from Dennis, Letter to author, November 10, 2018.

*Vivid prose*

is written in clear and vivid prose, all of it strengthened by Don's firsthand reports of museums, memorials, and civic actions where people remember and overcome the past. In vignettes, anecdotes, and analysis, Don demonstrates "that it is both possible and necessary for societies to face and to repent of certain evils in their past," and to make "firm, institutionalized forms of the collective commitment" never to repeat them again.[18] In *Honest Patriots*, this leads to chapters about past evils and contemporary repentance in textbooks, memorials, museums, and civic actions in Germany, South Africa, and the United States.

In his telling, the past and present are not always neatly divided. While he retains a historian's respect for the facts, and a reporter's knack for an illuminating scene or anecdote, he also has an ethicist's appreciation for the difficulty of establishing the present's obligation to the past. In Don's research, public memorials inform him as much as conventional historical research. Some of the most harrowing events he describes are in the German memorials to the Holocaust, particularly one in the Schöneberg neighborhood of Berlin, Germany that conveys—with images and text—the process of excluding Jews from German society that began with a ban on Jews becoming actors and culminated in genocide. In South Africa, he finds in Cape Town the District Six Museum, dedicated to commemorating and understanding, in human scale, a mixed-race neighborhood that was razed under apartheid. In the United States, he delves into the destruction of the African American community of Rosewood, Florida in 1923 (and the killing of at least six black residents), and the assault on African Americans in Tulsa, Oklahoma that destroyed a thriving black business community and took scores of lives.[19]  *Tulsa*

Don's studies of high school history textbooks are particularly valuable. He is impressed by German history courses' rigor and their insistence that German students study the rest of the world. He also appreciates South African efforts to create textbooks that will include all the nation's peoples and perspectives, fostering a societal sense of empathy absent under apartheid. And he charts, in the evolution of U.S. history textbooks, the emergence of a broader definition of who is an American, who matters in American history, and the relationship between the United States' highest ideals and its darkest realities.

As much as he believes that a proper repentance can heal peoples and check their readiness to do wrong, he is well aware that patriots do

18. Shriver, *Honest Patriots*, ix.

19. Shriver, *Honest Patriots*, 141–52. For recent figures on the Tulsa race riot, see Ellsworth, "Tulsa Race Massacre."

not always prevail. South Africans of color testified about their sufferings to their country's Truth and Reconciliation Commission, but whites did not respond with candor of their own in anything like equal numbers. Germans struggled to come to grips with the full meanings of Nazism, and did so only under the pressure of a total defeat of the Nazi regime that created a pressure for critical reckoning. Statues of Confederate generals on horseback still define Richmond, Virginia—even if the great African American athlete Arthur Ashe is now honored alongside them. Americans still argue over the subject of reparations for slavery, and one of the strongest parts of *Honest Patriots* is Don's discussion of the debate over forms that reparations might take, and why the debate is so vexed.

Even as Don describes painful history, he leaves the door open to collective memory that brings about social change. Nowhere is this more evident than in his book's subtitle: "Loving a Country Enough to Remember Its Misdeeds." He says that it took some time for him to find the right synonym for social "sin" in the book's title. That word, he thought, might not suit every reader's grasp of the traumas of twentieth-century history. "Flaws," suggested structural weaknesses; "evils," was too general; "crimes," perhaps too legal. Ultimately, he chose "misdeeds" because it was a word that quietly designates wrongs of many dimensions.

Donald Shriver is a Christian of broad-minded spirit. He believes in human beings' freedom to desist from collaboration with evil, to repent, and to forgive. Such ability offers, "hope for a future less evil than our pasts."[20] He recognizes that hatred and oppression scar not only the victims, but the haters and oppressors themselves. Turning away from doing wrong surely helps the victim, but it also begins the task of healing the one who does wrong. Those who seek to repent, he argues, can find direction in the Hebrew Bible, the Christian New Testament, and secular systems of thought. The pathways are many, he concludes, but the destination is the same: "repentance is an act of hope."[21]

As much as Don argues that we must confront the past "for the sake of ridding the present and future of its lingering effects," he does not suggest this course because it will provide us with lives of spiritual ease.[22] Indeed, throughout the book, when Don gets closer to his own history, his questions get tougher—not just with regard to Virginia, but when they touch on his later life in New York.

20. Shriver, *Honest Patriots*, x.

21. Shriver, *Honest Patriots*, x.

22. Shriver, *Honest Patriots*, 5.

Towards the end of *Honest Patriots*, he describes sitting on the porch of his summer home in Chatham, New York, and looking west across the Hudson River to watch the sun set on the Catskill Mountains. "My government assures me that I own this hillside with its view of the Catskills," he writes.[23] "But the Mohicans assure me that, in a deeper sense, it owns me, that it is a gift for which the only human response is: 'Thank you.' Remembering how we whites treated those original inhabitants of this land, I am inclined to add: 'Forgive us our trespasses.'"[24]

In the ten years that have passed since the publication of *Honest Patriots*, the political mood in the United States has shifted at least twice. The book was conceived under the shadows of 9/11, was published during the Iraq war, and marked its fifth year in print during the relative optimism of the Obama years. It is now at odds—in spirit and in recommendations—with a president who vows to "make America great again." Concern about economic inequality, hostility to globalization and immigration, and the rise of white nationalism are all much more evident internationally now than they were when *Honest Patriots* first appeared. Don says that the mood in the United States in 2018 leaves him feeling like an "auslaender," an optimistic liberal undergoing an internal exile during the Trump presidency.

The feeling is understandable, but it does not mean that Don's kind of honest patriotism will be forever exiled. As the historian David Blight has observed, the relationship between history and memory is complex. History, in Blight's view, is secular, scholarly, and guided by evidence. Memory, which Blight says can be understood as "the heritage or identity of a community," is more akin to a sacred worldview, rooted in the spiritual.[25] We remember individually and collectively, Blight observes, but there is always more memory available than history.[26]

In the United States, Blight argues, two forms of memory have dominated understandings of the primal conflict of the Civil War: the white supremacist view embodied in the Ku Klux Klan, and the reconciliationist view, expressed in popular culture and memory, that emphasizes the martial valor of boys in blue and gray. Neither of these has much room for Don Shriver.

But there is a third school of memory, Blight argues, a memory of the struggle for emancipation that has yet to be fully achieved for all Americans. It was born in African American resistance to slavery, embodied in

---

23. Shriver, *Honest Patriots*, 230.
24. Shriver, *Honest Patriots*, 230.
25. Blight, "Historians and 'Memory.'"
26. Blight, *Race and Reunion*, 1–5, and Blight, "Historians and 'Memory.'"

abolitionism, and carried forward into the civil rights movement that Don joined in the 1960s. It is focused not on the United States as an example of political and governmental perfection, but on the eventual redeeming of the promise of "life, liberty and the pursuit of happiness." It necessarily recognizes that American history includes a long record of denying freedom to many of our country's inhabitants, even as it also includes long struggles to overcome that legacy and form "a more perfect union."

It is this memory of the promise of emancipation and the struggle to realize it—birthed in the Declaration of Independence and invigorated by Dr. Martin Luther King—that can help chart a course from a scarred past to a better future. In this journey Americans of all sorts have much to learn from African Americans, whose feelings about our country are a complex mix of anger at centuries of wrongs, hopes for the future, and pride in under-recognized contributions to our commonwealth. As Don Shriver concludes, white Americans who study the stories of slaves and their descendants can emerge with "a new depth of chastened respect for anyone who not only loves a country in spite of it grievous misdeeds but loves it enough to remember the misdeeds and to work for their remedy."[27]

*Honest Patriots* begins with an epigram authored in 2004 by the minister and peace activist William Sloane Coffin. "There are three kinds of patriots," Coffin says, "two bad, one good. The bad are the uncritical lovers and the loveless critics. Good patriots carry on a lover's quarrel with their country, a reflection of God's lover's quarrel with the world."[28] By this measure, Don Shriver is both an honest patriot and a good patriot.

## BIBLIOGRAPHY

Blight, David W. "Historians and 'Memory.'" *Commonplace: The Journal of Early American Life* 2.3 (April 2002). http://commonplace.online/article/historians-and-memory/.

———. *Race and Reunion: The Civil War in American Memory*. Cambridge: Harvard University Press, 2001.

Dennis, Everette E. Letter to Robert W. Snyder, November 10, 2018.

Dennis, Everette E., and David L. Stebenne. "Requiem for a Think Tank: The Life and Death of the Gannett Center at Columbia, 1984–1996." *Harvard International Journal of Press/Politics* 8 (2003) 11–35.

Earle, John R., Deane D. Knudsen, and Donald W. Shriver Jr. *Spindles and Spires: A Restudy of Religion and Social Change in Gastonia*. Atlanta: John Knox, 1976.

27. Shriver, *Honest Patriots*, 204.

28. Shriver, *Honest Patriots*, 4.

Ellsworth, Scott. "Tulsa Race Massacre." In *The Encyclopedia of Oklahoma History and Culture*, edited by Dianna Everett. Oklahoma Historical Society. Accessed March 23, 2020. https://www.okhistory.org/publications/enc/entry.php?entry=TU013.

Glass, Brent D., and Michael Hill. "Gastonia Strike." In *Encyclopedia of North Carolina*, edited by William S. Powell. Chapel Hill: University of North Carolina Press, 2006. https://www.ncpedia.org/gastonia-strike.

*New York Times*. "At Year's End." December 31, 2001, A10.

Oates, Joyce Carol. "Words Fail, Memory Blurs, Life Wins." *New York Times*, December 31, 2001, A10.

Pope, Liston. *Millhands and Preachers*. New Haven: Yale University Press, 1942.

"Religion." Grawemeyer Awards, 2015. http://grawemeyer.org/religion/.

Shriver, Donald W., Jr. *An Ethic for Enemies: Forgiveness in Politics*. New York: Oxford University Press, 1995.

———. *Honest Patriots: Loving a Country Enough to Remember Its Misdeeds*. New York: Oxford University Press, 2005.

# 18

# Work and Ethics

*Ronald Stone*

The extraordinary life of Donald W. Shriver Jr. is profoundly summarized in his 2010 book, *On Second Thought*.[1] Choosing themes of his life he probes deeply into the major trajectories of his work. This approach has advantages over the more usual memoir in that he can deeply investigate subjects rather than being limited by chronological development. The chronological approach is limited by exactly where one is in any given year. The subject approach permits the analysis of a problem from the fuller perspective of ones' conclusions on the theme.

Shriver is a comprehensive Christian ethicist whose Presbyterian "work ethic" called him to investigate the important crises of his day and to risk judgments on those subjects. His conclusions have been grounded in the great Christian themes of forgiveness, love, hope, and faith. The theme of forgiveness, which distinguishes his work among ethicists, developed from his Harvard dissertation to fulfillment in *An Ethic for Enemies: Forgiveness in Politics* (1995). His love for books permeates his recorded life. Though

1. Shriver, *On Second Thought*.

156

he begins this love story with Socrates, clearly his work is dominated by his grounding in the Bible. He naturally inserts his Biblical themes into his contemporary discourse. But having originated in Methodism (which I share) he could never fall into a rigid biblicism, which has frozen some of his Presbyterian colleagues. Without any illusions of Methodist perfectionism he has been free to recognize the roles of tradition, experience, and human reason in the formulation of a powerful Christian ethic of freedom. The work ethic of the best of Methodism and Presbyterianism inspires both denominations after appreciating the word of God in Scripture to get up, as there is work for the neighbors' life to be undertaken.

In a short chapter he affirms the crucial friendships of Baruch for Jeremiah and Eberhard Bethge for Dietrich Bonhoeffer. Friendship was a major motif for his life. Those who worked with him closely knew the power of his friendship. His friend Henry Clark introduced me to Don in North Carolina, but as our careers took us to western Pennsylvania and New York City we were long-distance friends united in Presbyterian social action and love for Union Theological Seminary. Aristotle regarded friendship as based on attraction, helpfulness, and vocation. Shriver added another dimension as he on various occasions defended me from the criticisms of Wall Street supporters of Union, a misunderstanding by Ursula Niebuhr, and the New York City Presbytery. Through his defense he was also defending Union, but he could have thrown me under the bus and he refused to take the easy way out. The critiques of militarism and opposition to the expansion of Israel were at stake.

Another characteristic of Shriver's ethics is its church centeredness. He knows the Christian story is a community story. Too often theologians regard theology as grounded in their individual appropriations in Union's great towers. But it is messier than that as it is grounded in the political story of the church. Sometimes theologians and professors of religion cannot even find a satisfactory congregation. Thereby they become nearly as irrelevant as the political scientist who never touches actual politics or the social worker who is frightened by the society outside the office. Shriver frankly confesses how his Methodist congregation raised him up. This is my story as well. A Methodist Youth Fellowship and the Methodist Student Movement formed me, as did a theological seminary named Union. Shriver's youthful migration rings true. He laments deeply the loss of the Christian youth and student movements. Protestants neglected to raise many kids after our parents' generation, and we failed to maintain the ones we raised by neglecting our youth and college movements.

Writing about life in retirement at eighty-two years of age, the questions he ponders are the same he worked on in his profession. He hopes

God can continue to find joy in humanity and that humanity can overcome its tendencies to destroy itself and its environment. His vocation as an ethicist and citizen continues. In a final chapter he combines this vocation with a letter to grandchildren.

The sight of Donald Shriver and James Cone sharing a pew at Riverside Church witnesses to his career-long struggle to overcome racism in self, church, and society. His book reflects the passion he addressed to the issue. The poignant story he relates of his son's interruption of his education because of the conflict over his honoring of the martyrdom of Martin Luther King Jr. tears at the heart of any who have raised children of conscience through these tumultuous times. His books on the cities and on economics, class, and race in North Carolina have always displayed this sensitivity on race, as did his leadership at Union.

Shriver led Union Theological Seminary for sixteen years, from 1975 to 1991. They were years of financial constraints. Maintaining old, expensive buildings in New York City became impossibly expensive as other ecclesiastical organizations fled the city for more economic locations in Cleveland and Louisville. Union was forced to consider moving, or closing, or becoming a research institute without the expenses of students. The discord that rocked Union in the 1960s made solicitation of funds from those that had the money in the seventies and eighties difficult. Students occupying parts of the campus or picketing the campus for social justice did not enflame the generosity of Wall Street financiers or their families and heirs.

Union needed to create stability and continuity and Shriver managed that while raising prodigious amounts of money. Programs, staff, and faculty costs had to be reduced. So Shriver's options for creativity were muted as the institution had to reduce or drop programs of his predecessors. Union's freestanding nature denied it university or denominational support. Most denominations were abandoning financially their support for their colleges and seminaries at the time. In fact demographic facts were reducing proportionally the number of Protestants, and in particular New York City was shedding Protestants and their churches, which had traditionally supported Union. The trends against Union supported its decline. Even the ecumenical movement declined in worldwide importance, impacting the seminary, which had been central in initiating and leading it. It is really hard to lead when in retreat, but wise leadership of a retreat is as important as bold leadership when one's forces are easily advancing. Every city needs a progressive seminary. Even if they are small they provide consultation to churches, renewal to tired ministers, young faces for social ministry, and the resource library for the region. Most of all they provide the answer to the Puritans' fear of an uneducated ministry—demonstrated, for example, in the founding documents of Harvard College, which indicate that the founders feared the ministry of uneducated clergy after their own learned ministers passed. Uneducated religious leaders are truly disastrous.

The essence of the seminary was an intellectual community of Christians in an international city occasionally providing leadership in urban and international issues. Both the professional preparations for educated church leadership in the Master of Divinity degree and intellectual leadership for academia though doctoral studies were maintained. The Association of Theological Schools (ATS) recognized that most seminaries could not maintain both professional and doctoral educational programs; Union persisted in this vocation. The quality of the students and their professors was maintained while their numbers were reduced. Shriver managed to assist in the leadership of the ATS while also captaining Union. Along with other responsibilities he chaired the globalization project of ATS, building in requirements in international studies into the accrediting requirements of the agency.

Shriver had responded to the invitation to lead Union as a *call*. The Presbyterian theology of vocation does not demand success, but it promises power and consequently confidence in the most difficult times. For example: the participation in peacemaking is recognized as a *call* for Presbyterians even if their theological anthropology does not encourage optimism about the subject, and it promises hard trials. He hints at the cost to himself in *On Second Thought*. Gary Dorrien's essay in this series makes even clearer the obstacles to Union's survival that President Shriver faced.[2] Shriver's longer essay "The President as Pilgrim" recounts the struggle in more depth than the book's chapter on theological education.[3]

On answering the *call* to lead Union, he heard predictions of its demise. Those of us in the hinterland who loved Union heard of faculty divisions and financial weaknesses. The Board commissioned Shriver to reduce the deficit and to mend faculty relations while replacing central faculty members. He accomplished all three tasks in sixteen years under resistance and criticism. The threat to Union was real and he helped it to survive.

Beyond striving for Union's survival his work reveals commitment to institutions. He is not stuck with a focus on individual thinkers. He knows the call to understand and persevere in worthwhile institutions. His work at so many levels was dedicated to serving and strengthening structures. Social welfare institutions like social action and service organizations are continually threatened by predatory forces within capitalism. Forces supporting

2. Dorrien, "Hanging in There for a Good Cause."
3. Shriver, "The President as Pilgrim."

greed continually hammer at progressive churches or institutions like Union. Their survival must be protected and their missions advance. They often carry forward ideas whose time for realization has not arrived, which need to be carried into the future until the time is appropriate for their realization. Shriver's work for the social witness of the Presbyterian Church is only one example of his insight and commitment to this vital work.

Chapter 8 of his memoir essays celebrates the *German Requieum* led by Christoph von Dohnanyi, son of the resistance leader Hans von Dohnanyi, and the New York Choral Artists at Riverside Church to honor "Heroes of Conscience." The concert merged his great love of music to his recognition of Bonhoeffer as the greatest European theologian for him. He was able to dedicate the Bonhoeffer Room at Union and the fully funded Bonhoeffer Chair in theology and ethics with German financial help.

Shriver's theological understanding is multifaceted and complex and related to labor struggles in the South and at Union in his philosophy of education. He followed his Yale social ethics professor, Liston Pope, in writing about class, labor, and Christianity in Gastonia, North Carolina. I often used both Pope's *Millhands and Preachers* and Shriver's *Spindles and Spires* in economic ethics classes. The references to his theological ethics professor at Yale, H. Richard Niebuhr, are all positive in his reflections. Maybe he isn't quite so positive about the older brother Reinhold. From Harvard, the book warmly refers to his teacher, James Luther Adams. Gary Dorrien regards Adams as more fundamental for Shriver's thought than Dietrich Bonhoeffer. Perhaps, but in *On Second Thought* Bonhoeffer is the hero. As a Union man who taught all of H. Richard Niebuhr's books rather regularly and received Adams's gracious help at Harvard in the Paul Tillich Archives, I don't discern the influence of Tillich in Shriver's collected memoir essays. Tillich was determinative for H. Richard Niebuhr at an early stage and the object of Adams's work in his last decades.

Two of the causes of my vocation have been to explain and celebrate Paul Tillich's social philosophy and to defend Reinhold Niebuhr's role as an American-Christian political philosopher. With Roger Shinn's retirement it is probable that these causes were not defended well at Union while other great work was developed in feminism, ecology, Black theology, and other forms of liberation theology. While noting the problems of Union pride and the long shadows Tillich and Niebuhr threw over Union, Shriver may not in this book adequately celebrate their contributions to the Union ethos or their present viability.

In conclusion, all Union graduates, and future seminary administrators should read *On Second Thought* and his other reflections on theological education.[4] The presidency of Union was a stage of his vocation that was well done. Beyond his administration his writing has been important, with special recognition for the Grawemeyer Award–winning *Honest Patriots: Loving a Country Enough to Remember Its Misdeeds*. Ethicists, of course, will serve themselves well by reading the whole *corpus*.

## BIBLIOGRAPHY

Dorrien, Gary. "Hanging in There for a Good Cause: Donald Shriver's Presidency at Union Theological Seminary." In *Christian Ethics in Conversation: A Festschrift in Honor of Donald W. Shriver Jr., 13th President of Union Theological Seminary in the City of New York*, edited by Isaac B. Sharp and Christian T. Iosso. Eugene, OR: Cascade, 2020.

Shriver, Donald W., Jr. *On Second Thought: Essays Out of My Life*. New York: Seabury, 2010.

———. "The President as Pilgrim." *Theological Education* 32, supplement 3 (Spring 1996) 115–51.

4. Shriver, "The President as Pilgrim."

# 19

# A Lover's Challenge to America

*Eric Mount*

The title tells it. Donald Shriver's *Honest Patriots: Loving a Country Enough to Remember Its Misdeeds* (winner of the 2009 Grawemeyer Award in religion) confirms his career-long lover's quarrel with his homeland, with its history with Native Americans, with African Americans, with its enemies, with its fundamental sin of slavery/racism. The quarrel is more than a memory, however; it also a challenge to our nation and its leadership to live up to Abraham Lincoln's "better angels of our nature."

*Honest Patriots* (2005) is more than a memory in another sense. It is also the other half of a two-volume work that began a decade earlier with the predecessor, *An Ethic for Enemies: Forgiveness in Politics* (1995). In his sixteen books, more than a hundred essays, and numerous letters to the *New York Times*, he has carried on his lover's quarrel and challenge as a Christian social ethicist, but the combination of *An Ethics for Enemies* and *Honest Patriots* qualifies as the pinnacle of his formidable body of work.

It is in *An Ethics for Enemies* that he articulates another lover's quarrel with America and another challenge to his country's institutions and leadership. In this case, the object of his disaffection is our individualism, and his

*individualism*       162

hope is built on our sociality. What Shiver does in relating forgiveness and politics is show that forgiveness should not be limited to individual relationships and that racism should not be construed as limited to the prejudice of individuals. As it is spelled out in the following passages, the sociality of the self is the key on both counts.

## UNDERSTANDING THE SHRIVER PERSPECTIVE

Behind the individualization of an act of forgiveness lies the individualization of human victimization, guilt and responsibility, a model of human society that ignores the ripples that flow out from the initial victims to their literal kin to their political kin and thence to their moral kin. In point of fact, victimization and guilt have partners of greater and lesser degrees; and it is arbitrary to say in turn that such partnerships are candidates for neither forgiveness nor responsibility. Such arbitrariness flies in the face of the sociality of selves and the tragic as well as the redeeming consequences of that sociality.

In short, only in a context of perceived interconnectedness between participants in great traumatic political injustice can one go on to assert the symbolic, representative role of politicians in the enactment of a political form of forgiveness. An indefinite but real network of victims and agents calls for that role. Whether leaders accuse an enemy of crime, confess to crimes of their own people, or hold out hopes for a future reconciliation, they do all of this on behalf of one collective in addressing another. To deny this representative, symbolic role to politicians is to impoverish their service to a society's dealing with its past wrongs and its present corrective responsibility to the future.[1]

[T]here is a complementary diminishment on all sides of a human relation afflicted by racism. A self that stands up against such diminishment needs others to stand with; both the means and the end of personal worth require a society, a social means of support. The means and the ends of racism require the same. They both require society, citizenship, and politics. 'Strangely enough,' said Martin Luther King in 1961, 'I can never be what I ought to be until you are what you ought to be.' In individualistic Lockean America, it did sound strange. It was a truth that Americans all needed to learn, but which the culture of African

---

1. Shriver, *Ethic for Enemies*, 113.

Americans apparently taught them long centuries ago. If culture critics want to see demonstrations of what 'the social self' looks like in practice, they should look first at the history of African Americans.[2]

(They should, of course, look also at the history of Native Americans, who are eminently deserving of our national repentance, apology, and reparation, but the current focus of the national debate and Shriver's acknowledged major indebtedness to members of the African American community suggest the focus that has been adopted here.)

These passages expose the role of individualism as a primary barrier to the bridge Shriver attempts to build between personal religion and ethics, the usually assumed realm of "forgiveness and its twin repentance," and public theology and ethics, the realm of countervailing power and institutional resistance to reconciling initiatives.[3] American individualism is not just an inheritance of the medieval church's penitential system, Martin Luther's two kingdoms ethic (with its wedge between the duties of forgiving mercy and those of punitive justice), and Lockean contractarian philosophy. It has been reinvented and reinforced by the "go West" independence of the frontier experience and the current brand of individualism that distrusts all institutions. *Couples individualsm with "Social Self"*

Shriver counters this individualism with an understanding of "the social self" as developed by our mutual theological/ethical mentor H. Richard Niebuhr. This vision of interconnectedness refutes the mythology of the lone individual by illuminating the interpenetration of the self's various community memberships in the inner dialogue of one's personal identity even as it captures the richness of the diversity within communities unless they attempt to be authoritarian monoliths. At the root of the degree of difficulty of Shriver's project are competing anthropologies and competing senses of reality as filters operating in contrasting community contexts.

These quoted paragraphs also credit the experience of the African American community as Shriver's primary teacher in the project of these two volumes—whether about the social self or about the redeeming potential of forgiveness to ameliorate racist social conflict and discrimination. In his acknowledgments in *An Ethic for Enemies*, he states that, among all of the groups of people that moved him to write the book,

no one has influenced me quite as much as the company of friends, fellow Christians, ministers, and academic colleagues in the community of African Americans . . . Over the decades,

2. Shriver, *Ethic for Enemies*, 203.
3. Shriver, *Ethic for Enemies*, 6.

African Americans have been my teachers in matters of justice, forbearance, empathy, and the dream of a political order in America hospitable to all sorts and conditions of human beings. In their embodiment of that dream and their persistence in pursuing it, I count myself among their students.[4]

In today's setting his insights carry telling relevance for the discussion about the forgiveness offered by relatives of the slain at the Charleston Massacre and for the reawakened discussion of systemic or structural racism and reparations that is again informing and inflaming political discourse.

Add to these considerations the importance Shriver assigns to "the symbolic, representative role of politicians" in a society's dealing with past wrongs and assuming responsibility to enable a different future.[5] Our featured volumes, which treat Germany and South Africa as well as the United States, provide examples of both failure and success in assuming this symbolic role, and these reflections will cite others.

## AFTER CHARLESTON—THE QUESTION OF FORGIVENESS

The horrendous Charleston tragedy of June 17, 2015, was Dylann Roof's massacre of the "Charleston Nine" at a Wednesday night Bible study at Emanuel African Methodist Episcopal Church (a church that had been under attack by white supremacists for two hundred years). A self-professed white supremacist and evident admirer of the Confederate legacy, the twenty-one-year-old became argumentative after first being welcomed and then gunned down his nine victims. He justified his actions during the massacre by describing a necessary race war between white and black Southerners. When a young victim asked him why he was shooting the worshippers, he replied, "I have to do this because y'all raping our women and taking over the world." The questioner was then killed with five shots.[6]

Before his attack, he had published a manifesto citing his perverse rationale, defending slavery and the separation of the races, and picturing himself draped in the Confederate flag. He acknowledged drawing inspiration from the website of the Council of Conservative Citizens, a prominent white supremacist group. Its "statement of principles" declares that "the American people and government should remain European in their

4. Shriver, *Ethic for Enemies*, x, xi.
5. Shriver, *Ethic for Enemies*, 113.
6. Shapiro, "Key Moments in Charleston Church."

composition and character," and opposes "all efforts to mix the races of mankind."[7] In the course of his arrest and prosecution. Roof expressed no remorse, offered no apology, and begged no forgiveness. To him, his mass killing was unfortunate, but he believed he had to do it.

To the amazement of many, if not most, the families of the victims proceeded to offer forgiveness within days to the killer. To fathom such an action, we might recall Martin Luther King's response to a student question in an interview at Bennett College in Greensboro, North Carolina, on February 11, 1958. They asked him whether he could forgive those who lynched Emmett Till in Money, Mississippi, and the members of the Ku Klux Klan who mutilated a developmentally disabled black man in Birmingham. His answer explains both why he would have to forgive and why such an act would not indicate a failure to take the horror of the offense seriously.

> [I]f you really love on the basis of Christian concepts, forgive-
> ness is very difficult. It isn't easy. And when it comes so easy, it
> isn't forgiveness. There is pain and agony . . . Whether it is in
> social life or whether it's in individual relations. So for me not
> to forgive the people who killed Emmett Till or the people who
> mutilated the man in Birmingham, I am setting in my very per-
> sonality a structure of evil which can cause a disintegration in
> my personality. And so that it has both power of psychological
> integration as well as social integration.[8]

Put another way, his conviction is that "psychologists are telling us today that hatred not only hurts the hated but hurts the hater as much."[9] His actions definitely backed his words, but his attitude provokes as many questions now as it did then.

At a rally sponsored by the New Black Panther Party soon after the Charleston massacre, disdain was expressed for the stereotypical Christian forbearance narrative. "Do we forgive four hundred years of oppression and rape? NO!"[10] When lack of repentance on the part of the offender makes reconciliation impossible, it is arguable even on biblical grounds that forgiveness is incomplete. Don't both parties have to change to enable true forgiveness?

Nicholas Wolterstorff does a thorough examination of New Testament passages in "After Injustice: What Makes Forgiveness Possible," an article

---

7. Robinson, "The Roots of Racism Still Exist."

8. King, Interview by *Bennett Banner*.

9. King, Interview by *Bennett Banner*.

10. Wellington, "After the Charleston Massacre," 29.

excerpted from his book *Journey toward Justice: Personal Encounters in the Global South* (2013). His conclusion:

> Nowhere in the New Testament is Jesus reported as enjoining his listeners to forgive unrepentant wrongdoers. We are instructed to love our enemies, including those who have wronged us and are unrepentant. Neither do I know of any passage in the New Testament that says God forgives (justifies) even unrepentant wrongdoers.[11]

Wolterstorff questions whether it is even possible to forgive the unrepentant wrongdoer—"and if it is possible whether it is morally permissible."[12] It is one thing to be willing to forgive if the other repents; it is another to do so in the absence of repentance (which Shriver calls the twin of forgiveness). Wolterstorff is not sure it is possible; he questions whether he should if he could due to the moral seriousness of the offense.

A challenge to both the traditional rendition of Christian forbearance with its ever-ready forgiveness and the Christian form of what she calls "transactional" forgiveness (pardon for the offender who acknowledges the wrong done and repents) comes from Martha Nussbaum, *Anger and Forgiveness: Resentment, Generosity, Justice* (2016).[13] At the risk of dealing inadequately with the problem of evil, she targets anger as a deplorable element in human evolution. Anger is primitive and only momentarily appropriate in the face of injustice. If one does not quickly move beyond it to a more open future, it is decidedly inappropriate. When we demand repentance, we are compelling self-denigration in the offender. When we forgive unconditionally, it is still objectionable because of the self-righteousness of the person who magnanimously forswears retribution.

The relationship between forgiveness and repentance, which frames much of the Shriver examination of civil wrongs and the righting of them, grows increasingly problematic as we move from the sphere of the offenses of individuals to the sphere of institutional and systemic wrongs—in the case of the Charleston massacre by Dylann Roof, to the systemic and cultural racism that wraps itself and its witting and unwitting adherents in the Confederate flag. Shriver's tracing of forgiveness in the public realm conceives it as a painstaking and often unfinished process that seldom arrives at the reconciliation it seeks.

On the repentance requirement, Shriver observes that the forgiveness offered by civil rights leaders in Birmingham and elsewhere in the early

11. Wolterstorff, "After Injustice," 28.

12. Wolterstorff, "After Injustice," 28.

13. Nussbaum, *Anger and Forgiveness*, 10.

1960s was never unconditional (as it seems the forgiveness the Emanuel AME Church families and Martin Luther King cited earlier was). The willingness of many blacks to forgive the past was conditioned on white willingness to collaborate on building a new political future for all Americans. "No one, and no society," writes Shriver, "is ready for forgiveness without being ready for repentance."[14] In the concluding paragraphs of his chapter on "Justice and Forgiveness" in *An Ethic for Enemies*, he deals with the issue of unpaid debt and reparation:

> Whether we call it justice or rehabilitation or reparation is less important than that we call it the first order of our domestic national business . . . Until we make it that, African Americans have every right and obligation to reserve a certain portion of forgiveness in themselves for the day when that business has at last been tended to, that debt at last paid.[15]

His qualifier of the forgiveness offered by the Charleston families would appear to be seeing their gracious action as willingness to forgive, which is the beginning of a process that is only completed when justice is done and reconciliation is achieved.

One way to reconcile the words of Jesus from the cross ("Father, forgive them; for they do not know what they are doing," Luke 23:34 [NRSV]) and the immediate forgiveness offered to Dylann Roof by the families of those murdered in Charleston with the absence of repentance by Roof is to place him among those who do not fathom the magnitude of the evil they have done because of cultural and systemic racism. This racism has so warped his perception of the world that he has re-imagined a horrible evil as a sacred obligation. His "social selfhood" (to use an H. Richard Niebuhr/ Donald Shriver term) or identity was totally defined by one community membership, making him a fanatic. Michael Walzer calls this fanatical self a "singular self."[16] Roof, like all fanatics, became oblivious to other voices of other community memberships that might have summoned him to empathy for his fellow human beings.

When we look at some of the responses to the Charleston massacre, we find that America's reigning myth of individualism is equally adroit in its denial of individual racism or bigotry and its refusal to recognize systemic and institutional racism. As long as the massacre could be dismissed as the aberrant behavior of a mentally ill individual (possibly caused by overprescription of medication, according to Rick Perry) or a hate crime against

14. Shriver, *Ethic for Enemies*, 194.

15. Shriver, *Ethic for Enemies*, 216.

16. Walzer, *Thick and Thin*, 96–100.

Christians (Lindsey Graham) or an exceptional accident in an otherwise non-racist community, the surrounding culture could remain unindicted. Far-right radio host Jesse Lee Peterson claimed, on the one hand, that the Roof shooting was meant to start a race war and, on the other, that racism is not an issue in America today. He called identifying racism the real threat because white people are being made to feel guilty and to fear being called racist; which will lead to more violent race-based attacks like the one in Charleston.

Therefore, when President Obama, who tried unsuccessfully to conduct a post-racial presidency, took the occasion of the Charleston massacre to deliver his most candid remarks about racism to date, the radical right accused him of being racist, even the most racist of American presidents. He was accused of fomenting discord and even welcoming such incidents to give him another excuse for taking away America's guns. What he said was that race relations have improved, but that "we are not cured of racism," "our nation's original sin."[17] Slavery and Jim Crow discrimination are "still part of our DNA that's passed on."[18] When he led his audience in "Amazing Grace," he was offering hope for healing of a national sickness that afflicts us all in varied ways.

Charleston did not want to think such thoughts about itself. Nor did Southern culture. The tragedy brought an overwhelming outpouring of compassion for the victim's families and aroused an inspiring sense of unity among South Carolinians. This wanton attack was especially painful for a city that had had a black majority for decades. For generations, blacks in Charleston had defied the South's conservative political dominance by supporting Mayor Joseph Riley, a powerful white Democrat who throughout his forty-year mayoral dynasty had opposed the offensive Confederate symbol flying over the state capitol grounds in Charleston. It took the massacre, however, and perhaps Obama's case at the funeral for tearing down that flag, which he termed "a reminder of systemic oppression and racial subjugation," to convince Governor Nikki Haley and College of Charleston president and former state senator Glenn McConnell, both of whom had previously opposed removing the flag, to get the job done.[19]

Charleston had had a long-standing "cultural allegiance to the romanticized Old South" and a longstanding immersion in its culture of denial.[20]

17. Obama, interview by Maron, June 22, 2015; Obama, "Eulogy for the Honorable Reverend Clementa Pinckney."

18. Obama, interview by Maron, June 22, 2015.

19. Obama, "Eulogy for the Honorable Reverend Clementa Pinckney"; Ford, "Radical Response to Senseless Violence," 17.

20. Wellington, "After the Charleston Massacre," 27.

But its cultural racism observed a certain reserve. According to one local minister:

> When you get into the overall community, the White community in Charleston is still very patrician, very paternalistic, very polite. There's more polite racism in Charleston than I have ever seen. There's raging politeness in Charleston, so you don't dare say something inordinate . . . There are those lines that people don't like to cross.[21]

"Raging politeness" does have a ring to it, doesn't it?

This classy veneer helped reinforce the culture of denial in more places than Charleston and more regions than the South. It was often an unwitting accomplice in the resistance to facing up to racism. The Roof rampage served to convince leaders like Haley and McConnell that they could not hide behind individualistic diagnoses of Roof's mentality and menace. They had to look at the culture that shaped him, at groups like the Council of Conservative Citizens that formed him, at the traditions and institutions that perpetuated the attitudes and practices that characterized his white supremacist ideology. The effects were widespread. A *New York Times* reporter even wrote about a man getting his Confederate tattoo removed after he noticed the pained look on an African American woman's face after Charleston at the gym where he worked out.[22] Not all the reactions were so positive, even in the vicinity of the massacre. There was an immediate run on the sale of Confederate flags and related products that produced an early 200 percent increase in sales.

## BEYOND INDIVIDUALISM—THE QUESTION OF COLLECTIVE RESPONSIBILITY

Since resistance to being made to feel guilty is a leading perpetrator of the culture of denial, facing up to complicity in systemic and cultural racism can be aided by Shriver's distinction between feeling guilty and feeling responsible. Just as all Germans were not guilty of the horrors of the Third Reich, all Southerners and all Americans are not guilty of the sins of slavery, segregation, systemic discrimination, and oppression. But that does not mean that the sweep of complicity is not far reaching. Shriver regards "collective responsibility" as essential to forgiveness in politics and as necessary

---

21. Wellington, "After the Charleston Massacre," 27.
22. Robertson, "Flag Supporters React."

for genuine social change.[23] Concerning generations after the facts of the Third Reich or slavery and Jim Crow for examples, Shriver can speak of "inherited responsibility" in the absence of inherited guilt.[24] Even generations that were not contemporaneous with the Holocaust or with slavery need to remember the dreadful past and "to use that past as a negative measure of what they are responsible for not repeating in their present."[25]

Among the principles articulated in the chapter on South Africa in *Honest Patriots* (in the section on "Truth, Reconciliation, and Democracy") are these: "Some Must Represent Others" and "Some Power Must Call the Powerful to Account."[26] These reflect Shriver's claim in *An Ethic for Enemies* that "representative repentance" is a political vocation.[27] Someone who commands a hearing needs to be willing to remember the misdeeds of a nation or a society's past. These voices need communal backing to be heard. Still another of the principles speaks to the issue of collective responsibility (as opposed to collective guilt): "Some Are More Responsible, Some Less, but All Are Responsible."[28] Shriver gives us telling examples, none more telling than Dietrich Bonhoeffer and Willie Brandt.

If anyone could justifiably absolve himself of all guilt over the Nazi horrors, it was Bonhoeffer. He was the first among theologians to condemn the Nazis in 1933. He was involved in an unsuccessful plot on Hitler's life, and he was among the last to die in a concentration camp as a member of the German resistance. Yet he composed a poem about a sleepless night in prison in which he spoke for both himself and his fellow prisoners about their mixture of guilt and innocence in relation to those who held them captive. (Likewise, Brandt lived in Norway for all twelve years of the Nazi regime, yet he fell on his knees before the Warsaw monument to the victims of the ghetto.)

In Bonhoeffer's poem "Night Thoughts in Tegel," he speaks of being one of those who accuses others "who made us share the guilt," yet, he writes, "We learned to lie easily, To be at the disposal of open injustice."[29] He concludes the poem with a prayer:

> We saw the lie raise its head,
> And we did not honor the truth.

23. Shriver, *Ethic for Enemies*, 113, 114.
24. Shriver, *Honest Patriots*, 27, 195.
25. Shriver, *Ethic for Enemies*, 114.
26. Shriver, *Honest Patriots*, 114, 119.
27. Shriver, *Ethic for Enemies*, 107.
28. Shriver, *Honest Patriots*, 111.
29. Shriver, *Ethic for Enemies*, 115.

> We saw the brethren in direst need,
> And feared only our own death.
> We come before thee as men,
> As confessors of our sins.[30]

Supposedly forgiveness moves from wrong sufferers to wrong doers, but, says Shriver, "in human societies, and most of all in political conflict, it may have to go both ways."[31]

Shriver applauds the speech of Richard von Weizsacker, president of the Federal Republic of Germany, for his widely acclaimed speech to the Bundestag on May 8, 1985, (the fortieth anniversary of the end of the war) as a great example of public repentance. Though an active church leader who was perhaps informed by church expressions of penitence, he spoke as his nation's chief political leader. He concluded: "Let us . . . look the truth in the eye as well as we are able."[32] He did not mention forgiveness, but he remembered in detail who all of the sufferers were and what they had suffered. He refuted the idea that most Germans did not know what Hitler was doing; Hitler saw to it that they knew. He "made the entire nation the tool of his hatred."[33]

The president was the first West German leader to challenge publically the widespread claim that ordinary Germans were unaware of the Holocaust. He did not make a personal confession, but those in the hall knew that he had served on the Russian front at age nineteen, been wounded twice, and been a defense attorney at Nuremberg along with his father who had been chief secretary in the Nazi Foreign Office. In his list of what people had suffered, he ended with "the loss of all that one had mistakenly believed in and for which one had worked."[34] What he mainly did was leave no one's suffering in the war unrecognized and no one's complicity unindicted. He also addressed young Germans about their responsibility for a different future.

The point is that Weizsacker remembered and led a national expression of repentance using the confessional "we." At first he excited considerable discomfort among his fellow Germans, but the extremely positive international response soon quieted apprehensions about negative consequences for the defeated nation. Writes Shriver, "Whether in interpersonal

---

30. Shriver, *Ethic for Enemies*, 115.
31. Shriver, *Ethic for Enemies*, 7.
32. Shriver, *Ethic for Enemies*, 112.
33. Shriver, *Ethic for Enemies*, 110.
34. Shriver, *Ethic for Enemies*, 109.

relationships or in public life, the confession 'I was/we were wrong' lessens the compulsions of wronged parties to keep on insisting, 'Yes, you were wrong.'"[35] This example prompts a look at some avoided and appropriated opportunities by recent political leaders to acknowledge their people's misdeeds and their own. Again from Shriver's pen, we read: "As a political people, we would be better served by politicians who confessed our collective sins once in a while, even when our sins are enmeshed in the sins of others, as they certainly were in the Pacific War."[36] That is our next focus.

## AFTER PEARL HARBOR AND HIROSHIMA— THE QUESTION OF APOLOGY

Forgiveness and repentance in politics must begin with the recovery of painful memories, or should we say the recollection of a painful past. In Shriver's vision, remember and forgive is the right order, not forgive and forget. When he wrote *An Ethic for Enemies*, he labeled Hiroshima and Pearl Harbor "undigested memories," and this classic case of indigestion continues, but not without some notable gestures toward reconciliation to be treated later.[37]

In the final chapter of *Honest Patriots,* Shriver offers a list of public mourning markers that he hopes someday to see. He includes a tablet to be placed in the Washington memorial to World War II that "expresses grief for the millions of civilians killed by air power on both sides of that war."[38] (Other envisioned markers refer to American misdeeds in Korea and Vietnam.) In *The Irreversible Decision: 1939–1950*, social ethicist Robert C. Batchelder provides a detailed account of "The Evolution of Mass Bombing," which serves as a perfect backdrop for Shriver's telling lament about the firebombing of cities, the atomic bombing of Hiroshima and Nagasaki, and the loss of discrimination between military and civilian targets. Batchelder describes a seven-year span during which the "obliteration bombing of civilian areas" moved from being condemned by church leaders and decent people generally in 1937, through being regarded as only used by dictators in 1939, to being considered, between 1940 and 1944, as a "military

---

35. Shriver, *Ethic for Enemies*, 107.

36. Shriver, *Ethic for Enemies*, 138.

37. Shriver, *Ethic for Enemies*, 133.

38. Shriver, *Honest Patriots,* 269. See also 272 for an account of the obliteration city bombing and note 10 on 328 concerning the abandonment of discrimination of military and civilian targets.

necessity" and "a normal part of the procedure of war" by the general public and a majority of Catholic and Protestant church people.[39]

Early in the war, both President Truman and Churchill were insistent that bombing would only be precision bombing directed at military targets and avoiding direct attacks on civilians. As late as 1943, President Roosevelt told Congress that our bombing targets were "carefully selected" factories, munitions dumps, and shipyards, not tenements.[40] By late 1941, Great Britain switched from precision bombing to area bombing, and the distinction between the two regarding targeting civilians was soon lost. In light of the German devastation of cities, such as Rotterdam and Warsaw, obliteration bombing of cities became acceptable. After the U.S. entered the war, its targets soon shifted in similar fashion under the assumptions that nighttime obliteration of cities would shorten the war by destroying morale and avoid the costly losses of daytime precision bombing. Again whole cities came to be thought of as military targets. The firebombing that melted down Dresden and Hamburg is an example.

In the Pacific theatre, B-29 raids began in November 1944. Daytime high-altitude raids against aircraft factories proved to be imprecise and not very effective. General Curtis LeMay then turned to low-altitude, incendiary bombing of cities at night. These attacks escalated to the firebombing of Tokyo on the night of March 9–10, 1945. A wave of three hundred American bombers struck the capital city, killing one hundred thousand with nearly seventeen hundred tons of bombs, burning out more than fifteen square miles in the city's industrial and residential districts, destroying a fourth of the buildings, and making a million people homeless.[41] General LeMay bragged about the inferno caused by the napalm in the mist of the wooden frame buildings and canals with these words: "We scorched and boiled and baked to death more people on the night of March 9–10 than went up in vapor at Hiroshima and Nagasaki combined."[42]

There had been one incendiary bombing of Tokyo before this one, and there were two later in May covering fifty-six square miles between them, but this Operation Meetinghouse raid on March 9–10 has been judged to be the most destructive bombing raid of World War II and even of human history.[43] (The obliteration campaigns then moved to smaller cities—Nagoya, Osaka, and Kobe.)

39. Batchelder, *Irreversible Decision*, 181.
40. Batchelder, *Irreversible Decision*, 176.
41. Batchelder, *Irreversible Decision*, 71, 72.
42. Kristof, "Stoically, Japan Looks Back," A4.
43. Lendon and Jozuka, "History's Deadliest Air Raid"; Shriver, *Honest Patriots*, 272.

When President Truman decided to use the atomic bomb, he picked four targets, chosen in order of their importance as war production centers. They were Hiroshima, Kokura, Niigata, and Nagasaki. He referred to Hiroshima, the target of the first atomic bomb, as "a military base" chosen to avoid civilian deaths as much as possible.[44] Nevertheless, in Hiroshima, eighty to one hundred thousand civilians died on the night of August 6, 1945. The number of military deaths was small in comparison. After a forty-eight-hour delay, efforts to warn the Japanese scientific community, and the dropping of leaflets to warn the general populace (but leaving them no time to "petition the emperor"), the second bomb devastated Nagasaki.[45]

Although later deemed militarily unnecessary by American generals Eisenhower, MacArthur, and LeMay, and by Admiral William Daniel Leahy, the senior-most military officer on active duty during the war, and as not what sealed Japan's defeat, the use of the atomic bomb did bring about the Japanese surrender, as stated by Emperor Hirohito on August 15, 1945.[46] The obliteration bombing culminating in the atomic bombing has long been justified because of the lives it saved on both sides by avoiding an invasion of the mainland and the quicker end it brought to the war. Japan was already defeated and seeking help from Russia to get a negotiated settlement that would avoid "unconditional surrender" and allow them to keep their emperor, but there was stubborn resistance to surrender by extremists who still controlled the army before Hiroshima and Nagasaki.[47]

The shift in bombing strategy to the obliteration bombing of cities both before Hiroshima and Nagasaki and with them as targets drew few objections from religious leaders at the time. Batchelder cites editorials in the Catholic *Commonweal* and the Protestant *Christian Century* and a pair of individual Christian leaders. The Federal Council of Churches' Commission on the Relation of the Church to the War in the Light of the Christian Faith (which was made up of twenty-six distinguished Protestant theologians, including both pacifists and non-pacifists) took an ambivalent position in their 1944 report. While condemning "the massacre of civilian populations," the statement indicated that such repugnant tactics as "obliteration

44. Truman, *Year of Decisions*, 421; Batchelder, *Irreversible Decision*, 187.

45. Batchelder, *Irreversible Decision*, 41. Batchelder's note documents the uncertainty about the precise numbers of casualties at Hiroshima and Nagasaki. He adopts 70,000 for Hiroshima and 40,000 for Nagasaki with an equal number of injured for the purpose of his study. Estimates for Tokyo range between 80,000 and 130,000. The vast majority of casualties would have been women, children, and elderly since the able-bodied men were at the front.

46. Kuznick, "The Atomic Bomb."

47. Batchelder, *Irreversible Decision*, 127–32.

bombing of civilian areas" were regarded by some of the signers as "justifiable on Christian principles, if they are essential to the successful conduct of a war that is itself justified."[48]

After Hiroshima and Nagasaki, however, the Commission met again and unanimously condemned not only the atomic destruction of Hiroshima, but also the obliteration raids of Tokyo and elsewhere that preceded it. They expressed deep penitence for their earlier ambivalence and called their position "inexcusable." A number of Catholic moralists also registered their condemnation. In Batchelder's roll call, *Christian Century* refers to "America's Atomic Atrocity" as "wanton," *Commonweal* cries "Horror and Shame!" and the *Catholic World* calls Hiroshima "atrocious and abominable." Pacifists in both communions were of course adamantly opposed.[49] For a preponderance of the American population, however, justification of whatever means we decided to use continued to hold sway.

To dredge up these memories of American misdeeds is not to deny the savage atrocities committed by the Japanese forces in the war, including their treatment of prisoners of war, their long-suppressed record regarding "comfort women" from their Asian neighbors, their thirty-six years of colonial brutality to those neighbors, or the gravity of the deaths of 2,403 at Pearl Harbor, with the 1,178 wounded in addition.[50] Nor is it to indulge in a calculus of which nation did the most horrible things. The point is that remembering our national misdeeds is painful, but we need to acknowledge that our hands are far from clean. In the history that Shriver reviews, we Americans should take account of the American-led oil-embargo that preceded the Pearl Harbor attack, the mutual dehumanization of the propaganda between the two nations, replete with racist monkey images on our part, as well as the obliteration bombing of cities. And then there are Hiroshima and Nagasaki.

It is understandable that such second thoughts seldom get a hearing from anyone who was on the firing line at Iwo Jima, for instance, or positioned to be involved in an invasion of the Japanese mainland, while perhaps ignorant of the fact that our naval blockade would have forced surrender without the holocaust we unleashed with our bombing. What is most lamentable, however, is that many have accepted the official justifications of the war because of the racist depictions of our enemies by our propaganda.

Shriver provides some revealing statistics from 1991 about national sentiments in the two countries concerning making an apology. Forty

---

48. "The Relation of the Church to the War"; Batchelder, *Irreversible Decision*, 181.

49. Batchelder, *Irreversible Decision*, 115.

50. Black, "Pearl Harbor."

percent of Americans thought Japan should apologize for Pearl Harbor, and 55 percent of the Japanese thought so. When asked whether the U.S. should apologize for dropping the atomic bombs, only 16 percent of Americans answered "yes," while 73 percent of Japanese did.[51]

The only apologies offered by our leaders concerning World War II have been the passage of the Civil Liberties Act during the Reagan administration, apologizing to the Japanese Americans who were herded into relocation camps, and the statement of the chairman of the Joint Chiefs of Staff John Shalikashvili (in Dresden, February, 1995) concerning the "senseless" firebombing of that city fifty years earlier, killing at least thirty-five thousand and maybe as many as one hundred thirty-five thousand civilians.[52] The formal apology to the Japanese Americans included compensation of 82,219 Japanese American citizens who were interned in the camps with $20,000 per surviving victim.[53] There have been no apologies offered for the firebombing of Hamburg, Yokohama, and Tokyo that decimated civilian populations. In all, sixty-seven Japanese cites were bombed, killing an estimated four hundred thousand civilians.[54] Commitment to the just war/international law mandate to spare non-combatants insofar as possible had apparently been forgotten.

To a remarkable degree, it does seem that our nation and Japan have moved on as allies and trading partners from what some have called "the war without mercy." There have been gestures from both sides from individual civilians and groups on behalf of permanent peace. There have now been visits to Hiroshima and Pearl Harbor by national leaders after repeated avoidance. In May 2016, President Obama chose to visit Hiroshima as a gesture of sadness and peacemaking, but he offered no apology. Presidential candidate Trump saw no difference as he seized on another opportunity to attack the president's alleged weakness on Twitter.

On December 27, 2016, Prime Minister Shinzo Abe stood next to Obama at Pearl Harbor and offered "condolences" to the souls that died that day, but not apology. He placed a wreath of peace lilies at the memorial site. These were both notable gestures, especially for Abe, a conservative politician with strong ties to nationalist groups. He was the fourth Japanese leader to visit the memorial, but Shriver cites several examples of Japanese leaders, including an emperor, who sought to visit there and in some cases

51. Shriver, *Ethic for Enemies*, 144.

52. Shriver, *Honest Patriots*, 275.

53. Shriver, *Honest Patriots*, 200. Some references mention over 100,000 recipients, but the Department of Justice statistics use 82,219, "Ten Year Program to Compensate Japanese Americans."

54. Shriver, *Honest Patriots*, 272.

were at nearby meetings, but changed plans and stayed away apparently because of adverse opinion back home.

Still one has to wonder what it would take for representative apology and repentance to occur and for mutual forgiveness to reach its culmination in true reconciliation. There are at least signs of hope, but "undigested memories" remain.

## AFTER SLAVERY AND JIM CROW—
## THE QUESTION OF REPARATIONS

Shriver entitles his chapter in *Honest Patriots* about undigested memories of the African American experience in America "Old Unpaid Debt to African Americans." There, as in the powerful chapter on the treatment of Native Americans, he provides a reparations primer about the magnitude of our unpaid debt that must be paid before the past can be repaired. He was one of the few voices in support of reparations in 2005. Michigan Representative John Conyers Jr. had introduced a reparations study bill in the U.S. Congress every year from 1989 until his retirement in 2017, but it got scant attention until 2019 when Representative Sheila Jackson Lee of Houston and New Jersey Senator Cory Booker introduced similar bills, and several presidential candidates began supporting some form of reparations.

Ta-Nehisi Coates had triggered renewed attention with "The Case for Reparations" in *The Atlantic* (June 2014), providing impressive documentation of the great unpaid debt.[55] Conservative *New York Times* columnist David Brooks, after "mild disagreement" with Coates in 2014 that later turned to endorsement, authored "The Case for Reparations" in an op-ed in March 8, 2019, calling the racial divide "the original sin that hardens the heart" and keeps us from moving forward as one nation.[56] The issue of reparations has now definitely made a place for itself in our public discourse.

As Shriver, Coates, Brooks, and others have shown, the detailing of the debt cannot stop with slavery, which enabled much of white wealth. It runs through the Reconstruction and Jim Crow, convict leasing, vagrancy laws, debt peonage, staggering numbers of lynchings, residential segregation, discrimination under the New Deal in the administration of the G.I. Bill and Social Security, redlining, denial of loans, predatory lending, mass incarceration, and targeting by law enforcement and the court system.[57]

55. Coates, "The Case for Reparations."

56. Brooks, "Case for Reparations," A27.

57. Equal Justice Initiative, "Lynching in America," documents 4,084 lynchings of black people in twelve Southern states between 1877 and 1950. For coverage of *Chicago*

The debt also includes the wealth gap, the health gap, the employment gap, and the education gap.

Determining the forms that reparations should take is fraught with complications. It is hard if not impossible to come up with adequate reparations, and then there is the problem of winning broad acceptance and sufficient funding. Still Shriver does not let his readers shrug off the unpaid debt.

Acceptance may be growing, but that hurdle remains high. When we recall popular opinion against making apologies as a nation for our misdeeds cited earlier, we should not be surprised at the findings of a 2019 poll by the Associated Press-NORC Center for Public Affairs. Only 29 percent of Americans (15 percent of white Americans) favor reparations. Seventy-four percent of African Americans and 64 percent of Hispanic Americans are in favor. As for apologizing for slavery, 64 percent of white Americans oppose. Seventy-seven percent of African Americans and 64 percent of Hispanic Americans are in favor.[58]

In *Honest Patriots: Loving a Country Enough to Remember Its Misdeeds*, Donald Shriver does us the service of tracing the heroic efforts in Germany and South Africa to face the guilty past, apologize for it, change the damaged present, and promise a peaceful and just future. He also explores honestly the failures and successes of our history with Native Americans and African Americans. As he recognizes the difficulties national leaders face in making apologies, he does cite positive examples from the last century, including instances from presidents Reagan, G. W. Bush, and Clinton.

The important case that Shriver makes and the crucial challenge that he issues is that "it is possible and necessary for societies to face and to repent of certain evils in their past."[59] Whether about the systemic racism of our nation's past and present or "the war without mercy," (sometimes called "the Good War" because of the horrendous wrongs it challenged) waged by the Greatest Generation, as long as the memories remain undigested, the wreckage of the past lives on in the ruins of the present to hamper the construction of a just and peaceful future.

As noted earlier, the massacre at Emmanuel AME Church in Charleston brought a wave of soul-searching about the display of Confederate symbols and monuments as well as a surge of opposition to their removal. The violent clash in Charlottesville, Virginia (with its overt expressions of white supremacy and neo-Nazi mentality) over the moving of the statue of Robert

---

*Tribune*, NAACP, and Tuskegee Institute statistics and all lynchings in the U.S., see Seguin and Rigby, "National Crimes."

58. Williams and Nasir, "Poll Shows Gap," 14A.

59. Shriver, *Honest Patriots*, ix.

E. Lee has increased attention to conflicts over the appropriate place for Confederate monuments in many other cities.

Where else do we see current examples of the honest patriotism that remembers our misdeeds in the Shriver spirit? Since 2014 we have had the slavery museum on the Whitney Plantation near Wallace, Louisiana. A retired New Orleans lawyer and real estate magnate named John Cummings has stepped up to tell "the rest of the story." He bought the 250-acre plantation, spent $8.6 million of his own money, did prodigious research with expert assistance, and opened it as a museum depicting the actual experience of slaves. The names of the more than 350 slaves who farmed indigo and sugar there are engraved on black granite slabs that form the Wall of Honor. Other memorials list the names of the 107,000 slaves who toiled in Louisiana. Cummings believes that racism can be turned around through education. According to his Senegalese director of research, Ibrahima Seck, "If one word comes to mind to summarize what is in John's mind in doing this, that word would be 'reparations.' Real reparations. He believes there is something to be done in this country to make changes."[60] Visitors to the museum will have to own the history we would like to forget.

In 2018, the Memorial for Peace and Justice opened in Montgomery on the site of a former slave warehouse. Named "From Enslavement to Mass Incarceration," it commemorates some four thousand lynching victims in twelve states. Its developer is Bryan Stevenson, director of the Equal Justice Initiative, law professor, recipient of multiple prestigious awards, and author of the highly acclaimed *Just Mercy*, which chronicles his tangles with the racism of the criminal justice system. His efforts on behalf of those facing death sentences have spared 125 from execution. Desmond Tutu has called him "America's Nelson Mandela."[61] For Stevenson, the museum tells the story. Eight hundred steel columns are suspended from the ceiling, each one labeled with the name of a U.S. county and bearing the names of those who were brutally lynched there. Talk about lynching and segregation is unnecessary after you visit.

Such honest patriots as Cummings and Stevenson have stepped forward to address the challenges to America to repent and forgive, to apologize, and to repair the breach in our nation that Donald Shriver has laid bare. He has called us to the task of remembering what we have too often managed to forget or ignore or deny. The debts remain that require repentance and forgiveness, apology, and reparations before the reconciliation than make us whole can occur. In Shriver's language, we hunger for more

---

60. Amsden, "Building the First Slavery Museum in America."
61. Adams, "Bryan Stevenson: 'America's Mandela.'"

political leaders who are willing to assume "a symbolic, representative role" in telling the rest of the story about our nation's sins and finding a shared story that reflects our better angels.[62]

## BIBLIOGRAPHY

Adams, Tim. "Bryan Stevenson: 'America's Mandela.'" *The Guardian*, February 1, 2015. https://www.theguardian.com/us-news/2015/feb/01/bryan-stevenson-americas-mandela.

Amsden, David. "Building the First Slavery Museum in America." *New York Times*, February 26, 2015. https://www.nytimes.com/2015/03/01/magazine/building-the-first-slave-museum-in-america.html.

Batchelder, Robert C. *The Irreversible Decision, 1939–1950*. Boston: Houghton Mifflin, 1962.

Black, Brian. "Pearl Harbor." In *Encyclopedia of American Studies*, edited by Simon Bronner. Baltimore: Johns Hopkins University Press, 2018. https://search.credoreference.com/content/entry/jhueas/pearl_harbor/o.

Brooks, David. "The Case for Reparations." *New York Times*, March 8, 2019, A27.

Coates, Ta-Nehisi. "The Case for Reparations." *The Atlantic*, June 2014, 54–71.

Equal Justice Initiative. "Lynching in America: Confronting the Legacy of Racial Terror." 3rd ed. 2017. https://lynchinginamerica.eji.org/report/.

Ford, Lacy. "A Radical Response to Senseless Violence." *Presbyterian Outlook*, February 13, 2017, 16–17.

King, Martin Luther, Jr. Interview by *Bennett Banner*. Bennett College, Greensboro, NC, February 11, 1958. Martin Luther King, Jr. Papers Project. https://kinginstitute.stanford.edu/king-papers/documents/interview-bennett-college/.

Kristof, Nicholas D. "Stoically, Japan Looks Back on the Flames of War." *New York Times*, March 9, 1995, A4.

Kuznick, Peter. "The Atomic Bomb Didn't End the War." *U.S. News and World Report*, May 27, 2016. https://www.usnews.com/opinion/articles/2016–05–27/its-time-to-confront-painful-truths-about-using-the-atomic-bombs-on-japan.

Lendon, Brad, and Emiko Jozuka. "History's Deadliest Air Raid Happened in Tokyo during World War II and You've Probably Never Heard of It." *CNN*, March 8, 2020. https://www.cnn.com/2020/03/07/asia/japan-tokyo-fire-raids-operation-meetinghouse-intl-hnk/index.html.

Nussbaum, Martha. *Anger and Forgiveness: Resentment, Generosity, Justice*. New York: Oxford University Press, 2016.

Obama, Barack. Interview by Marc Maron. *WTF with Marc Maron*, podcast episode 613, June 22, 2015.

———. "Remarks by the President in Eulogy for the Honorable Reverend Clementa Pinckney." College of Charleston, Charleston, SC, June 26, 2015. https://obamawhitehouse.archives.gov/the-press-office/2015/06/26/remarks-president-eulogy-honorable-reverend-clementa-pinckney.

"The Relation of the Church to the War in the Light of the Christian Faith." *Social Action* 10, no. 10 (December 15, 1944) 5.

---

62. Shriver, *Ethic for Enemies*, 113.

Robertson, Campbell. "Flag Supporters React with a Mix of Compromise, Caution and Outright Defiance." *New York Times*, June 23, 2015. https://www.nytimes.com/2015/06/24/us/politics/supporters-of-confederate-battle-flag-watch-as-symbol-is-stripped-from-public-eye.html.

Robinson, Eugene. "The Roots of Racism Still Exist." *Oakland Tribune*, June 23, 2015.

Seguin, Charles, and David Rigby. "National Crimes: A New National Data Set of Lynchings in the United States, 1883 to 1941." *Socius: Sociological Research for a Dynamic World* 5 (2019) 1–9.

Shapiro, Emily. "Key Moments in Charleston Church as Dylann Roof Pleads Guilty to State Charges." *ABC News*, April 10, 2017. https://abcnews.go.com/US/key-moments-charleston-church-shooting-case-dylann-roof/story?id=46701033.

Shriver, Donald W., Jr. *An Ethic for Enemies: Forgiveness in Politics*. New York: Oxford University Press, 1995.

———. *Honest Patriots: Loving a Country Enough to Remember Its Misdeeds*. New York: Oxford University Press, 2005.

"Ten Year Program to Compensate Japanese Americans Interned during World War II Closes Its Doors." U.S. Department of Justice, February 19, 1999. https://www.justice.gov/archive/opa/pr/1999/February/059cr.htm.

Truman, Harry S. *Year of Decisions*. Garden City, NY: Doubleday, 1955.

Walzer, Michael. *Thick and Thin: Moral Argument at Home and Abroad*. Notre Dame: University of Notre Dame Press, 1994.

Wellington, Darryl Lorenzo. "After the Charleston Massacre: A Black Southerner Reflects." *The Crisis* 122 (2015) 26–29.

Williams, Corey, and Noreen Nasir. "Poll Shows Gap on Reparations for Slavery Era." *Courier-Journal*, October 26, 2019, 14A.

Wolterstorff, Nicholas. "After Injustice: What Makes Forgiveness Possible." *Christian Century*, November 13, 2013, 26–29.

———. *Journey toward Justice: Personal Encounters in the Global South*. Grand Rapids: Baker Academic, 2013.

# 20

## Travels with Donald

*Joseph V. Montville*

When Donald Shriver invited me to contribute to this collection, my mind went to the partnership we shared with four other colleagues as faculty for the annual training seminars in 2001 for chaplains in the US Navy, Marine Corps, and Coast Guard. Each session was a week long, and took place in major military bases throughout the United States, and some in the Pacific region. I was assigned to the Naval Base in Rota, Spain for one session. The contract was arranged by our close friend and colleague Douglas M. Johnston Jr., then founder and president of the International Center for Religion and Diplomacy in Washington, DC.

The training sessions' subject was the role of religion in peacemaking and how chaplains might contribute not only in their ministry with officers and enlisted personnel, but possibly in assisting the missions, especially abroad, in creating positive environments for relating to host communities for the military commands they served. When we were assigned to the same team, Donald, his wife, Peggy, who accompanied him on each seminar, and I frequently dined together at the end of our workday. Donald had noted in the acknowledgments section of *Honest Patriots: Loving a Country Enough to Remember Its Misdeeds* (2005) that, as a Christian ethicist, it had become clearer to him that his chief scholarly companions are the historians. In return I note that, as a political psychologist, my chief scholarly companions are historians. *Honest Patriots* won the 2009 Grawemeyer Award for outstanding book on religion and peacemaking.

Many of our dinner table discussions were drawn from Don's 1995 book, *An Ethic for Enemies: Forgiveness in Politics*. And many more came to be elaborated in *Honest Patriots*. All of our training team members agreed that focusing on the American tradition of racism would be central to our task. The Chief of Navy Chaplains during our mission was Rear Admiral Barry Black, an African American Seventh-day Adventist minister, who was extremely gifted intellectually and spiritually, and since 2003 has been the highly respected first black chaplain of the United States Senate. But our small team of trainers was about to put a test to him that he would not soon forget.

## RITUALS OF BLOOD

I had been building a library on the Civil War and Southern history, and one of the most powerful studies was Harvard sociologist Orlando Patterson's *Rituals of Blood: Consequences of Slavery in Two American Centuries* (1998). Patterson was born in Jamaica and he was particularly shocked by the savagery of the post-Reconstruction period of lynching indeed up to and including the murder of fourteen-year-old Emmett Till in Mississippi in 1955. Patterson is a cultural and historical sociologist, which enabled him to go analytically deep into the psychology of murder through ritual sacrifice. He researched vast numbers of contemporary newspaper accounts of lynchings to put together his study.

What our team felt was especially relevant for our training curriculum was Patterson's focus on the fundamentalist Christian rationalization for ritual murder of freed slaves. His descriptions of the lynchings themselves were painful for all of us to read—but necessary to make the argument that, although there were several examples of lynchings in the federalist states, the overwhelming number were in the former Confederate states. I'll cite one example from *Rituals of Blood*. This was the murder in Georgia of Sam Holt, an Afro-American farm laborer who had been charged with killing his white employer during a quarrel over wages.

> In the presence of nearly 2000 people, who sent aloft yells of defiance and shouts of joy, Sam Holt was burned at the stake in a public road. Before the torch was applied to the pyre, the Negro

was deprived of his ears, fingers, and other portions of his body with surprising fortitude. Before the body was cool, it was cut to pieces, the bones were crushed into small bits and even the tree upon which the wretch met his fate was torn up and disposed of as souvenirs.

The Negro's heart was cut in small pieces, as was also his liver. Those unable to obtain the ghastly relics directly, paid more fortunate possessors extravagant sums for them. Small pieces of bone went for 25 cents and a bit of liver, crisply cooked, for 10 cents.[1]

Patterson cites lynchings in which the small portions of the burned parts of victims were consumed, like Holy Communion.

Attempting to provide a broader social-psychological context to understand the phenomenon of human sacrifice, Patterson cites the case of the Tupinamba, a pre-Columbian, hunter-gatherer tribe who lived on the Brazilian coastal strip near today's Sao Paulo. They were among the most primitive tribes known, vastly different from the advanced capitalist economy of the Old South. But they shared two social features with the Old South. They were extremely militaristic and possessed of a high standard of honor. Slaves were few among the Tupinamba, and they were treated fairly well by their masters. But if a slave attempted to escape, he became a symbol of danger to the entire community and had to be sacrificed to the gods.

Patterson writes that in times when entire societies seem to be at risk, the greatest demand exists for the greatest sacrifices. The whole way of life looks to be in peril. Patterson writes that this was the situation that the Old South faced after the end of slavery and the forced system under Reconstruction to completely transform its social structure. But this period immediately after Reconstruction came to be the worst fifty years for the freed slaves, who were made to pay the extreme propitiatory price for the South's forced transformation in increasingly savage rituals of human sacrifice.

In one of his most powerful analyses, Patterson contextualizes the post-Reconstruction lynching epidemic in a period in which

[white] Southerners were faced with a vast mass of domestic enemies, an army of masterless slaves in their midst. Add to this the bitterness of defeat in war by a people obsessed with their sense of martial superiority. Add further the fact that the reason for this collective loss of honor was the very army of masterless slaves among them. Add also the economic insecurities of the

1. NAACP, *Thirty Years of Lynching*, 13, quoted in Patterson, *Rituals of Blood*, 194–95.

times, the frenzy of violence that the Civil War had unleashed, and finally, the fundamentalist religious fanaticism of the region, one finds in the masterless slaves of the postbellum South the perfect scapegoats, the ultimate sacrificial victims. Throughout the South, among all classes the preoccupation with the ex-slaves became obsessive. The hatred, fear, loathing, and horror of Afro-Americans attained levels of emotional, political and religious intensity that are hard to imagine.[2]

Citing the Southern theologian James Sellers, Patterson writes that he argues persuasively that Euro-American supremacy and commitment to segregation was for the South, "a religion, a theology. It is, in fact, the unrepentant Southern kingdom of God."[3] The freed slaves in this theology were the embodiment of Satan. Patterson offers a brief history of this phenomenon of what he calls two religions competing for ascendancy in Christendom.

He writes that the religion that Jesus preached was—and is—"a radical gospel, both spiritually and socially. Spiritually, its program is a loving reengagement with a living God, a call to spiritual watchfulness, and an existential experience of the divine through fellowship and love of other human beings."[4] But the radical gospel represented in the life and teachings of Jesus was almost entirely replaced early in Christian history by a religion—invented mostly by Paul—that focused instead on "his death and its sacrificial meaning."[5]

There were numerous failed attempts during the two-thousand-year history of Christianity to revive the message of Christ, the Jewish peasant, but they never survived the political hierarchies, supported by the Church of Rome and then the Reformation. Then, Patterson writes, a religion developed during the mid-twentieth century that "came fairly close to the gospel of love, fellowship, commitment, and radical engagement that he preached," namely, "the revitalized Afro-American Christianity that took shape in the church-directed protest movements culminating in the Southern Leadership Conference led by Martin Luther King Jr."[6]

Patterson makes the striking comparison between the religion of the African-American church, which represents "Christianity in its most pristine, most liberating, and most authentic form, returning, at last, to the

2. Patterson, *Rituals of Blood*, 192.
3. Patterson, *Rituals of Blood*, 207.
4. Patterson, *Rituals of Blood*, 229.
5. Patterson, *Rituals of Blood*, 229.
6. Patterson, *Rituals of Blood*, 230.

religion not *about* Jesus, but of Jesus," and the "Southern religion of the Lost Cause."[7] With the "fundamentalist lynch mob's sacrificial feasting on Afro-American blood and . . . the negrophobic and supremacist iconoclasm of the burning cross," in the religion of the latter, Patterson writes, "we find Christianity at its most destructive, its most socially cannibalistic, and its most demonic, on a par with the Crusades, the Thirty Years' War, and the Nazi terror."[8]

At this point I should note that Patterson was clearly indignant as a result of his research into lynchings and the post-Reconstruction reaffirmation of white supremacy in the former Confederate states. And his passion is evident in his writing. I think of how offended my late friend and colleague Bishop Krister Stendahl, former dean of the Harvard Divinity School, who immersed himself in the writings of the Apostle Paul, would likely have been at Patterson's dismissal of Paul. But the author's rage is genuine.

## THE IMPACT OF ORLANDO PATTERSON'S *RITUALS OF BLOOD* ON THE CHAPLAINS

The Navy officers in charge of the curriculum had agreed to distribute limited pages from the book, for copyright reasons, but the material the chaplains saw was powerful. Yet we managed to have broad and open discussions of the impact of slavery on the captured Africans brought to the colonies against their will. And discussion of the retrogression in the post-Reconstruction South as the white leadership effectively negated the liberation of African-Americans.

I recall an intense exchange during a break with a Navy chaplain who spoke passionately about the Confederate battle flag. He told me that the flag portrayed St. Andrews Cross, the symbol of Scottish nationalism, which was rarely discussed, but clearly powerful in the creation of Southern identity. It is well known that Andrew Jackson's mother used to tell him stories of the English brutality against the Scots. That memory was imported to the English colonies and their descendant Southern states.

Another memory that I cherish was of a plenary discussion of American racism when a young, African-American Coast Guard chaplain stood up and said with obvious pride that she was a direct descendent of President William Henry Harrison. After the plenary concluded, she walked by me in the middle of a conversation I was having with two other chaplains. She

7. Patterson, *Rituals of Blood*, 231.
8. Patterson, *Rituals of Blood*, 231.

was still grinning, and I grabbed her and gave her a big hug—I just could not resist.

A final note for this limited record, I proposed to the Scottish nationalist chaplain that we visit the Jefferson Davis Presidential Library and Museum in Biloxi. My thought was to acknowledge the symbolic power to many Southerners of the Confederate presidency with a gesture of respect. The chaplain was very excited by the idea and made the arrangements for busses to take us to the site. It must be noted that such a visit was not on the agreed program, and the Navy captain, a Southern Baptist clergy woman who was in charge of the seminar—and who was chafing at the decision of the Southern Baptist Convention to forbid female ministers to lead congregations because of literal interpretations of the Bible that said women should be subordinate to men—was very worried that our adventure to the Jefferson Davis Library would make headlines and cause her embarrassment, possibly hurting her career. To her great credit she allowed the trip to go. And we Yankee trouble-makers—usually me but with willing accomplices—were able to send a message to the Southerners among us that we respected their innate human value including their memories. (The Davis Library and Museum were destroyed by Hurricane Katrina in 2005, and the entire complex rebuilt.)

I should note also that Don Shriver and I were constantly discussing the best ways to acknowledge the memories and feelings of losers in ethnic and sectarian conflicts, and of which he wrote later with eloquence and deep insight in his prize-winning *Honest Patriots: Loving a Country Enough to Remember its Misdeeds*.

## FAST FORWARD TO 2018 AND THE PROJECT: *THE CIVIL WAR AT 150 YEARS: DEEP WOUNDS YET TO HEAL*

This effort is named for a book chapter I contributed to the collection edited by Daniel Rothbart of the George Mason University School for Conflict Analysis and Resolution (S-CAR), entitled *Systemic Humiliation in America: Finding Dignity within Systems of Degradation* (2018). President Vartan Gregorian of the Carnegie Corporation of New York read a draft of the chapter and decided to offer a one-time, one-year special category grant to S-CAR with me as project director to develop public policy analyses and recommendations generated by our work in three two-day workshops. As this is being written, the project is two-thirds completed.

From its inception Donald Shriver has been a key adviser for this project. He was instrumental in advising on the structure and goals of the workshops and especially valuable in recruiting Rev. James Forbes, former chief minister at the Riverside Church in Morningside Heights, New York, and neighbor of the Union Theological Seminary, which Donald headed for many years. In the second of the three planned two-day workshops of the project, June 30–July 1, held at S-CAR's residential research and conference center, Point of View, in Mason Neck, Virginia, there was a major breakthrough in our exploration of healing tasks associated with the social and psychological wounds incurred in colonial America, the slave economy, the pre-war lead up to 1861, the savagery of the war itself, Reconstruction, post-Reconstruction, and the re-imposition of Southern white control over freed slaves with Jim Crow policies and lynching of blacks by crowds usually of families of men, women, and children, often led by Christian preachers as described above.

James Forbes heard the presentation by Nancy Isenberg, professor of history at Louisiana State University, a brilliant writer, meticulous researcher, and author of the groundbreaking *White Trash: The 400-Year Untold History of Class in America*. The book is the most detailed and insightful study of the poor white demographic expelled from England and Ulster to the American colonies in the seventeenth century as indentured servants to work the land and relieve the perceived burden of their existence on the home country. The story is critical to the project's goals because it establishes the history of a people who were treated as contemptible, barely human beings: the men, the women, and the children they produced.

Isenberg introduces her organizing theme thus:

> Historical mythmaking is made possible only by forgetting. We have to begin, then, with the first refusal to face reality: most colonizing schemes that took root in seventeenth- and eighteenth-century British America were built on privilege and subordination, not any kind of proto-democracy. The generation of 1776 certainly underplayed that fact. And all subsequent generations took their cue from the nation's founders.[9]

Isenberg takes her readers back to the sixteenth century and the writings of Richard Hakluyt the Younger (1552–1616), who wrote a study for Queen Elizabeth entitled "Discourse of Western Planting" (1584). Hakluyt said that the open, wasteland of America—undeveloped—and opened to exploitation by England, would require large numbers of English "waste people," to be the body of physical labor, to cut down trees, dig the earth

9. Isenberg, *White Trash*, 5.

for minerals, raise olives, and all other forms of manual work. The bulk of the labor exported was to come from the swelling numbers of poor and homeless, perceived as serious burden on the English economy. Among the first waves of workers were convicts. Because they owed England for their crimes, they would not be paid, but be required to work off their debts through producing goods for export to England.

In the mid-sixteenth century, the English poor were routinely condemned as "thriftless" and "'idle' . . . Compared to swarms of insects . . . [like] a subterranean colony of dirty and disfigured 'monsters' living in 'caves'"—all of which makes it hard to "resist the conclusion that the children of the poor were regarded as recycled waste."[10]

Even in virtuous New England, in the 1630s, New England governor John Winthrop wrote in "A Model of Christian Charity,"

> that some were meant to rule, others to serve their betters: 'God Almightie in his most holy providence hath soe disposed the Condition of mankind, as in all times some must be rich some poore, some highe and eminent in power and dignitie; others meane and in subjeccion.' Lest there be any doubt, Governor Winthrop despised democracy, which he brusquely labeled 'the meanest and worst of all forms of government.' For Puritans, the church and state worked in tandem; the coercive arm of the magistracy was meant to preserve both public order and class distinctions.[11]

*White Trash* is a treasure trove of meticulously documented research that is critical to establishing the historical record of the systemic, structural degradation of poor whites exported to the New World to rid them from England, Scotland, and Ulster. And in her last pages, Isenberg concludes that

> white trash is a central, if disturbing, thread in our national narrative. The very existence of such people—both in their visibility and invisibility—is proof that American society obsesses over the mutable labels we give to the neighbors we wish not to notice. "They are not who we are." But they are who we are and have been a fundamental part of our history, whether we like it or not.[12]

---

10. Isenberg, *White Trash*, 22, 24.

11. Isenberg, *White Trash*, 30.

12. Isenberg, *White Trash*, 321.

## BACK TO DONALD AND JIM FORBES

I went into considerable detail on *White Trash* because, as a political psychologist, I have frequently cited in public discussions what I call "the iron laws of human nature":

> There is impressive evidence of the dominance in universal human needs not only for food, shelter, and physical safety, but also for recognition, acceptance and respect, the iron laws of human nature. The most persistent evidence of the sources of continued antagonism and inclination toward violence comes from documentation of wounds to the self-concept or self-esteem of identity groups—ethnic, religious, linguistic, indeed, whatever trait a group considers its most noteworthy characteristic.[13]

Nancy Isenberg's book is not only carefully researched history. It is also the basis for designing a healing strategy for one of the most enduring wounds not only of the Civil War but of four hundred years of hurt.

Thus, I was very moved after Nancy's presentation when Jim Forbes came up to me in the corridor to say that her talk for him was worth the entire trip from New York to Virginia. She opened his eyes to the sustained pain that a major segment of the American population has been enduring since before even the first twenty Angolan slaves landed in Jamestown in 1619. And at the end of the workshop on July 1, Katrina Browne, who made the powerful feature-length documentary film *Traces of the Trade: A Story from the Deep North*, which recounts the history of her slave-trading ancestors in Bristol, Rhode Island; Lisa Pruitt, professor of law at UC Davis, who had presented on her five generations of Arkansas family; and I were speaking with Jim Forbes and wondering if Jim, when he moves to Raleigh this fall and begins working with Rev. William Barber, might collaborate on a TV project on our healing themes. Jim responded enthusiastically to the idea.

This was a major breakthrough for the project, because it laid the basis for an alliance of morally powerful African-American religious leaders and white Americans who would bring genuine southern memory and emotional authenticity and a Northern witness to the hypocrisy of slave traders, profiteers, and slave owners in New England.

13. Montville, "Reconciliation as *Realpolitik*," 368.

## THE REVEREND DR. WILLIAM BARBER

Reverend Barber is a pastor of Greenleaf Christian Church, in Goldsboro, North Carolina. In a thorough profile of Barber by Jelani Cobb, a staff writer for *The New Yorker*, entitled "The Southern Strategist," published May 14, 2018, Barber was called "an indispensable figure in the civil rights landscape, and, perhaps, the individual most capable of crafting a broad-based political counterpoint to the divisiveness of Trumpism."[14] Cobb noted that Barber wears a stole that reads, "Jesus was a Poor Man."[15]

For the past three years, Cobb notes, Barber has been working with the Reverend Liz Theoharis, codirector of the Kairos Center at the Union Theological Seminary in New York, which was Don Shriver's base as president until his retirement. This center has been working to revive Dr. Martin Luther King Jr.'s most radical project, the Poor Peoples' Campaign. The campaign aims to establish full employment, a guaranteed basic income, and access to capital for small and minority businesses.

At the same time, Rev. Barber was launching his Moral Monday movement in North Carolina, enlisting a broad-based alliance of Christians, Muslims, Jews, non-believers, blacks, Latinos, poor whites, feminists, environmentalists, and others to protest the conservative agenda of the North Carolina state legislature. His new project is called a National Call for Moral Revival. The demands include federal and state living-wage laws, equity in education, an end to mass incarceration, a single-payer health system, and the protection of the right to vote. Jelani Cobb reports that Rev. Barber texted him photos of recent Poor Peoples' Campaign rallies in Appalachia with hundreds of people, most of them white, in the audience.

At the 2016 Democratic National Convention, Rev. Barber said, "I worry about the way that faith is cynically used by some to serve, hate, fear, racism, and greed."[16] And finally, he said, "We must shock the nation with the power of love, we must shock the nation with the power of mercy. We can't give up on the heart of our democracy, not now, now ever."[17] He received a standing ovation.

The point of our excitement about the potential of the alliances being generated by the Healing the Wounds of the Civil War project is that its aim has been to assemble the finest scholars of the period with conflict resolution activists who can meet and plan new initiatives. Rev. Jim Forbes

14.  Cobb, "Southern Strategist," 68.
15.  Cobb, "Southern Strategist," 68.
16.  Barber, "Remarks at Democratic National Convention."
17.  Barber, "Remarks at Democratic National Convention."

is in his own right a dynamic preacher who will be a strong partner for Rev. Barber. If we can help Lisa Pruitt, Katrina Browne and, possibly, Nancy Isenberg find ways to work with these two powerful African American leaders, there are impressive possibilities ahead.

## MOURNING LOSSES AND HEALING WOUNDS, FINAL THOUGHTS

In *Honest Patriots* Don Shriver reports on numerous incidents of government and citizen action in Germany, South Africa, and the United States to symbolically acknowledge historical crimes and find ways to honor the memory of the victims—all of the victims. He devotes important space to the creation of the Hope in the Cities program in Richmond, Virginia. Ben Campbell, director of an East End ecumenical center, was one of the lead designers of what was to become "a unity walk through history," in Richmond, in 1993.

I was particularly interested in this story because I had met with Campbell at a restaurant in Fredericksburg, Virginia, about half the distance between McLean in northern Virginia where I lived and Richmond. Dick Ruffin, who was then the executive director of Initiatives of Change in the U.S., had arranged the meeting and participated in it to brainstorm about the Richmond initiative. It was there that I suggested the idea of "a walk through history," which is a concept that came to me at a meeting with visitors from Northern Ireland to the University of Virginia's Center for the Study of Mind and Human Interaction, founded by Professor Vamik Volkan, a member of the UVA medical faculty and a world-renowned psychoanalyst. I was a member of the Center's faculty.

Ben Campbell listened very carefully to my thoughts gleaned from several years of conflict resolution work with Egyptians and Israelis, in Northern Ireland, the former Yugoslavia, the Baltic States and Russia, and other ethnic and sectarian conflicts. As Don Shriver reports in *Honest Patriots*, Campbell said that "Richmond was ground zero for race relations in the United States."[18] He noted that in 1857 gross income of $4 million came to the city from the slave trade. Mayor Walter Kenney, Susan and Robert L. Corcoran, the Richmond representatives of Initiatives of Change at the time, the African-American Baptist minister Paige Chargois, and other citizen activists joined Campbell in the organizing committee.

I wish I could take credit for the brilliant plan the Richmond group designed for the Unity Walk through History in Richmond. As a participant

18. Shriver, *Honest Patriots*, 137.

I could only marvel at how cleverly they plotted the two-mile walk for all the participants, including guests from abroad. There were key stops on the trek for newly disembarked African slaves on the James River docks to the holding areas, and to the auctions blocks. Shriver notes that the path led to Church Hill, on the east side of town, still the site of the historic St. John's Episcopal Church, where Patrick Henry gave his famous "Give Me Liberty, or Give Me Death" speech. A costumed actor actually gave the speech, the irony of which was sharpened by the screams of other costumed actors dressed as slaves because one of their fellow slaves had just jumped to her death in a deep well, holding her two infant sons, because she did not want to raise them into slavery.

For me the most moving event of the walk was to another hilltop over-looking the James River docks. We had been given clusters of gladiolas to carry, which were then collected and transported to the opposite shore of the James. The flowers were then cast on the waters of the James as a memo-rial gesture to the souls of the African captives who died in the crossing of the Atlantic. Precious human beings whose names would never be known.

There is another story from the Richmond experience that will always stay with me. This was of Rev. Paige Chargois, who had called publicly for empathy for the need for some whites to honor the courage and suffering of their Confederate forebears. I recall Paige telling the story of her visit to the home of a leader of the Confederate Ladies organization in Richmond, and her description of the emotions she struggled with as she sat across from her gracious hostess and saw the large Confederate battle flag on the wall. And to her everlasting credit, she accompanied a leader of the Richmond Sons of the Confederacy to visit then Governor Jessie Ventura of Wisconsin to kindly request the return to Virginia of a Confederate battle flag captured by Wis-consin Union troops. As Paige tells the story, Ventura showed little sympathy and declined the request, saying Wisconsin won the flag fair and square.

In the final chapter of *Honest Patriots*, Don Shriver deals with the con-cept of apology by leaders whose countries have inflicted painful losses on other countries and peoples. He tells of a remarkable gesture by President Harry Truman on visit to Mexico City in March 1947.

> On an unscheduled stop at Chapultepec Castle, he laid a wreath on the monument of six Mexican army cadets who killed themselves rather than surrender to the American army that conquered the city one hundred years before. Numerous local Mexicans rejoiced in the presidential gesture. A local newspa-per proclaimed: 'Rendering Homage to the Heroes of '47 Heals an Old National Wound Forever.' A cab driver exclaimed, 'To think that the most powerful man in the world would come and

apologize.' Back home Truman avoided the word 'apology,' saying simply, 'Brave men don't belong to any one country. I respect
bravery wherever I see it.'[19]

Continuing on the subject of acknowledement, contrition, and forgiveness, Shriver reports that, on February 14, 1995, General John Shalikashvili,
chairman of the Joint Chiefs of Staff

> stood before thousands in the Kreuzkirche in Dresden and
> apologized for the senseless firebombing of the city fifty years
> ago to the day . . . Dresden was a museum city with little military
> significance. Not profoundly different from terrorist strategies
> in 2004, civilians were the intended targets of the British and
> American bombs which killed "at least 35,000 people and per-
> haps 135,000."[20]

Shriver continues on this news item writing that the general's apology reflected the reaffirmation of the just war doctrine developed in the 1990s
in the face of the massive retrospectively war crime bombings of civilian
centers in Germany and Japan.

As my travels with Donald have continued this year, we have discussed
the idea of memorials to victims of the slave trade in America and, more
broadly, to the victims of our incredibly savage Civil War. Don would like to
see a memorial to the first African slaves from Angola sent to Jamestown in
1619. I support this proposal.

I have been developing the idea of a Civil War memorial, to be authorized by Congress, and to be built in northern Virginia, that honors all of
the dead Confederate and Union, white and black troops lost in the war.
The purpose is to acknowledge the preciousness of all of these human beings who gave their lives in the mercilessness of the combat. It would be
especially focused on the Confederate losses, which have not been nearly
recognized by the Union. This is where my political psychology orientation
comes in. Winners in a war spend little time mourning the dead on the
losing side. Yet the losses in the Civil War were so cruel and the impact on
families in the South was so devastating that I believe it would be potentially
very impactful on the psychology of Southerners who have felt humiliated
and degraded by the victorious Union generals and political leaders, John
Wilkes Booth's assassination of Abraham Lincoln notwithstanding.

---

19. Shriver, *Honest Patriots*, 274.
20. Shriver, *Honest Patriots*, 275.

These ideas are works in progress, but it strikes me as thoroughly appropriate to include them in this collection of memoires and tributes to my colleague and friend Donald W. Shriver.

## BIBLIOGRAPHY

Barber, William. "Rev. William Barber FULL REMARKS at Democratic National Convention." *C-Span*, July 28, 2016, Philadelphia, Pennsylvania. https://www.youtube.com/watch?v=aw3PUghqlAA.

Cobb, Jelani. "The Southern Strategist." *The New Yorker*, May 14, 2018, 68–75.

Isenberg, Nancy. *White Trash: The 400-Year Untold History of Class in America*. New York: Viking, 2016.

Montville, Joseph V. "Reconciliation as *Realpolitik*: Facing the Burdens of History in Political Conflict Resolution." In *Identity, Morality, and Threat: Studies in Violent Conflict*, edited by Daniel Rothbart and Karina V. Korostelina, 367–92. New York: Lexington, 2006.

NAACP. *Thirty Years of Lynching in the United States, 1889–1918*. New York: National Association for the Advancement of Colored People, National Office, 1919.

Patterson, Orlando. *Rituals of Blood: Consequences of Slavery in Two American Centuries*. Washington, DC: Civitas/CounterPoint, 1998.

Shriver, Donald W., Jr. *Honest Patriots: Loving a Country Enough to Remember Its Misdeeds*. New York: Oxford University Press, 2005.

# 21

## Remembering—Berlin and Virginia

*Helmut Reihlen and Erika Reihlen*

I will call this subject: repentance in politics.

—DONALD W. SHRIVER JR.[1]

Donald Shriver and Helmut Reihlen became acquainted in 1991 as they strove together to establish the Bonhoeffer chair. Donald Shriver as the President Emeritus and Professor of Ethics at the Union Theological Seminary in New York City and Helmut Reihlen as the President of the Synod of the Evangelical Church in Berlin Brandenburg.

In the following years the Reihlens and Shrivers became friends. When Donald Shriver publishes his 1995 book, *An Ethic for Enemies: Forgiveness in Politics*, he thanks Helmut and Erika Reihlen for their friendship.[2] In his dedication of February 3, 1995, he writes, "With gratitude for five years

---

1. Shriver, *Honest Patriots*, 13.
2. Shriver, *Ethic for Enemies*, x.

of deepening colleagueship and friendship that embodies many themes of this book." Helmut and Erika had spent nights on end doing proofreading.

For his next book, *Honest Patriots: Loving a Country Enough to Remember Its Misdeeds*, Shriver comes to Berlin for half a year. In the spring of 1999 he becomes a Fellow of the American Academy. His study subject: "Dealing with the Nazi Past in the Third Generation." Accompanying him is his wife, Peggy L. Shriver, theologian and author. Together the two undertake journeys into the recent and older history of the region: to Wittenburg and Wörlitz, to Sachsenhausen, Brandenburg, and Friedensdorf—and to the *Steglitzer Kreisel*, where they learn about Erika Reihlen's Preschool Program for Dental Health.

In the following years the Shrivers' visits to Berlin increase. There is reason enough, such as the Bonhoeffer Congress in August 2000 and the Meeting of the International Society of Political Psychology in July 2002, where Helmut and Erika Reihlen present a lecture on the scandal-ridden story of the Steglitz Mirror Wall.

And again and again, Donald Shriver asks to be shown the places that commemorate the "misdeeds" of the Germans. "Beyond all calls of duty," notes Shriver in the dedication of *Honest Patriots*, Helmut and Erika apply their time and energy looking for historical sources, memorials and translations, so that Donald Shriver can gain an understanding of the battle of three generations of Germans over the proper handling of their past.[3] There he describes what can be seen of Germany's engagement with the dark chapter of its past. He also turns his eye to South Africa and the work of the Truth and Reconciliation Commission that was confronted with the legacy of the Apartheid regime day after day, and where each side had a chance to speak, the victims and the perpetrators. Shriver's conclusion: both countries are ahead of white America in coming to terms with the "evil" past.

In the United States, Shriver also discovers attempts to come to terms with the fate of the Native Americans. This applies even more so for the almost three-hundred-year-long history of slavery. Shriver wants to know if and how patriotism is possible under the conditions of a history that—theologically speaking—carries "evil" within it.

It leads the Shrivers, in 2003, to their Berlin friends for the third time. In October of the previous year, Helmut and Erika Reihlen were in the United States, and occupied with the review of the chapter of *Honest Patriots* that was concerned with Germany.

Shriver is impressed by the rich memorial landscape he discovers with the Reihlens on his forays through Berlin and Germany: museums,

3. Shriver, *Honest Patriots*, viii.

monuments and memorials, history books, "authentic sites" such as concentration camp memorials, documentation and research institutes—most of them arisen and designed in the last thirty years.

In Berlin it is hardly possible to miss the evidence of Germany's National Socialist past. There is no city tour that does not also include evidence of the time when the Germans plunged the world into war and murdered the European Jews. "A single day of touring modern Berlin," says Shriver in *Honest Patriots*, "will dispel any American's suspicion that Germans in general have forgotten all about the Nazis."[4] Shriver's guided city tour through Berlin is a journey through the official German memory of the crimes of National Socialism. Tourists who cross Berlin with the Bus 100 can already discover at a normal bus stop on the Kurfürstenstaße where the office of Adolf Eichmann was. A plaque originally planned for advertising, now contains information on the Topography of Terror, giving detailed information about his role in the extermination of the European Jews. And also the curved steel wall from Richard Serra behind the Berlin Philharmonic does not escape him. The Berlin Junction commemorates the "euthanasia" victims. Not far away at the German Reichstag, forty slate slabs stand with the names of the members of the Reichstag who were murdered by the Nazis. At Bebelplatz next to the State Opera is the "memorial" Library of Micha Ullman to be seen, a pane of glass on the ground with a view of an empty bookshelf, sunken deep below. Before it, two recessed bronze plaques with the citation of Heinrich Heine: "This was but a prelude, wherever they burn books, they will also, in the end, burn human beings."

Towards Potsdamer Platz are the excavated remains of the former Gestapo Headquarters, maintained by the Topography of Terror. Not far is the Jewish Museum by Daniel Libeskind that opened its doors in 1999, and gives the visitors, through its architecture, an oppressive and disoriented sense of space.

Then on the Oranienburgerstraße in Berlin Mitte, the rebuilt part of the New Synagogue, a reminder of the pogrom night (Night of Broken Glass) of November 9, 1938. And also the commemorative plaques and the *Stolpersteine* (Stumbling Blocks), the bronze tablets embedded in the footpaths before the houses of former Jewish residents with their name, their year of birth, the deportation site, and the date of their murder.

And not least, erected in 2005, the Holocaust Memorial by Peter Eisenman, 2,711 stelae on twenty thousand square meters for the murdered Jews. Berlin campaigns for it with a quote of Willy Brandt: "Our dignity demands

4. Shriver, *Honest Patriots*, 15.

an extremely great expression of commemoration to the murdered European Jews."[5]

Shriver also visits Bayerischen Platz with its eighty signs on lampposts: a reminder of the once lively Jewish community in Schöneberg. On each sign a public proclamation from the thirties and forties testifies to how these German citizens, through laws and decrees, were gradually segregated and ostracized.

Shriver and his wife also find themselves at the House of the Wannsee Conference. Here on January 20, 1942, the Nazis agreed upon their plans for the "Final Solution to the Jewish question in Europe" with the high-ranking heads of the German ministerial bureaucracy. Since 1992, it is a Museum and Educational Site, the documentation center for "National Socialism and its Consequences." Shriver was particularly impressed by how much the Holocaust had found its way into the history books. Since the end of the Second World War, the subject had developed from a "non-subject" to becoming a central part of history classes. It has gone so far that students in recent times moan about too great an emphasis on National Socialism in their classes at school. Shriver quotes a student who felt morally overburdened by the constant presentation of the "evil" in history class, "Are you trying to crush us with knowledge of that past?"[6]

Shriver can reconstruct, almost in entirety, the controversy around the Steglitz Mirror Wall, from the accounts and experiences of Helmut and Erika Reihlen.[7] After all, he sat in the public as the two of them spoke about the story of the Mirror Wall before the International Society of Political Psychology at Berlin's Hotel InterContinental. The Mirror Wall is a memorial with 1,723 names from the total of fifty-five thousand people of Jewish background deported from Berlin. It gives the information that, in 1933, of the 3,186 Steglitzers considered to be Jews, by 1945 less than 150 still lived in Steglitz. It also gives the information that, in the courtyard of the building at Duppelstraße 41, not visible from the street, the former Synagogue can be found, which today is used as an office building.

In 1991, the district council announces an architectural competition for a memorial in the middle of bustling Hermann Ehlers Platz that should commemorate the fate of the Jewish citizens of Steglitz and establish a connection to the small Synagogue in the neighborhood. In 1992, the group of Wolfgang Goschel, Joachim von Rosenberg, and Norbert Burkert wins the bid. Their idea is impressive: An 11.5-meter-long and 3.5-meter-high wall

5. https://www.holocaust-denkmal-berlin.de/.

6. Shriver, *Honest Patriots*, 55.

7. Reihlen and Reihlen, "The Mirror Wall Berlin-Steglitz."

out of reflective stainless steel with the names, birthdates, addresses, the destinations and date of deportations of Berlin Jews. Anyone who steps up to the wall should be a participant in the events written "on its face." In the following two years, a public debate takes place over the pros and cons of the Mirror Wall, originating in Steglitz, but soon spreading to all of Berlin and throughout entire Germany. Words like, "memorial hysteria," make the rounds or, "Not only the Jews suffered in the war," and, "The majority doesn't want it." After month-long discussions, after flyer campaigns on the side of various organizations and groups, it emerges that the district council of Steglitz does not stand behind the award-winning design. In 1993, the decision comes down to indeed realize the Mirror Wall, but in a smaller form. The compromise accepted by the artists: reducing the length of the Mirror Wall to nine meters. This does not stop quite a few of the opponents from calling for a further reduction, which in turn the artists do not accept. So in 1994 the district council comes to the decision to completely cancel plans to go ahead with the Mirror Wall. Particularly embarrassing in this: the alliance of the CDU (Christian Democratic Union) and the FDP (Free Democratic Party) with the radical right-wing Republicans.

The decision of the Steglitz district council sets off a harrowing echo in both the national and international press. The petty bourgeois resentment that is expressed in Steglitz threatens to disgrace the German capitol that wants to present itself as a liberal-minded metropolis in which human rights are a priority.

Now the Berlin Senate steps in with a plan. It revokes the decision of the Steglitz district council, exercising its right to override decisions of Berlin districts when they harm the essential interests of the federal state of Berlin. The Mirror Wall is a culturally meaningful event for all of Berlin, and therefore is in the focus of worldwide concern for Germany's relation to its past, is the reason given. In fact in Berlin in 1994, it was about more than just the politics of one city district. Berlin had a reputation in the world as a place of freedom and did not want to jeopardize this. The districts are also obligated to this objective, whether they wish it or not.

On June 7, 1995, on the lively Hermann Ehlers Platz, the memorial is officially opened, accompanied by song from the cantor of the Jewish community in Berlin, the 'Estrongo Nachama.

Donald Shriver is impressed: the Shoah belongs conspicuously to the reasons of state of the reunified Germany. To go through the center of Berlin, to the professor of applied ethics, means to encounter the great and the sordid in its history. As he writes, "Without doubt, Berlin is a city that remembers."[8] This gives Germans the opportunity to regain their dignity, when subsequently, at any rate, they provide a place for the victims in their national memory.

Again and again, Helmut and Erika Reihlen describe to their friend their feelings and observations in relation to the "politics of memory" in Berlin and Germany. For example, about the difference that it makes to speak about an anonymous, abstract crime or to be confronted with the birthdates and names of former neighbors. "This hurts," they say, "but suppression of an evil past hurts more." It is important to them that the memory of the failures of the forefathers becomes a tangible part of the history that history books, memorials, and public holidays tell of. Because only when an event has become an object of the commonplace historical awareness can a society find distance to it and shed what otherwise adheres to it like a foul smell. If morally reprehensible events succeed in being raised in the everyday awareness of the general public, the danger is lessened that they could repeat themselves.

The Steglitz Mirror Wall, since 1995, is anchored in the everyday life of the citizens of this district. For Helmut and Erika Reihlen it performs here a process of active atonement. Though far too late for the victims, nevertheless, it is important for the reconciliation of a society with the survivors and their descendants, and not least with itself and its forefathers.

> So now the wall stands there, in the middle of pulsating commercial and social life. These years after its inauguration it is an accepted part of Steglitz. Market merchants protect it. Not a single bit of graffiti has besmirched the wall to date. Often people put flowers there. Our grandchildren ask us what it is all about; and we may find ways of telling them how the Lord finally, in spite of our sins, brought us out of Egypt. Our grandchildren listen. They look into the mirror and make faces. And they go on sucking on their ice cream cones.[9]

In 2004, Erika Reihlen experienced how the Mirror Wall history was brought to life. In November, to remember the 1938 pogrom night, the ecumenical community of Steglitz organized a procession to the Mirror Wall. In Berlin in the previous year, the Ecumenical Church Congress had focused on the site for the ecumenical community. The location at the Mirror Wall is ideal because three Christian congregations exist here in the immediate vicinity: the Catholic Rosary Church, the Evangelical Matthäusgemeinde,

---

8. Shriver, *Honest Patriots*, 18.
9. Shriver, *Honest Patriots*, 44.

and two streets away the Baptist Church. Erika Reihlen is on the organizing committee.

The gathering begins at Hermann Ehlers Platz with meditative words about the place of prayer that it was. In the rear courtyard, the small former synagogue is hidden. The synagogue building is looked at and at the Mirror Wall texts are read. There are street names from the neighborhood recognized by all in which those deported had lived.

Two to three hundred people have come. As Erika Reihlen presents her text, a parish priest steps up to speak. He conveys greetings from Hansi and Alfred Silberstein from New Zealand, who knew about the procession. The siblings Hansi (born 1925) and Alfred (born 1927) Silberstein were deported to Auschwitz from their home at Holsteinischen Straße 34 in Steglitz. That they survived was a great surprise and a moving moment in the evening, not only for Erika Reihlen. And that there are more people who knew the Silbersteins, she discovers at the snacks after the procession at the Baptist community center. A neighbor tells her about reciprocal visits to Berlin and New Zealand and of their intention to send Erika Reihlen's photo documentation of the Mirror Wall to the Silbersteins in New Zealand.

The Mirror Wall—this place is a gift, and Erika Reihlen feels this especially strongly on this day. She establishes contact with the Silbersteins and treasures a photo that shows the two, who were deported and yet saved, in front of the Mirror Wall.[10]

*Honest Patriots* appeared in 2005; two years later, in October 2007, it was published in German. It's title: *Honest Patriots: Patriotism and Coming to Terms with the Past*. Once again Helmut and Erika Reihlen help with the completion of the manuscript.

In this year the Shrivers visit Berlin for the sixth time. This time they will also see an original part of German history: the Martin Luther Memorial Church in Berlin Mariendorf. Built between 1933 and 1935, it is a symbol for the compliant adapting of a part of the evangelical church to the ideology of the National Socialist state. Art and architecture create a connection here between National Socialistic and Christian symbolism. A German mother stands beside a German soldier before the baptismal font. At the pulpit, an SA trooper, a Hitler youth, and a Wehrmacht soldier can be seen, and in the center of the space: Jesus on the cross as muscular hero and triumphal figure.

Peggy Shriver cannot forget this church. "Empire Christ" is the title of the poem that she writes after her visit to the Martin Luther Memorial Church:

10. Reihlen and Reihlen, "Church Congress as Preliminary Church."

Jesus stands, not hanging, on
this altar's gleaming crucifix,
his muscled arms out-stretched
like wings,
the nails not tearing his
pierced flesh,
simply holding wooden planks
in place upon his straining back,
upright against his pinioned feet.
Like a huge metallic bird,
his body arches toward the sky
jaw defiantly thrust out
in unscathed triumph over death.
With close-cropped hair, bold eyes,
athletic torso, gymnast's legs,
this Teuton christ in polished steel
evokes no mourning, only awe.

What a tempting crucifix
for any empire-seeking state!
This sleek messiah promises
no blood, no suffering nor grief—
a triumph through no tragedy—
resurrection with no death—
a god-like human with no God.

I ponder this seductive christ
and Jesus' wise, forgiving love,
his humble birth, self-giving will.
That Nazi cross has power still.[11]

In October 2007, Helmut and Erika Reihlen travel again to the United States. This time the Shrivers want to give the two "an object lesson in American history." Together they visit Virginia and its cities of Jamestown, Williamsburg, Richmond, and Charlottesville. Erika Reihlen writes:

Don Shriver's book about the 'Honest patriots' had at home in Berlin already prepared us for the fact that we would receive a

11. Shriver, "Empire Christ."

vivid view of the guilt-burdened American history. Just as we
as children made the acquaintance of no Jewish families, so too
Donald Shriver had no contact in his childhood with families
with a Native American background.[12]

As Don Shriver showed Jamestown to his friends it was just celebrating its four hundredth birthday as the first colony of the English settlers. The
Jamestown Settlement Museum began remembering though also, in the last
few years, another story: the story of the Powhatans, the Native Americans
of eastern Virginia without whose help the white settlers would not have
survived their first winter in the new world. But soon thereafter, the same
settlers ensured that the Powhatans and their children and grandchildren
almost completely vanished from the area. By the end of the seventeenth
century the population had dropped from five thousand to six hundred.

To acknowledge that the Native Americans were the actual first residents of Virginia and not the English settlers is to a great extent new for the
generation of Donald Shriver (born 1927). A photo shows Helmut Reihlen
and Donald and his wife Peggy L. Shriver before the hut of a Powhatan village that is a part of the museum. The museum also reminds us of the arrival
of the first African slaves to Virginia in 1619. And also with this history, a
white from the southern states who came of age in the second half of the
twentieth century had hardly ever been confronted with it. Again and again,
Donald Shriver talks about how, as a young man in the 1950s, he took part
in a Christian youth conference. There, for the first time, he met with blacks
who treated him as "an equal." Only then did he realize that until then he
had thought of blacks as "not equal." Later, in the 60s, he became an activist
of the Civil Rights Movement and fought for the rights of blacks.

Then they move on to Colonial Williamsburg, an almost completely
reconstructed town from the eighteenth century, which for a time (1699–
1780) was even the capitol city of the independent commonwealth of Virginia. Today Colonial Williamsburg is a Living History Museum in which
not only the houses and their furnishings but also people in the dress of the
eighteenth century are to be seen. In this it is not only about a true to the detail recreation of the past, but above all the tradition and bringing to life of
the "American experiment" that, with the rebellion of the thirteen colonies
against the English state power and the Declaration of Independence of July
4, 1776, brought it into being. Actors playing historical figures discuss human rights and democracy with the public. "Don Shriver and Helmut Reihlen asked questions, for example, about the consistency of the defending of
the right to freedom (Jefferson) with the simultaneous slavery of persons,"

12. Reihlen, "USA 2007."

writes Erika Reihlen about this interactive theater.[13] And then further: "The answers to the questions that were true to their time were impressive with their exceptionally good historical knowledge and sense of humor."[14]

After this they head to Richmond, today's capitol city of Virginia. At every turn now they come across Thomas Jefferson (1743–1826), lawyer, Enlightenment philosopher, politician, architect, and universal scholar. Born near Charlottesville, the city where he will later found the University of Virginia, the author of the American Declaration of Independence is a "moderate opponent" of slavery. Yet, like so many of his contemporaries, he also feared the freeing of slaves—once suggesting that remaining with slavery was like holding "the wolf by the ear . . . we can neither hold him, nor safely let him go."[15]

No less than Berlin, Richmond is a city that remembers.[16] "But many once-suppressed tributaries of the history are now visible in the public mainstream of this city. Like few cities in the United States, Richmond can now host a civic conversation that involves virtually the whole of the American story."[17]

What Donald Shriver means with this, the Reihlens discover on the city tour passing the Saint John's Episcopal Church where Patrick Henry on March 23, 1775, made the Liberty or Death speech in which he called for an armed battle against the English colonial rulers. The site of the speech: the House of Burgesses that in 1775 was in close proximity to and within earshot of the slave market. Like Jefferson, Patrick Henry, the later governor of Virginia, had divided feelings and sometimes even perhaps a guilty conscience regarding slavery, without this becoming a political problem for his generation. It remains in place during the nineteenth century.

That Richmond publicly reflects the history of slavery is a development that first began in the mid-eighties of the twentieth century. In 1993, a people's initiative developed a historical city tour that brought to light the imprint of the slave trade in the city. Thus well-known old squares gained with this, all at once, a two-fold significance. As centers of civic trade, they were also slave markets.

On Monument Avenue there is a sculpture of Arthur Ashe: a tennis champion from Richmond of African American origin who died young in 1993 of AIDS. Since the beginning of the eighties, he was active in the

13. Reihlen, "USA 2007."

14. Reihlen, "USA 2007."

15. Jefferson, Letter to John Holmes, April 22, 1820.

16. Shriver, *Honest Patriots*, 133.

17. Shriver, *Honest Patriots*, 140.

battle against AIDS and for the education of black children and youth. His memorial stands now in a stately row with the equestrian statues of former Confederate generals. An extension to the monumental memory of the city, comments Donald Shriver. So to the historical figures of war, Ashe adds a civilian history: that of a hero of the sport of tennis who committed himself to the integration of African Americans into US society.

Finally Donald Shriver takes his guests to the American Civil War Center, also called the Tredegar Museum because it occupies the building of the old Tredegar Iron Foundry. The American Civil War Center, which officially opened its doors on October 7, 2006, laid out a new approach by which the old Museum of Confederacy would be completely redesigned. The objective would be to present the American Civil War of 1861–1865 from the point of view of all who took part: the Confederates, the Northern States, and also the blacks who were freed from the yoke of slavery in the wake of the victory of the Northern States under Abraham Lincoln.

The new concept for the museum came at the end of a long development, a process awakening awareness, in which the view of Southerners of their history extended to include the history of African Americans. For the first time, an active role was conceded to African Americans in the history, so they were no longer treated only as objects, but came to the fore as active subjects—a standpoint that helped to give blacks back their dignity.

Don Shriver gives the last word in *Honest Patriots* to Helmut and Erika Reihlen:

> America will achieve leadership in self-restraint and critical self-reflection. The problems ahead of us in the global village are too big even for the strongest nation in the world to handle alone. Gratitude and contrition make honest patriots, and such patriots are best qualified to be responsible World Citizens.[18]

Apparent also here is the Christian understanding of politics, underpinned by an "Ethics of Remembering."

In 2009 Donald W. Shriver received the prestigious Grawemeyer Award in Religion for his book *Honest Patriots*. The purpose of the prize "is to honor and publicize annually creative and constructive insights into the relationship between human beings and the divine, and ways in which this relationship may inspire or empower human beings to attain wholeness, integrity or meaning."[19]

18. Shriver, *Honest Patriots*, 285.

19. http://grawemeyer.org/religion/

Shriver had set the politics of memory in countries like Germany and South Africa in an explicitly Christian context of repentance and atonement. That this Christian dimension of politics is also a possibility for modern societies to morally develop further, connects him to the political and theological thought of Dietrich Bonhoeffer that had also influenced Helmut and Erika Reihlen. And so it is a nice conclusion to this trip in which Helmut and Erika Reihlen take part in the Bonhoeffer Lectures at the Union Theological Seminary in New York. The topic: "Ending Poverty: World Poverty & Moral Responsibility." The ethos of these lectures, observe Helmut and Erika Reihlen when looking back, anticipated the optimistic and visionary position of the "Yes we can" of Barack Obama. What Obama, during his candidacy for President, indefatigably repeated had already been in the air, as it were. We remain humans, made so as the Bible soberly describes it. The innovative spirit of people, though, has laid the biological and technological foundation to overcome hunger and extreme poverty on earth. We, the people in the better off and in the poor countries of the earth, must truly want it and apply this will in methodical action is the conclusion of the Bonhoeffer Lecture. We have arrived at a point in world history in which the dreams of the Bible for peace between peoples and the end of world hunger could become reality. We and our children and grandchildren remain obligated to take advantage of these opportunities given to us.

## BEFORE THE MIRROR WALL

What is left to say about that which was and about that which is to come? Helmut and Erika Reihlen talk about the transience of all life, which they more and more frequently see—for the years of our lives "pass quickly, and we are gone," as it says in Psalm 90:10 (ESV). Erika Reihlen quotes Walther von der Vogelweide: "Owê war sint verswunden alliu mîniu jâr!—ist mir mîn leben getroumet, oder ist ez wâr?"[20]

They look back on the development of Germany and Europe since the war ended and Helmut Reihlen happily reflects, "That we experienced it all and could do our part as well!" He remembers the first united East-West celebration on June 17, 1990, in the Schauspielhaus at Gendarmenmarkt. Manfred Stolpe gave a speech about the creation of a free, productive, and socially just state in western Germany convinced this was one of the preconditions for German unity.

20. "Oh woe, where have all of my years gone—has my life been a dream, or is it true?" Vogelweide, "Owê," 115.

Erika Reihlen remembers a remark of Johannes Rau: Germany is "surrounded by friends."[21] They all follow the same set of values for the state. "We are a tremendously lucky generation," adds Helmut Reihlen. Goals that Helmut and Erika Reihlen advocated for, such as confronting the National Socialist past, the equality of men and women, fair conditions of access to education, and the equal status of capital and labor, today belong to the crossparty consensus.

Helmut and Erika Reihlen influenced the shape of German society before and after unification. They embody a new generation of German middle-class that have learned from National Socialism and worked towards a Germany of parliamentary democracy that turned towards human rights, the social market economy, and responsibility in relation to natural resources. This middle-class connects the high esteem of family, work discipline on the job and the honoring of open-mindedness, the readiness to learn, and social and critical engagement, intertwined in the Jewish-Christian tradition.

For Erika Reihlen, the symbol of the historical experience that defines this new reorientation is Herman Ehlers Platz with the Mirror Wall and the Haus Wolfstein, which lays hidden behind a row of houses. Until the November pogrom of 1938, the original horse stable was used as a synagogue. There is a line of sight to it, consciously left open from Hermann Ehlers Platz. It goes through the hair salon on the ground floor of the building at Düppelstraße 41 that was erected at the beginning of the nineties. Only when one bends down can one see, through the interior of the salon, the plaque in Hebrew text at the synagogue entrance.

At the Mirror Wall, Erika Reihlen points out the names of the siblings Hans and Alfred Silberstein, then the block of twenty-six names with the same address: Lichterfelde East, Heindersdorferstraße 40. They were the residents of a retirement home, around eighty years old when they were deported. The streets listed on the Mirror Wall are named the same today as they were then. A truck drives up and stops quite close to the Mirror Wall. The market stalls at Hermann Ehlers Platz were just being dismantled. Glaring sunlight makes the Mirror Wall almost invisible. One must find the right angle to read the 1,723 engraved names. Erika Reihlen points out two of them: Ella Weinberg and Otto Morgenstern. They were Christian. Ella Weinberg was baptized in the Evangelical Johannes Church in Lichterfelde, for twenty years the congregation of the Reihlens. Otto Morgenstern was the Director of Studies at the Schiller Gymnasium in Lichterfelde, municipal councilor, and founder of the nearby Schlosspark Theater. *Stolpersteine*

21. Cohen, "Germany Celebrates," A14.

were laid in front of their building. A gesture of commemoration that is important to Erika Reihlen.

What do Erika and Helmut Reihlen wish for the future? Many of the dreams they had for their life have become true. Both hope for an old age true to Psalm 103:2: "Bless the LORD, O my soul, and forget not all his benefits" (KJV). Together as long as possible, healthy enough not to be a burden to one another, long enough to be able to share still for a while in the lives of their children and grandchildren, listen to music, experience landscapes and art. And a comforted dying.

Perhaps Erika Reihlen will write a book with all the stories she has gathered from the time with her children and grandchildren, with the preschool children and her little dental patients. From this, she cannot get enough.

## BIBLIOGRAPHY

Cohen, Roger. "Germany Celebrates a Decade of Unity with 'a Bit of Pride.'" *New York Times*, October 4, 2000, A14.

Jefferson, Thomas. Letter to John Holmes, April 22, 1820. The Thomas Jefferson Papers, Special Collections, University of Virginia Library. Transcription available online at Founders Online, National Archives, https://founders.archives.gov/documents/Jefferson/98-01-02-1234.

Reihlen, Erika. "USA 2007." Travel Diary. In the authors' possession. 2007.

Reihlen, Helmut, and Erika Reihlen. "Church Congress as Preliminary Church and What Remains When It Goes: An Example." In *Quo vadis Kirche? Gestalt und Gestaltung von Kirche in den gegenwärtigen Transformationprozessen: Joachim Track zum 65. Geburtstag,* edited by Susanne Munzert and Peter Munzert, 195–99. Stuttgart: Kohlhammer, 2005.

———. "The Mirror Wall Berlin-Steglitz." Lecture presented before the International Society of Political Psychology, Berlin, Germany, June 18, 2002.

Shriver, Donald W., Jr. *An Ethic for Enemies: Forgiveness in Politics.* New York: Oxford University Press, 1995.

———. *Honest Patriots: Loving a Country Enough to Remember Its Misdeeds.* New York: Oxford University Press, 2005.

Shriver, Peggy L. "Empire Christ." In the authors' possession. 2008.

von der Vogelweide, Walther. "Owê war sint verswunden alliu mîniu jâr!" In *Der große Conrady: Das Buch deutscher Gedichte von den Anfängen bis zur Gegenwart,* edited by Karl Otto Conrady, 115. Düsseldorf: Artemis & Winkler, 2008.

# 22

# A Long Partnership

*Stephen Phelps*

Early in July of 2018, at a retreat center in Virginia where more than a dozen participants were teaching and reflecting on the enduring wounds and meanings of the American Civil War, during a break, I was giving Don Shriver a lesson in using dictation software.

In his tenth decade, with feet and fingers slowed in recent years, and no match for his un-slowed mind, Don instantly grasped that the software could serve as a channel to send out still more gifts from his intellect and passions for social ethics and social action. His first question when I proposed we give the software a try: "Will it understand my southern accent?"

I first heard Don's southern accent almost thirty years ago in the company of Peggy, of course, and of a friend who just that particular Sunday happened to be visiting me and my congregation in a hamlet more than one hundred miles up the Hudson Valley. This hamlet of my first pastorate happens also to be the crossroads in the Taconic Hills where the Shrivers' elder son Gregory had built for them a bungalow some years earlier. Many present readers came to know the place.

This occasion was the Shrivers first time at the church during my dozen years serving there. I had not studied at Union Theological Seminary (nor had I seen photographs of its president), so I did not know whom I was greeting at the door of the simple Christopher Wren-style church—but my visiting friend had studied there. From beneath the brim of her huge summer hat, she inquired, "Dr. Shriver?" My friendship with Don and Peggy began that day and has since traversed ever-changing landscapes of vocation, relationship, hope, and thought cast toward justice.

While reflecting on Don Shriver, other contributors will also have noted that he cannot be thought of in the singular so much as in the Don-and-Peggy. Several years ago, they composed a memoir of their marriage. The unpublished manuscript revealed that the couple had separate printers, or at least separate printer preferences, as their interwoven texts carefully inscribed memories of the patterns and the unusual junctures of their great life. The word great today carries mixed messages about out-sized achievement and effect, though I believe Don and Peggy have had that. Here I mean rather to express an existential sense of greatness, that Don and Peggy from their beginning and always since have each considered the other of absolute and greatest significance, and therefore held and hold and behold their marriage as a being itself worthy of great attention. In principle, every human has this capacity for what is great, though by many and by much, it is ignored.

A few years into our friendship, there came the occasion one Sunday morning to celebrate during the worship service the wedding of two beloved members of the community, both well-advanced in their eighties. When "till death do us part" is to be uttered with a certainty and poignancy quite unlike that spoken by a couple of young years, Sunday worship is the right setting to hear and affirm it. My sermon spoke some high-minded words about love, marriage, and precious time, and afterward, the Shrivers invited me up for lunch at Thistlestop, the cottage nestled on a slope of their wooded height of land looking out to the Catskill Mountains.

Two things I remember from that conversation. One, together they let me understand—I cannot recall how or with what words they managed both to say it—that marriage, even forty years on, was more fun and more delightfully physical than the careful, reserved sermon of the morning seemed to allow. Two, Don said—others will have heard him say the like more than once—"I was certainly not the smartest man Peggy might have chosen, but I was smart enough to see that I should ask her to marry me, and that is the smartest thing I ever did." (Apologies to Don for whichever of those words sound not quite as he put it.) Fully as much as the compelling and closely reasoned ethics of Dr. Donald W. Shriver Jr. and the irresistible invitations to love and compassion in the poems of Peggy Ann Leu Shriver, the marriage of this man and this woman has furnished to me and to uncountable others a book to read, to enjoy, someday to close, yet even then to open again for edification, delight, and direction.

The church in Spencertown grew remarkably in those years, in spirit, in numbers, in generosity. *An Ethic for Enemies* was published in those years and Don centered more than one public conversation at the church on its themes. Peggy published *Pinches of Salt* in those years, and read from that volume and other poems during church gatherings and once, at least, when I was on vacation, during the space reserved for the preaching of the Word. There Peggy was ordained as an elder in the Presbyterian tradition, and, in years after I had been called to serve a church in Buffalo, *Honest Patriots* was published, *The Dancers in Riverside Park* was published, and the congregation in town, as I learned during regular visits to Thistlestop, continued to invite these good friends to share insights from their travels and writings.

As often as I applied for a pastoral position with a congregation I found compelling, Don and Peggy served as references. Not long after the Sunday morning wedding service described above, I was one of two candidates in each of two congregations' search processes on the Upper West Side of Manhattan. So supportive were these Shrivers! I recall the immense, cold cavern of a Manhattan sanctuary where I was to preach for the benefit of a search team. In the biz, this arrangement is called a "neutral pulpit." In most ways, it makes a travesty of the purposes of preaching, since the preacher has no sound reason to speak to these people—all twenty of them, in the event—but only to those five from the search committee endeavoring to evaluate the preacher. However, Don and Peggy were there. Although their home church was The Riverside Church, they made it their purpose to join with me that day, which certainly made the pulpit feel less neutral. And, as always, there came specific, probing, supportive comments and questions about that particular sermon from these particular friends in that oddly unparticular place, just as had always come from them in our accustomed place up in the country.

I was not called to either of the two congregations in Manhattan. Over the coming years, recommendations from the Shrivers supported me in a few other searches, and when those searches turned toward other candidates, Don would comment not just whimsically that he wondered how he might improve his batting average—or perhaps his pitch—in support of my preaching. Not seldom, he shared with me the written account offered to others of his experience of the character and quality of my own preaching. His word had no small part in sustaining my sense of call to a pulpit of greater influence.

During the ten years I served a church in Buffalo, I was deeply involved in a ministry at Attica Prison. More than two hundred times, I participated in an open-ended inward-looking conversation with about a dozen men and three or four other volunteers. In the same years, the Shrivers were also becoming more active in prison ministries and advocacy for reform of criminal justice systems. When I moved to New York City in 2009, after the Buffalo congregation had sold its properties and joined with a larger church, it was the Shrivers who linked me up with my first job in the city, teaching church history for New York Theological Seminary's Master's program at Sing Sing Correctional Facility.

About eighteen months after my arrival in New York, and not least with the strong support and recommendations of Dr. and Mrs. Shriver, I was asked to serve as Interim Senior Minister of The Riverside Church. Thus did I become for a second time pastor to the Shrivers! Not pastor only, needless to say—but how often we have smiled at the remarkable turn of events.

Any reader not familiar with Don's main work of the last thirty years will benefit from a brief summary. He has been concerned with the question of how a society deals with and fails to deal with its history of injustice, its guilt, its denial, and the possibility of its reconciling, both with its past and with the people whom it has feared and oppressed and is still oppressing. Can there be a more urgent ethical question? Don's decades of inquiry into possible national responses to the history of oppression have prefigured all the acts of the cultural and political drama, which, since 2016, so unhappily portend a tragic Act V. I cannot overstate how thrilling and deepening for my own soul and wit was the continuing conversation with Don and Peggy Shriver in their home and at the church through the three years of my ministry at Riverside and in the years since. I conclude with a story from my work at Riverside.

Among the first sermons I delivered there was one called "Shall the Fundamentalists Win? (Reprise)." It took its title from the famous sermon by Harry Emerson Fosdick, circa 1922, yet observed how the meaning and function of fundamentalism shape-shifted across the century while retaining a peculiar lock on much American interpretation of scripture and of history. At the door from the nave, Don offered a thoughtful commentary on Fosdick and his times.

The sermon of the following week, called "Soul Service and Social Service," claimed a priority, albeit not a superiority, for the individual Christian's inward preparation for the indwelling of the Spirit when considered in relation to preparations to help the wounded world. Again Don stopped at the door from the nave of the great cathedral, but now with a word of caution—the necessary caution, I might call it—lest any take what the sermon called "soul service" as the sole concern of the godly. "Since no one is ever fully prepared to serve this world," he observed, "your counsel of 'soul service' might excuse inexcusable delay."

The third sermon, delivered near the birthday of Abraham Lincoln, drew on the surprising recent discovery at the Smithsonian Institution of embroidery inside the waistcoat designed at President Lincoln's request for the occasion of his second inaugural address. There, unseen for 150 years, is emblazoned in black thread on black silk an eagle clutching olive branches and arrows, above the words "One Country, One Destiny." Drawing on the story of the birth and bitter enmity of the twin brothers Jacob and Esau, my sermon raised for the congregation the possibility of Americans becoming one nation by reconciling both with our past and with the people whom we have oppressed and are oppressing. At the door from the nave that day, as throughout all these long years of life and love and reflection and action, Don and Peggy expressed with profound hope that words like those of the morning might become flesh.

# 23

# An Ethicist for Our Time or All Time

*David W. Blight*

As I have long since learned, Donald W. Shriver Jr. will never high-hat you, never spend much of your or his time on mundane matters, never engage you without making you think and likely feel an idea in new ways. Don is a deeply moral man, in both training and in his personal make-up. I always feel humbled by his combination of moral and historical sensibility. He is a thinker of conscience, and one always steeped in learning, both biblical and in the greatest intellectual traditions of the open, pragmatic academic community. With roots in Virginia and then educated first at Davidson College in North Carolina, Don is one of my favorite examples of many white Southern progressives I have known. There is nothing quite like the passion, the seriousness, the devotion to social justice of white Southern liberals who understand deeply in their family bones the system of white supremacy they had to face and overcome. Don was transformed by the prophetic traditions of both the Old and New Testament; but he was also transformed by history itself, by the civil rights movement, which altered America and his South forever. He has done it utmost to continue that altering with his own life.

I have learned firsthand from Don in face-to-face encounters, conferences, and by private means where I am the student, the eager learner sitting at the feet of wisdom. That is now an old-fashioned notion—taking time to read and then listen slowly to a voice both prophetic and steeped in understanding the ways of fallen man's human nature. Whenever I have talked with Don I feel a little like I got closer to meeting Reinhold Niebuhr, perhaps Paul Tillich, and who knows, maybe Isaiah himself. Don has been a pastor, a scholar, a teacher, and an institutional president at Union Theological Seminary. And for many of us he has also been a mentor, sometimes at a distance and sometimes in person. When I was in the middle of writing my biography of Frederick Douglass, I struggled to understand just how deeply steeped my subject was in the Bible, particularly the Old Testament Hebrew prophets. I called on Don and he invited me to lunch. After he finished laughing at my question—"What should I read about the Old Testament?"—he got serious and named several theologians, especially Walter Brueggemann. And indeed, I dove into Brueggemann, his curricular guides to the Hebrew prophets, to the Exodus story, and especially his writing about the nature of prophecy.

I was looking for justification for using the word "prophet" in my title for the book. The more I read Brueggemann, and other theologians such as Abraham Heschel and Robert Alter, I began to see that Douglass's oratory and his voluminous writing in the nineteenth century were indeed within the greatest traditions of the meaning of a prophet. Heschel wrote that the true prophet is he or she who can speak words about our condition "one octave too high for our ears," and whose words are intended to "shatter" us, to trouble our pretentions and our hypocrisies.[1] And in Brueggemann's *The Prophetic Imagination* I read that true "hope is the decision to which God invites Israel [meaning the people of the Old Testament], a decision against despair, against permanent consignment to chaos (Isa. 45:18), oppression, barrenness, and exile."[2] And in *The Practice of Prophetic Imagination*, Brueggemann argues that the true prophet "staggers and offends" us even as his words and stories also "open vistas of possibility where we had not thought to go and where, in fact, we are most reluctant to go."[3] Don guided me to readings that buttressed my own developing conviction, based on years of historical research and writing, that one of the deepest roots of all hope is a serious and abiding sense of tragedy. In one long lunch in New York with Don I turned a corner in a biographical and scholarly

1. Heschel, *Prophets*, 10, 12.
2. Brueggemann, *Prophetic Imagination*, 68.
3. Brueggemann, *Practice of Prophetic Imagination*, 25.

conundrum. Don helped me grasp Douglass's prophetic voice. He then became one of the most astute readers of the biography I will ever enjoy. Approximately every six chapters or so, as Don was reading the book, he would write me substantial email messages—almost like a reading diary—telling me his observations and reactions to the work. I felt honored to say the least. We should all have such an engaged and careful reader.

When Don published his remarkable book *Honest Patriots: Loving a Country Enough to Remember Its Misdeeds,* in 2005, the United States was mired in the middle of the Iraq War, the Bush administration's Justice Department had looked the other way at various schemes of voter suppression conducted by the Republican party, Barack Obama had just begun his one term in the U.S. Senate, Donald Trump was a largely irrelevant New York tabloid mogul, and no one could have predicted a roiling debate over Confederate flags and memorials such as we have seen in recent years. Evangelical Christians were a backbone of the American right, and hardly anyone even thought about Russia rising to be a nemesis of American politics. At that point, since September 11, 2001, American culture had endured a thoroughgoing struggle once again over what it meant to be patriotic in America. In the "global war on terror" we were supposed to "support the troops." The days of tearful jubilation and open expressions of African American patriotism around the election of the first black president were still in a near future no one would have predicted. The Patriot Act was in full force.

In Don's book we are treated to a rigorous examination of how three important countries—the US, South Africa, and Germany—have or have not faced their collective pasts. The book exudes deep reading in the historical literatures of all three countries, and as Don generously admits, he has become most comfortable with historians in addition to his usual comrades in theology and ethics. Don wrote a lasting work about the nature of social remembering and forgetting, about how people are capable of great obfuscation of their pasts in order to serve social order, regimes, and power in any given present. But he also wrote about how we humans can—sometimes by will, often by compulsion—face our past. *Honest Patriots* is a book rooted in Don's Christian conviction that humans can exercise repentance, gain knowledge, learn responsibility and forgiveness, and therefore find redemption. These are large and weighty issues in the world as it has evolved in Don's lifetime from the pre-World War II South into which he was born, all the way through to our own time. He wrote a book about memory—the thing we cannot live with or without.

The third chapter of *Honest Patriots,* "Old Unpaid Debt to African Americans," ought to be required reading as the reparations debate rises again in our current political culture. Don knows what a vexed issue this

*The nature of social remembering and forgetting*

can be in society, but he argues that we have no choice but to use history to understand history and then to overcome its stranglehold on our moral imaginations. In a conclusion he calls, strikingly, "Being Human While Being American," born it seems of the crisis over the devastating war in Iraq, Don makes a moving case for humility as the basis of the policies of a superpower. Don admits that finding justice, domestically or internationally, in relation to the past is always as torturous as it is necessary. He leaves us, though, well-warned and informed with a Niebuhrian caution as we seek justice in history: "We must hope that the justice and benefit will outweigh the injustice and harm, but we will never have an excuse for clothing that hope in the drapery of arrogance."[4] True patriotism, we learn from Don, can only come from forthright encounters with all our deeds, the good, the bad, and the ugly. His book is a prescription for hope drawn from tragedy and an honest confrontation with the past.

## BIBLIOGRAPHY

Brueggemann, Walter. *The Practice of Prophetic Imagination: Preaching an Emancipating Word*. Minneapolis: Fortress, 2012.
————. *The Prophetic Imagination*. Philadelphia: Fortress, 1978.
Heschel, Abraham J. *The Prophets*. Vol. 1. New York: Harper & Row, 1962.
Shriver, Donald W., Jr. *Honest Patriots: Loving a Country Enough to Remember Its Misdeeds*. New York: Oxford University Press, 2005.

4. Shriver, *Honest Patriots*, 285.

# Conclusion

## A Response to These Essays

*Donald W. Shriver Jr.*

My first reaction to these essays is to say that, as a whole, they make me glad that against much resistance to the idea, I managed to say yes to the 1975 invitation of Union Seminary to become its thirteenth president.

My second response is the memory of a bit of advice offered me by Dean James Laney as I was about to leave Atlanta and Emory for New York and Union: "You will find that nothing you would like to do at Union can be done by you alone." I knew that, but it was a wise reminder, one I was frequently to quote to others and myself.

Not every reader will understand why, when a member of the Board of UTS first asked me in 1975 if I would agree to be interviewed for the presidency, I did resist the idea. I had just ended ten years at North Carolina State University after my work on a PhD at Harvard. I had just become a professor of ethics and society at Emory's Candler School of Theology. I was aware that UTS was looking for a new president, but the idea of my filling that post was remote from my imagination. Union had hardly ever had a non-graduate of the school as president. For a Southern Presbyterian to think of the position seemed very unpromising, especially given the news that big financial problems were looming there. The new president needed Wall Street-type friends, right? As a graduate of the "other" Union in Virginia, I had long felt that my calling might be to a teaching ministry in the South. Moreover the financial needs of this northern seminary seemed beyond my competence to understand or address.

220

Then came to Atlanta that search committee with different ideas, and thus began a conversation set in motion especially by two of my Harvard professors, Robert Bellah and James Luther Adams, the one a Presbyterian sociologist, the other a Unitarian professor of Ethics. So the search committee and I talked and talked. I had been settled in Atlanta for scarcely two-and-a-half years. I had just begun to develop interdisciplinary academic work at Emory in line with my ten years of work at North Carolina State. Why cut short a beginning-to-feel-at-home in that city whose leaders were eager to build a "New South"?

An answer came from those conversations: I told them that I had liked New York since the time in 1939 when my parents took me out of seventh grade in Norfolk for a week to go with them to the New York World's Fair. For a twelve-year-old it was a great educational move on their part. My parents had spent their honeymoon in New York in 1925, and in the thirties they had returned two or three times on their anniversaries. In the 1939 visit we stayed at a hotel thirteen streets south of Union, to which my father had already developed some connection. The only one of five brothers to enroll in college, my father studied law at the University of Virginia. A visiting UTS-NY professor of Bible had taught a course at UVA that left an imprint on my father by introducing him to scholarly study of the Bible that flowered into his sixty years as a Sunday school class teacher in his Norfolk Methodist church. Never quite convinced to follow his mother's hope for his becoming a Methodist minister, he began teaching Uniform Lessons to young and adult classes in our local Methodist church. It was my regular experience to see him spend every Saturday afternoon studying for next morning's lesson. He certainly influenced me to become a lover of the Bible.

From that 1939 family visit to New York, I became fascinated enough with the city that, by age eighteen as an army draftee, I volunteered for an assignment to Fort Monmouth, NJ, fifty miles by rail to weekends in the city. A visit to the Riverside Church afforded me a glimpse of Union and the future site of the new Interchurch Center across the street. The latter would become familiar to me in committee meetings to which the Southern Presbyterian Church would one day send me as a representative in the fifties. In the 1940s, George Abernathy, a Michigan-born philosophy teacher at Davidson College in North Carolina, had urged me to acquaint myself with the books of Reinhold Niebuhr. Little did I anticipate that in October 1953, on my way to a world ecumenical youth conference in India, I would be rooming two nights with a friend on the seventh floor of Hastings Hall at UTS and would be introduced personally to Niebuhr, who presented to me a signed copy of his recent book, *The Irony of American History*. I would read it on the deck of the H.M.S. Queen Elizabeth on my way across the

Atlantic during the first leg of my trip to Asia. Five months later, returning from Asia, I was back home with a plan to join my future wife Peggy for her first visit with me to Norfolk. (A five-month absence was not the best plan for celebrating our engagement of the previous October!) From then until 1975 New York became a place I would visit for meetings connected to Peggy's and my election as officers of the United Christian Youth Movement, an outgrowth of my increasing devotion to an ecumenical definition of the church.

In the years 1947–51, I had enjoyed being a history major at Davidson. History fitted my interests in theology and ethics, which I pursued at Union Seminary in Richmond and in a year at Yale Divinity School. There, in classes taught by Reinhold Niebuhr's brother Richard, I engaged the emerging field of Christian social ethics in the work of both Niebuhrs. By 1956, I was serving a small Presbyterian congregation in North Carolina when I was invited by UTS-VA to apply for a Rockefeller Doctoral Fellowship for theology students open to careers in theological education. Having succeeded in that application, I undertook renewed study of ethics and social sciences at Harvard. I little suspected that five years later I would be wrestling with an invitation to join the faculty of Harvard Divinity School, an invitation that would compete with my new engagement in foundation-supported interdisciplinary studies at North Carolina State University. Over many a lunchtime in 1964, Peggy and I wondered together: Was HDS the better locus for working out a vocation for teaching social ethics than might be offered me, say, at the "other" Union in Richmond, Virginia? Far from my mind was any ambition to join a faculty at 120th street and Broadway. Turning down a Harvard appointment was hard, but imagining an appointment to UTS-NY was harder.

When that possibility heaved above my vocational horizon in 1975, I had to wrestle seriously with the possibility that UTS-NY was ready to appoint a southerner as its new president.

As Gary Dorrien's essay in this collection makes eloquently clear, prestigious Union was now in an institutional wrestle with contemporary forces challenging its very survival, a possibility that occupied many conversations in national seminary circles. In one of them a professor of religion opined to a colleague, "We think that the library of the Hartford Seminary may be up for sale. Would your school be interested?" "No," came the reply. "We think we might wait for the Union library to come on the market."

When that search committee from New York turned serious about its interest in me, Peggy and I began some of the longest lunchtime discussions of our lives together. Always active in church and community service, she had recently been elected as one of three staff of the new Southern

Presbyterian Office of Review and Evaluation, with responsibilities for assessing the work and leadership of agencies of the whole denomination. Her new job was central to our long lunchtime discussions in 1975 over our mutual calls. We reached a critical point in those discussions when Peggy drew on her own grasp of church history in concluding: "In the long run Union Seminary is more important to the church than the O.R.E. of the Southern Presbyterian Church. I think we should seriously consider that call to New York." (As one or two authors in this collection point out, the wife of the proposed thirteenth president of UTS indeed had a major role in his deciding to accept that appointment. I am pleased to observe that one test of a genuine marriage is the obligation of both partners to ponder vocations mutually. In our case, mutual theological commitments were important bases for decision-making about job offers.)

Happily the Protestant church world was entering a new era of women's leadership in the churches and in theological education. Soon after our arrival at Union, Peggy was offered a post in the offices of the National Council of Churches. The job resembled the post she was leaving in Atlanta, so she soon became the first full-time-employed wife of a UTS president.

The first year or two of our new life at UTS were destined to be anything but joyful. The university world in 1975 was still enduring waves of student protests against the growing American investment in the Vietnam War. Union students and faculty were among the most active participants in the protest at Columbia University. I had already a fund of experience in this national upset at N.C.S.U. Our elder son, age fifteen, had insisted on joining local college students in the protests. But the upset at Union was powered by a pervasive theological passion that for me was a new, difficult dimension of being an educator. Our academic registrar James Hayes helped me adjust to it all when he once remarked to me that, "there are two things around here that we admire in you, Mr. President: your marriage and your capacity for absorbing hostility." I hoped that he perceived that the two were related: without Peggy I might not have been so "absorbent" of that hostility.

Gary Dorrien's essay is an accurate account of these early rigorous years of my time at UTS. I was fortunate to have the restraining wisdom of certain members of the UTS student body, faculty members, and board who believed with me that the word "administration" is not necessarily a synonym for an oppressive power structure responsible for ideological, political, and economic endorsement of the evils of war. Union's connection to the war and a neighboring university's responsibility for supporting or opposing it was complicated by our budget crisis and reputation for raising Niebuhrian public outcries for justice. The latter were not an encouragement of large financial help from wealthy New Yorkers, like the ones who had financed the UTS move from Park Avenue to Morningside Heights in the early twentieth century.

In my early years as president and ethics professor I found great personal stabilities in classroom teaching that confirmed for me that Union was still attracting students of theological depth with the capacity to address social-political issues of great complexity. An aid to appreciation of these traits of UTS students came in the Board's and my decision to pursue "educational evaluation" after the model of Peggy's work in the Presbyterian Church in Atlanta. As Mac Gatch points out in his essay, we undertook this under the guidance of educator Malcolm Warford, one of seven new faculty members whom we were able to appoint in the seventies in the wake of many recent departures from the faculty. Among the new appointments were four African Americans and an internationally known Japanese Christian theologian, Kosuke Koyama. The four included preacher-extraordinary James Forbes; James Washington, church historian and chronicler of the still vigorous Civil Rights Movement; Cornel West, young philosopher fresh from Princeton; Mary Pellauer, called to explore the challenges to women in the new openness to women's leadership in churches; and urban sociologist Samuel Roberts.

Union was beginning to attract unprecedented numbers of black and women students, and some of them had understandable suspicion of a new president with Southern roots. My support of women's ordination in the P.C.U.S and my participation in the Civil Rights Movement were well known to students and faculty who took care to study my past. Welcome to some was a Southern accent that I shared with the growing number of black students in contrast with many a New Yorker who heard that accent as a mark of ignorance!

The same suspicion haunted our necessary budget cuts during my first two years. Anxiety about institution-saving economies led a leader of the local UTS union of non-academic employees to circulate a letter opining that, as a southerner, "our new president can't be expected to sympathize with unions," a sad evidence of ignorance of my support of the union cause in North Carolina and my opposition to the Taft-Hartley Law. Ironically, when I visited the local NYC leaders of union 32B, which our local maintenance workers were considering to represent them, those citywide union leaders were better acquainted with my union-friendly background than were many of our UTS staff. The irony was compounded by the fact that this was the institution whose most famous theologian was a longtime friend of unions.

In the midst of these rancorous discussions, some faculty credited (or accused) me of being a Niebuhrian, a credit I preferred to share with my admiration of the other Niebuhr, H. Richard. From him I had acquired some of the approach to human conflicts that seemed to multiply in my first attempt to balance the UTS budget.

The wisdom of the Hebrew proverb—"A soft answer turneth away wrath" (KJV)—persisted for me in those angry first months of my attempt to be president of UTS. That proverb matched a proclivity natural to me in my upbringing as a Southerner and as a learner from the examples of my Iowa-born wife Peggy, plus the immemorial patience of my new UTS friends in the Black community. The "other" Niebuhr, H. Richard, fortified me with his consistent references to listening to critics, learning from them, and conversing with them in an adventure toward consensus that can only emerge from conversation. On my side of it all, I was learning that we clergypeople are not inclined to wrestle with questions of economic scarcity, especially in an institution accustomed to depend on the luxuries of a large endowment that was being eaten away by two-digit inflation.

Various faculty, old and new, plus numerous members of our Board, brought understanding and helps in the conflicts. I think especially of two board chairs, Walter Burke and Thomas Johnson; Dean Robert Handy and faculty members Raymond Brown, James Forbes, Cornel West, Kosuke Koyama, and Will Kennedy. The latter said to me once that his membership in the Finance Committee helped educate him as a professor of education to the necessity of tradeoffs in the building of an institution's budget. Inviting one's critics into partnership for facing financial problems can be a step away from destructive to constructive conflict. I always hoped that how we undertook that budget discussion would help prepare future ministers and teachers to enter into the same process in their future service to the church and other institutions. Once our graduates had to wrestle with the financial challenges of a local church, they were more sympathetic with the same at their seminary.

By 1975 the word "institution" had acquired a great cloud of negative associations in the discussions of many theologians, ethicists, and university students. I have long believed that anything worth our human doing is worth organizing. The beginnings of the Christian movement as described in Acts 2:42 would have been only a beginning if the apostles had not paid organized attention to perpetuating the story of Jesus through "teaching and fellowship . . . the breaking of bread and the prayers." (NRSV) Soon they authorized the office of deacon for the ordinary service of waiting on dinner tables. I used to say to the critics of our perpetual attention to budgets at UTS that "you have to pay attention to the budget if you believe in the daily human importance of breakfast." Food and shelter are requirements for our survival and our neighbor's. One does not have to be a materialist to insist on that.

Theologically one does have to insist that humans do "not live by bread alone, but by every word that comes from the mouth of God." (Matt 4:4 [NRSV]) The faith on which the Jewish and Christian communities are founded arose in their experience of being addressed by a word of God worth all possible human effort to preserve it for future generations: that Word was a treasure to be preserved in fragile "earthen vessels" that we call "institutions." One might say that we humans ourselves are such earthen vessels. Preserving us in life together is the purpose of institutions, which are only as valuable as what and who they preserve.

In his essay Professor Dorrien pays me the tribute of a comparison with one of my mentors—James Luther Adams, whose favorite maxim was, "you shall know them by their groups," i.e., their social connections. My twenty-one-year connection with UTS-NY is probably, most observers will say, my major life work, which has only been possible by the efforts of thousands of people who affirm the importance of a Union Seminary. Most of those thousands believed that the preservation of the Christian faith and its message were worth the work of preserving this earthen vessel of a school. Jim Laney was right: an institution begins and continues in collaborations.

At NCSU I had practiced this wisdom by helping to turn it into academic collaborations across disciplinary boundaries, e.g., in asking my friend Patrick McDonald, professor of engineering mechanics, to join me in a seminar for engineering students on "Ethical Issues in Engineering." That precedent came with me to Morningside Heights in similar collaborations with faculty members of four professional schools—the Jewish Theological Seminary (with Professor Gordon Tucker); the Columbia School of Business (with Professor James Kuhn); the Columbia University Schools of Law and International Affairs in their and Barnard College's program on Human Rights; the Columbia University School of Journalism (with Professor James Carey). Added to this was collaboration with UTS's own Professor of the Sociology of Religion, Samuel Roberts, on "ministry in cities." With the exception of Professor Tucker, death has now claimed all of these colleagues, much to my grief that they could not appear among the authors of these essays.

Dietrich Bonhoeffer, once a student at UTS-NY, confronted Nazism in that faith and in the confidence that the life of humanity itself was at stake in organized resistance to the evils of Nazism. One of the high points in my twenty-one years at UTS was the concert memorializing that resistance on April 5, 1996, in the Riverside Church. The date was close to the fifty-first anniversary of Bonhoeffer's murder in Flossenberg. The event was organized by our UTS board member Joseph Robinson, first oboist of the NY Philharmonic, and by orchestra Director Christoph von Dohnanyi, nephew of Bonhoeffer. With orchestra members drawn from around the world, including survivors of the Holocaust and choral conductor Joseph Flummerfelt, the concert featured Brahms, Beethoven, and the memorial by Schoneberg, "Survivor from Warsaw." In the full audience that afternoon were many faculty and students from our neighbor, the Jewish Theological Seminary, almost all of them with relatives destroyed in the Holocaust.

The concert reminded me that since my birth in 1927 I had lived through some of the most terrifying years of human history. I am a member of the generation of draftees whose life may have been saved by my country's bombing of Hiroshima. Of German ancestry, I greatly admire the above testimonies of Ismar Schorsch and Robert Pollack, whose reconciliation with modern Germany is an exemplary hope for our human future. Having written and traveled extensively as president of UTS, I have reasons for both hope and despair over that future. Our concert in honor of the resisters to Nazism was graced by the presence of Bonhoeffer's biographer Eberhard Bethge and his musician son, a cellist with the orchestra.

Thinking about that concert and the threats to human life that Bonhoeffer and other heroes of faith were resisting in the 1940s, I pondered a few lines from a novel written in the midst of World War II: *The Journal of Albion Moonlight*. As one remembers the evils committed by us humans against each other in the twentieth century, "The question is not: do we believe in God? but rather: does God believe in us?"[1]

In an essay on Psalm 8 and the theology of Dietrich Bonhoeffer, Marilynne Robinson poses a similar question in her definition of theology: "Great theology is always a kind of giant and intricate poetry, like epic or saga. It is written for those who know the tale already . . . and who attend to its retelling with a special alertness because the story has a claim on them and them on it."[2] It is also a story that they believe has to be told often to fellow human beings who pray, "Lead us not into temptation but deliver us from evil." The evil from which the twentieth century and the twenty-first need to be delivered grows out of the temptation to deny the worth of human life. One of the terrifying phrases in the Nazi ideology was its concept of "leben unwertes leben"—lives unworthy of life, a classification that induced millions of us to kill millions of others.

The notion that some of our human neighbors are trash, waste, and only worth killing is a great curse of some contemporary American political speech. Contrasting to that speech is the language of Christian faith. The

1. Patchen, *Journal of Albion Moonlight*, 10.
2. Robinson, "Dietrich Bonhoeffer," 116.

workday purpose of us academics in seminaries is to teach each other to speak that language persuasively.

Once, a few years before his death, I asked my friend professor James Cone, "What is it that keeps African Americans like you 'keeping on keeping on' in your persistent undermining of racism in American and other societies?" His answer: "The Gospel of God's love for us all."

That love is at the base of the existence of theological schools. When we spend our wealth and energies to preserve such a school as an earthly human container of something we deem precious, we are trying to sustain its capacity to celebrate a gift we have received: God's almost incredible affirmation of the worth of us human beings. From time to time we are all assaulted by doubt that we are worth such high estimate of ourselves. Seminaries exist to protect us from the ravages of such doubt.

Like most of the writers of these essays, I have been honored with helping one of those institutions to persevere in that witness.

## BIBLIOGRAPHY

Patchen, Kenneth. *The Journal of Albion Moonlight*. New York: New Directions, 1961.
Robinson, Marilynne. "Dietrich Bonhoeffer." In *The Death of Adam: Essays on Modern Thought*, 108–25. New York: Picador, 2005.

# Contributors

**M. Craig Barnes**, President and Professor of Pastoral Ministry, Princeton Theological Seminary. His publications include *Body and Soul: Reclaiming the Heidelberg Catechism*, *The Pastor as Minor Poet*, and *Searching for Home*.

**David W. Blight**, Sterling Professor of American History, Yale University. He is the author of the Pulitzer Prize–winning *Frederick Douglass: Prophet of Freedom*.

**Bill Crawford**, Retired Minister, Presbyterian Church (USA). He previously served for many years as the senior minister of Larchmont Avenue Church in Larchmont, New York, and recently served as Dean of Students for Union Theological Seminary in the City of New York.

**Gary Dorrien**, Reinhold Niebuhr Professor of Social Ethics, Union Theological Seminary in the City of New York. His publications include *Kantian Reason and Hegelian Spirit: The Idealistic Logic of Modern Theology*, the Grawemeyer Award–winning *The New Abolition: W. E. B. DuBois and the Black Social Gospel*, and *Social Democracy in the Making: Political and Religious Roots of European Socialism*.

**James A. Forbes Jr.**, Harry Emerson Fosdick Distinguished Professor Emeritus, Union Theological Seminary in the City of New York. He is the President and Founder of the Healing of the Nations Foundation and a Senior Scholar and Fellow of the Drum Major Institute.

**Milton McCormick Gatch Jr.**, Professor Emeritus of Church History and Director Emeritus of the Burke Library, Union Theological Seminary in the City of New York. He previously served as academic dean, provost, and director of the Burke Library at Union Theological Seminary.

**Thomas S. Johnson**, Retired Chairman and Chief Executive Officer, GreenPoint Financial Corporation. He previously served for fourteen years as a trustee and for nine years as the chairman of the board of Union Theological Seminary in the City of New York.

**Serene Jones**, President and Johnston Family Professor for Religion & Democracy, Union Theological Seminary in the City of New York. Her publications include *Calvin and the Rhetoric of Piety*, *Trauma and Grace*, and, most recently, her memoir *Call It Grace: Finding Meaning in a Fractured World*.

**Joseph V. Montville**, Board Chair and Senior Fellow, Center for World Religions, Democracy, and Conflict Resolution, George Mason University. He is the editor of *Conflict and Peacemaking in Multiethnic Societies* and the originator of "Track II," non-official diplomacy.

**Eric Mount**, Nelson D. and Mary McDowell Rodes Professor Emeritus of Religion, Centre College. His publications include *Covenant, Community, and the Common Good* and *Professional Ethics in Context: Institutions, Images, and Empathy*.

**Stephen Phelps**, Retired Minister, Presbyterian Church (USA). He previously served for many years as a minister throughout the New York region and as the interim senior minister for the Riverside Church in the City of New York.

**Robert Pollack**, Professor of Biological Sciences and Director of the University Seminars, Columbia University. His publications include *Signs of Life: the Language and Meanings of DNA*, *The Faith of Biology and the Biology of Faith*, and, most recently, *The Course of Nature* with his wife, the artist Amy Pollack.

**Larry Rasmussen**, Reinhold Niebuhr Professor Emeritus of Social Ethics, Union Theological Seminary in the City of New York. His publications include the Grawemeyer Award-winning *Earth Community, Earth Ethics*, and, most recently, *Earth-Honoring Faith: Religious Ethics in a New Key*.

**Erika Reihlen**, Former President, Deutscher Evangelischer Kirchentag, Germany. A pioneering children's dentist, she and her husband, Helmut, have served as leaders in the German Evangelical Church Assembly for many years.

**Helmut Reihlen**, Retired Director, Deutsches Institut für Normung (DIN), Berlin, Germany. He previously served as Chairman of the Synod of the Evangelical Church of Berlin-Brandenburg and of the council of the Diakonisches Werk Berlin (Church Social Welfare Commission).

**Hays Rockwell**, Retired Ninth Bishop of the Episcopal Diocese of Missouri. The former rector of St. James' Church on the upper east side of Manhattan, he previously served as a member of the board of Union Theological Seminary in the City of New York.

**Ismar Schorsch**, Chancellor Emeritus and Rabbi Herman Abramovitz Distinguished Service Professor of Jewish History, The Jewish Theological Seminary. He is the author of *Canon Without Closure: Torah Commentaries*, and, most recently, *Leopold Zunz: Creativity in Adversity*.

**Roger Sharpe**, Former North Carolina State Senator, former Professor, East Carolina University. He is the author of *Ceremony of Innocence: A Memoir*, and the executive producer of the documentary *The Boy Who Heard Lincoln at Gettysburg*.

**Lionel Shriver**, Novelist and Journalist. Her publications include the Orange Prize–winning bestseller *We Need to Talk about Kevin*, the National Book Award finalist *So Much for That*, and the *New York Times* bestselling *The Post-Birthday World*.

**Robert W. Snyder**, Professor of Journalism and American History, Rutgers University. He is the author of *Metropolitan Lives: The Ashcan Artists and Their New York*, and, most recently, *Crossing Broadway: Washington Heights and the Promise of New York City*.

**Ronald Stone**, John Witherspoon Professor Emeritus of Christian Ethics, Pittsburgh Theological Seminary. His publications include *The Ultimate Imperative: An Interpretation of Christian Ethic, Politics and Faith: Reinhold Niebuhr and Paul Tillich at Union Seminary in New York*, and, most recently, *Reinhold Niebuhr in the 1960s: Christian Realism for a Secular Age*.

**David Kwang-sun Suh**, Professor Emeritus of Theology at Ewha Womans University, Seoul, South Korea. He is the author of *The Korean Minjung in Christ*, and the co-editor of *Asian Christian Spirituality: Reclaiming Traditions*.

**Dean K. Thompson**, President and Professor of Ministry Emeritus, Louisville Presbyterian Theological Seminary. He is coeditor of *Mentoring: Biblical Theological and Practical Perspectives*, *Essays on the History of the Household of Faith*, and coauthor of *Go Therefore: 150 Years of Presbyterians in Global Mission*.

**Phyllis Trible**, Baldwin Professor Emerita of Sacred Literature, Union Theological Seminary in the City of New York. Her publications include *God and the Rhetoric of Sexuality*, *Texts of Terror: Literary-Feminist Readings of Biblical Narratives*, and *Rhetorical Criticism: Context, Method, and the Book of Jonah*.

**Janet Walton**, Professor Emerita of Worship, Union Theological Seminary in the City of New York. She is the author of *Art and Worship: A Vital Connection*, and, most recently, *Feminist Liturgy: A Matter of Justice*.

**Cornel West**, Professor of the Practice of Public Philosophy, Harvard University, Professor Emeritus of Philosophy and Christian Practice, Union Theological Seminary in the City of New York. He is the author of *Race Matters*, *Democracy Matters*, and, most recently, *Black Prophetic Fire*.

136 - 2 Shriver books
146 - Honest Patriots
  — Could criticism & celebrate
    be combined?
227 "Does God believe in us?"
  — leben unwertes leben"
  Nazi ideology


— New aspects of the me
— admire
— example